Everything Crochet ™

Edited by CAROL ALEXANDER and CONNIE ELLISON

Annie's Attic ®

EDITORS Carol Alexander, Connie Ellison
ART DIRECTOR Brad Snow
PUBLISHING SERVICES DIRECTOR Brenda Gallmeyer

ASSISTANT EDITOR Sara Meyer
ASSISTANT ART DIRECTOR Nick Pierce
COPY SUPERVISOR Deborah Morgan
COPY EDITORS Emily Carter, Mary O'Donnell, Amanda Scheerer
TECHNICAL EDITOR Susanna Tobias

PRODUCTION ARTIST SUPERVISOR Erin Augsburger
COVER & BOOK DESIGN Greg Smith
GRAPHIC ARTISTS Jessi Butler, Minette Collins Smith
PRODUCTION ASSISTANTS Marj Morgan, Judy Neuenschwander

PHOTOGRAPHY SUPERVISOR Tammy Christian
PHOTOGRAPHY Scott Campbell, Matthew Owen
PHOTO STYLISTS Martha Coquat, Tammy Liechty, Tammy Steiner

Library of Congress Control Number: 2011904091
ISBN: 978-1-59635-361-9

welcome!

from the editors

Most crocheters would love to have that one special, go-to-over-and-over-again crochet reference book that answers those nuts-and-bolts questions that aren't addressed in the average "tutorial" crochet book. Questions like, "How do I figure the stitch multiple in this afghan pattern so I can change the size to suit my needs?" Or, "If a sweater pattern only goes to size X-large, but I need to make it in a bigger size, how do I enlarge the pattern for a proper fit?" And especially, "If I want to substitute a different yarn for the one called for in a pattern, how do I know which type of yarn will work and which won't?"

In this comprehensive, one-of-a-kind crocheters' handbook, you'll find the answers to these and many, many more questions or problems that every crocheter encounters at one time or another. For the beginner, basic stitch techniques are covered with easy-to-follow lessons and diagrams to get you started. From there, you'll find helpful information on a host of subjects, including how to: read patterns, master seaming, evaluate gauge, convert measurements, fix crochet mishaps, work with color, block projects and add professional touches to your crochet.

In addition, you'll learn how to do a variety of crochet stitches and techniques that go beyond the basics, such as mosaic crochet, Swedish embroidery, tambour crochet, Fair Isle, felting, crocheting with thrums and locks, flatwork bead crochet, doing cross-stitch on crochet, crocheting on fabric, and even how to process and crochet with pet hair.

At last, here is that one, must-have guidebook that will become a much-used and treasured staple in any crocheter's library. Whether you're a beginner or experienced stitcher, you'll find answers to many of those bewildering and frustrating problems you're sure to encounter in your crochet experience.

Carol & Connie

Carol Alexander

Connie Ellison

c o n t e n t s

chapter one
stitch basics

It's easy to learn the basic stitches with our large, easy-to-follow, step-by-step illustrations and practice swatches that you can crochet as you go along. It's like having a crochet guru right there beside you giving you special helps and hints as you learn!

Chain Stitch (abbreviated ch)

Note: Instructions are given for right-handed crocheters. Left-handers will work the opposite. For special helps for left-handed crocheters, see page 61.

Crochet usually begins with a series of chain stitches called a beginning or foundation chain. Begin by making a slip knot on the hook about 6 inches from the free end of the yarn. Loop the yarn as shown in Fig. 1.

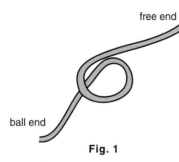

free end

ball end

Fig. 1

Insert the hook through center of loop and hook the free end (*Fig. 2*).

Fig. 2

Pull this through and up onto the working area (*see Fig. 1 on page 68*) of the hook (*Fig. 3*).

Fig. 3

Pull the free yarn end to tighten the loop (*Fig. 4*).

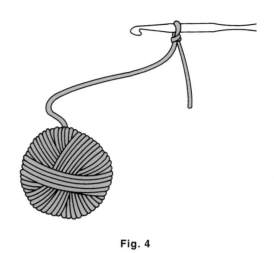

Fig. 4

It should be firm, but loose enough to slide back and forth easily on the hook. Be sure you still have about a 6-inch yarn end.

Hold the hook, now with its slip knot, in your right hand (*Fig. 5*).

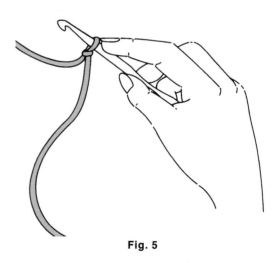

Fig. 5

Now, let's make the first chain stitch.

Step 1: Hold the base of the slip knot with the thumb and middle or index finger of your left hand; thread yarn from the skein over the middle or index finger (*Fig. 6*) and under the remaining fingers of your left hand (*Fig. 7*).

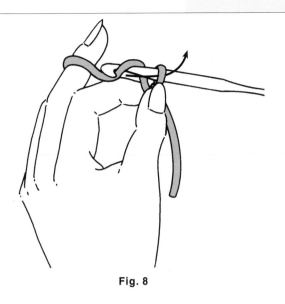

Fig. 6

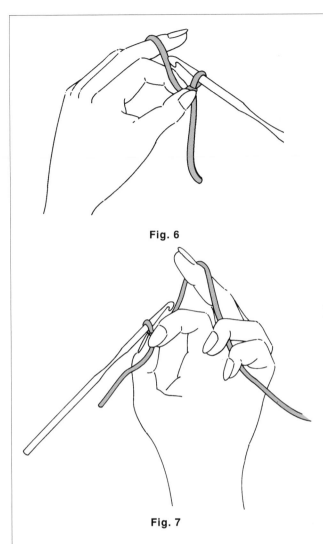

Fig. 7

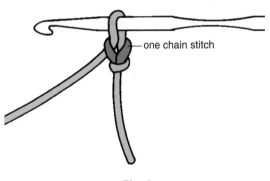

Fig. 8

Draw hooked yarn through the loop of the slip knot on the hook and up onto the working area of the hook *(see arrow on Fig. 8)*; you have now made one chain stitch *(Fig. 9)*.

— one chain stitch

Fig. 9

Your middle finger will stick up a bit to help the yarn feed smoothly from the skein; the other fingers help maintain even tension on the yarn as you work.

Hint: As you practice, you can adjust the way your left hand holds the yarn to however it is most comfortable for you.

Step 2: Bring the yarn over the hook from back to front and hook it *(Fig. 8)*.

Step 3: Again, bring the yarn over the hook from back to front *(Fig. 10)*.

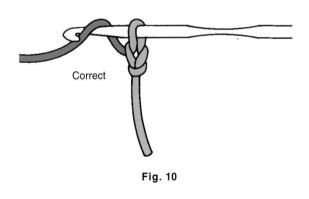
Correct

Fig. 10

Note: Take care not to bring yarn from front to back (Fig. 11).

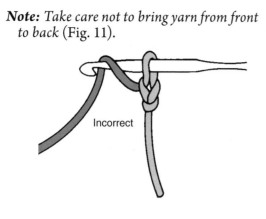

Fig. 11

Hook it and draw through loop on the hook: You have made another chain stitch *(Fig. 12)*.

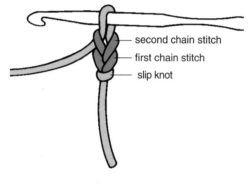

second chain stitch
first chain stitch
slip knot

Fig. 12

Repeat step 3 for each additional chain stitch, being careful to move the left thumb and middle or index finger up the chain close to the hook after each new stitch or two *(Fig. 13)*. This helps you control the work.

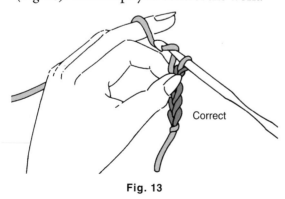

Correct

Fig. 13

Note: Fig. 14 shows the incorrect way to hold the stitches.

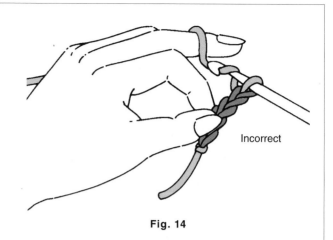

Incorrect

Fig. 14

Also, be sure to pull each new chain up onto the working area of the hook.

The working yarn and the work in progress are always held in your left hand.

Practice making chains until you are comfortable with your grip on the hook and the flow of the yarn. In the beginning your work will be uneven, with some chain stitches loose and others tight. While you're learning, try to keep the chain stitches loose. As your skill increases, the chain should be firm—but not tight—with all chain stitches even in size.

Hint: As you practice, if the hook slips out of a stitch, don't get upset! Just insert the hook again from the front into the center of the last stitch, taking care not to twist the loop *(Fig. 15)*.

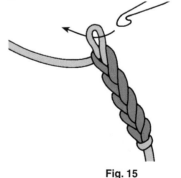

Fig. 15

When you are comfortable with the chain stitch, draw your hook out of the last stitch and pull out the work back to the beginning. Now you've learned the important first step of crochet: the beginning chain. ■

Working Into the Chain

Once you have learned to work the beginning chain, you are ready to begin the stitches required to make any project. These stitches are worked into the beginning chain. For practice, make six chains loosely.

Hint: When counting your chain stitches at the start of a pattern—which you must do very carefully before continuing—note that the loop on the hook is never counted as a stitch, and the starting slip knot is never counted as a stitch (*Fig. 16*).

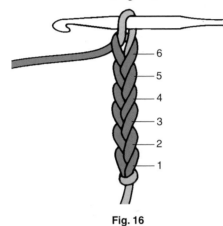

Fig. 16

Now stop and look at the chain. The front looks like a series of interlocking "V"s (*Fig. 16*), and each stitch has a bar at the back (*Fig. 17*).

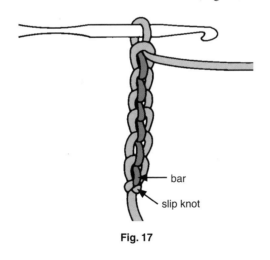

Fig. 17

You will never work into the first chain from the hook. Depending on the stitch, you will work into the second, third, fourth, etc., chain from the hook. The instructions will always state in which chain you will work.

When working a stitch, insert hook from the front of the chain, through the center of the "V" and under the corresponding bar on the back of the same stitch (*Fig. 18*).

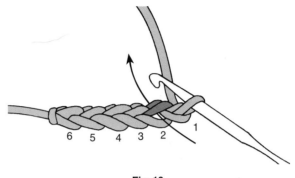

Fig. 18

Excluding the first chain, you will work into every chain, unless the pattern states differently, but not into the starting slip knot (*Fig. 18a*). Be sure that you do not skip that last chain at the end. When you finish, you should have one less stitch than you have chains. ▪

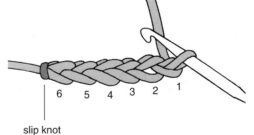

Fig. 18a

Single Crochet (abbreviated sc)

Most crochet is made with variations on just four different stitches: single crochet, half double crochet, double crochet and treble crochet. The stitches differ mainly in height, which varies based on the number of times the yarn is wrapped around the hook before the hook is inserted in the indicated chain, stitch or space. The shortest and most basic of these stitches is the single crochet.

WORKING ROW 1

Step 1: Chain six, skip first chain from hook. Insert hook in the second chain through the center of the V and under the back bar of the chain. Bring the yarn over the hook from back to front (*Fig. 19*). Draw yarn through chain and up onto the working area of the hook. You now have two loops on the hook (*Fig. 20*).

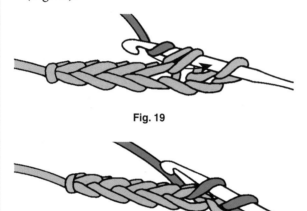

Fig. 19

Fig. 20

Step 2: Again, bring yarn over the hook from back to front, and draw it through both loops on the hook (*Fig. 21*).

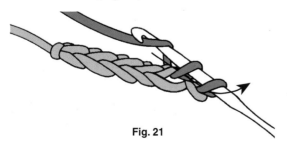
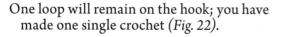

Fig. 21

One loop will remain on the hook; you have made one single crochet (*Fig. 22*).

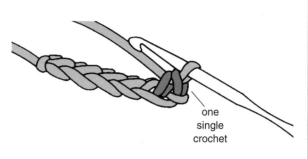

one single crochet

Fig. 22

Step 3: Insert hook in next chain as before, yarn over the hook from back to front, and draw it through the chain stitch. Yarn over the hook the yarn again and draw it through both loops. You have made another single crochet.

Repeat step 3 in each remaining chain, taking care to work in the last chain, but not in the slip knot. You have completed one row of single crochet and should have five stitches in the row. Fig. 23 shows how to count the stitches.

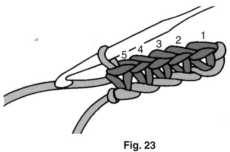

Fig. 23

Hint: As you work, be careful not to twist the chain; keep all the V's facing you.

If included in a pattern, the instructions would read as follows:

Row 1: Ch 6, sc in 2nd ch from hook and in each rem ch across, turn. (*5 sc*)

Note: *To save space, a number of abbreviations are used. For a list of abbreviations used in patterns, see page 30.*

WORKING ROW 2

To work the second row of single crochet, you need to turn the work in the direction of the arrow (counterclockwise), as shown in Fig. 24, so you can work back across the first row.

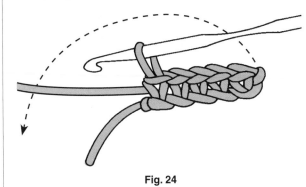

Fig. 24

Do not remove the hook from the loop as you do this *(Fig. 24a)*.

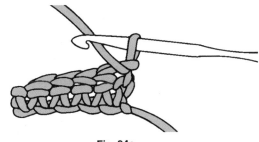

Fig. 24a

Now you need to bring the yarn up to the correct height to work the first stitch. So, to raise the yarn, chain one (this is called a beginning chain).

This row, and all the following rows of single crochet, will be worked into a previous row of single crochet, not into the beginning chain as you did before. Remember that when you worked into the starting chain, you inserted the hook through the center of the V and under the bar. This is only done when working into a starting chain.

To work into a previous row of crochet, insert the hook under both loops of the previous stitch, as shown in Fig. 25, instead of through the center of the V.

The first single crochet of the row is worked in the last stitch of the previous row *(Fig. 25)*, not into the beginning chain. Work a single crochet into each single crochet to the end,

taking care to work in each stitch, especially the last stitch, which is easy to miss *(Fig. 26)*.

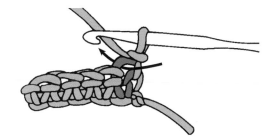

Fig. 25

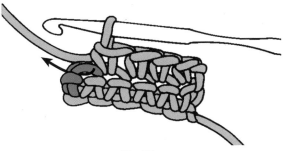

Fig. 26

Stop now and count your stitches; you should still have five single crochets on the row *(Fig. 27)*.

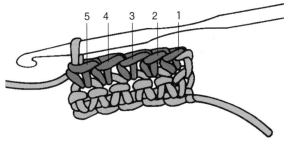

Fig. 27

Hint: When you want to pause to count stitches, check your work, have a snack or chat on the phone, you can remove your hook from the work—but do this at the end of a row, not in the middle. To remove the hook, pull straight up on the hook to make a long loop *(Fig. 28)*. Then, withdraw the hook and put it on a table or other safe place (sofas and chairs have a habit of eating crochet hooks). Put work in a safe place so loop is not pulled out. To begin work again, just insert the hook in the big loop (don't twist the loop) and pull on the yarn from the skein to tighten the loop.

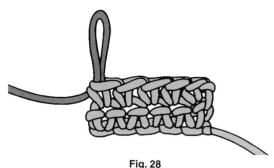

Fig. 28

To end row 2, after the last single crochet, turn the work counterclockwise.

Here is the way instructions for row 2 might be written in a pattern:

Row 2: Ch 1, sc in each sc across, turn.

WORKING ROW 3

Row 3 is worked exactly as you worked row 2. Here are the instructions as they would be given in a pattern:

Row 3: Rep row 2.

Now wasn't that easy? For practice, work three more rows, which means you will repeat row 2 three more times.

Hint: Try to keep your stitches as smooth and even as possible; remember to work loosely rather than tightly and to make each stitch well up on the working area of the hook. Be sure to turn at the end of each row and to check carefully to be sure you've worked into the last stitch of each row.

Count the stitches at the end of each row; do you still have five? Good work.

What if you don't have five stitches at the end of a row? Perhaps you worked two stitches in one stitch, or skipped a stitch. Find your mistake, then just pull out your stitches back to the mistake; pulling out in crochet is simple. Just take out the hook and gently pull on the yarn. The stitches will come out easily; when you reach the place where you want to start again, insert the hook in the last loop (taking care not to twist it) and begin.

FASTENING OFF

It's time to move on to another stitch, so let's fasten off your single crochet practice piece, which you can keep for future reference. After the last stitch of the last row, cut the yarn, leaving a 6-inch end. As you did when you took your hook out for a break, draw the hook straight up, but this time draw the yarn cut end completely through the stitch. Photo A shows an actual sample of six rows of single crochet to which you can compare your practice rows. It also shows how to count the stitches and rows.

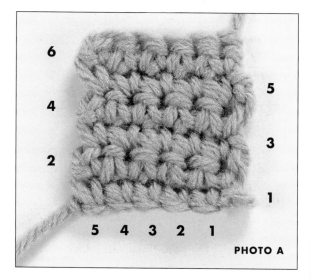

PHOTO A

Now you can put the piece away, and it won't pull out (you might want to tag this piece as a sample of single crochet). ▪

Double Crochet (abbreviated dc)

Double crochet is a taller stitch than single crochet. To practice, work the first row of double crochet as follows:

WORKING ROW 1

Step 1: Chain 14, bring the yarn over the hook from back to front, skip the first three chains from the hook, then insert the hook in the fourth chain *(Fig. 29)*.

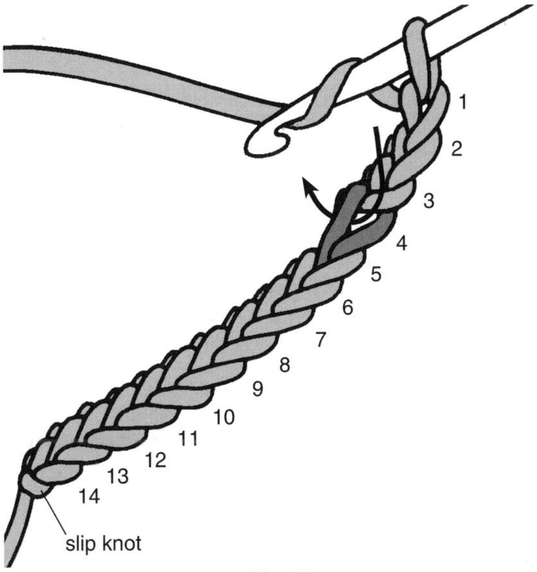

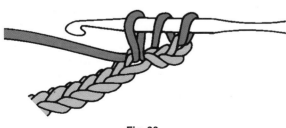

Fig. 29

Remember not to count the loop on the hook as a chain. Be sure to go through the center of the V of the chain and under the bar at the back; do not twist the chain.

Step 2: Bring the yarn over the hook from back to front and draw it through the chain stitch and up onto the working area of the hook; you now have three loops on the hook *(Fig. 30)*.

Fig. 30

Step 3: Bring the yarn over the hook from back to front and draw through the first two loops on the hook *(Fig. 31)*. You now have two loops on the hook *(Fig. 32)*.

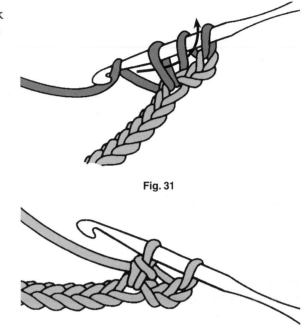

Fig. 31

Fig. 32

Step 4: Bring the yarn over the hook from back to front and draw through both loops on the hook *(Fig. 33)*.

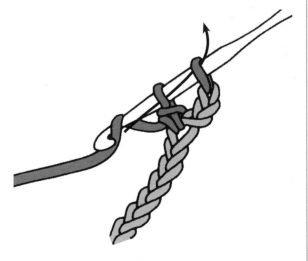

Fig. 33

You have now completed one double crochet; one loop remains on the hook (*Fig. 34*).

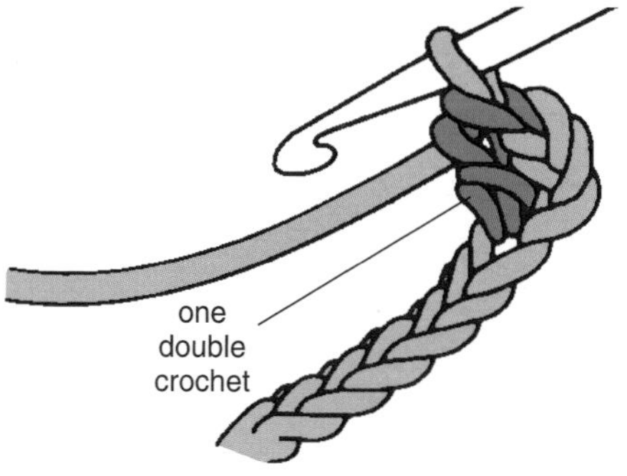

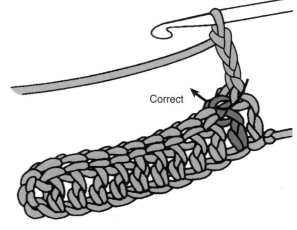

one double crochet

Fig. 34

In remaining chains, work as follows:

Step 1: Bring the yarn over the hook from back to front and insert the hook in the next chain.

Step 2: Bring the yarn over the hook from back to front and draw it through the chain and up onto the working area of the hook; you now have three loops on the hook.

Step 3: Bring the yarn over the hook from back to front and draw through the first two loops on the hook. You now have two loops on the hook.

Step 4: Bring the yarn over the hook from back to front and draw through both loops on the hook.

You have now completed one double crochet; one loop remains on the hook.

After working in each chain across, count your double crochet stitches. There should be 12 of them, counting the first three chain stitches you skipped at the beginning of the row as a double crochet (*Fig. 35*).

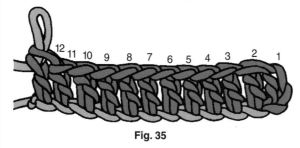

Fig. 35

Hint: In working double crochet on a beginning chain row, the three chains skipped before making the first double crochet are often counted as a double crochet stitch.

Turn the work counterclockwise before beginning row 2.

Here is the way the instructions might be written in a pattern:

Row 1: Ch 14, dc in 4th ch from hook (*beg 3 sk chs count as first dc*) and in each rem ch across, turn.

WORKING ROW 2

To work row 2, you need to bring the yarn or thread up to the correct height for the next row. To raise the yarn, chain three (this is called the beginning chain).

The three chains in the beginning chain just made count as the first double crochet of the new row, so skip the first double crochet and work a double crochet in the second stitch. Be sure to insert hook under top two loops of stitch; Fig. 36a and 36b indicate the correct and incorrect placement of this stitch.

Correct

Fig. 36a

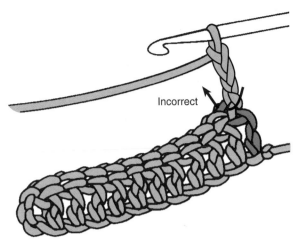

Incorrect

Fig. 36b

Work a double crochet in each remaining stitch across the previous row; at the end of each row, be sure to work the last double crochet in the top of the three skipped chains from the previous row. Be sure to insert hook in the center of the V (and back bar) of the top chain of the beginning chain *(Fig. 37)*. Stop and count your double crochets; there should be 12 stitches. Now, turn.

Fig. 37

Here is the way the instructions might be written in a pattern:

Row 2: Ch 3, dc in each dc across, turn. *(12 dc)*

WORKING ROW 3
Row 3 is worked exactly as you worked row 2.

In a pattern, instructions would read:

Rows 3–6: Rep row 2.

For practice, work three more rows, repeating row 2. At the end of the last row, fasten off the yarn as you did for the single-crochet practice piece. Photo B shows a sample of six rows of double crochet and how to count the stitches and rows. ▧

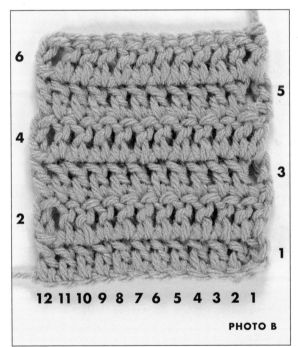

PHOTO B

Half Double Crochet (abbreviated hdc)

Just as its name implies, this stitch eliminates one step of double crochet and works up about half as tall.

WORKING ROW 1

Step 1: Chain 13, bring yarn once over hook from back to front, skip the first two chains, then insert the hook in the third chain from the hook (*Fig. 38*).

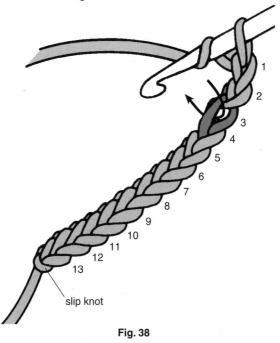

Fig. 38

Remember not to count the loop on the hook as a chain.

Step 2: Bring the yarn over the hook and draw it through the chain stitch and up onto the working area of the hook. You now have three loops on the hook (*Fig. 39*).

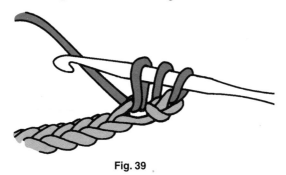

Fig. 39

Step 3: Bring the yarn over the hook and draw it through all three loops on the hook in one motion (*Fig. 40*).

Fig. 40

You have completed one half double crochet; one loop remains on the hook (*Fig. 41*).

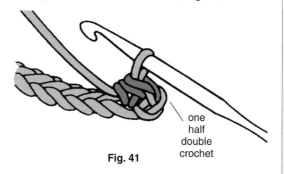

one half double crochet

Fig. 41

In the next chain, work a half double crochet as follows:

Step 1: Bring yarn over hook from back to front, insert hook in next chain.

Step 2: Bring the yarn over the hook and draw it through the chain stitch and up onto the working area of the hook. You now have three loops on the hook.

Step 3: Bring the yarn over the hook yarn and draw it through all three loops on the hook in one motion.

Repeat the previous three steps in each remaining chain across. Stop and count your stitches: You should have 12 half double crochets, counting the first two chains you skipped at the beginning of the row as a half double crochet (*Fig. 42*).

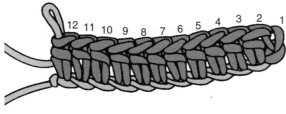

Fig. 42

Turn your work.

If included in a pattern, the instructions would read as follows:

Row 1: Ch 13, hdc in 3rd ch from hook (*beg 2 sk chs count as first hdc*) and in each rem ch across, turn. (*12 hdc*)

WORKING ROW 2

Like double crochet, the beginning chain counts as a stitch in half double crochet (unless your pattern specifies otherwise). Chain two, skip the first half double crochet of the previous row; work a half double crochet in the second stitch (*Fig. 43*) and in each remaining stitch across the previous row. At the end of the row, turn your work.

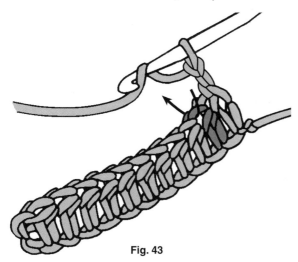

Fig. 43

Here is the way the instructions might be written in a pattern:

Row 2: Ch 2, hdc in each hdc across, turn. (*12 hdc*)

WORKING ROW 3

Row 3 is worked exactly as you worked row 2.

For practice, work three more rows, repeating row 2. Be sure to count your stitches carefully at the end of each row. When the practice rows are completed, fasten off.

Here is the way the instructions might be written in a pattern:

Rows 3–6: Ch 2, hdc in each hdc across, turn. Fasten off at end of last row. (*12 hdc*)

Photo C shows a sample of six rows of half double crochet and how to count the stitches and the rows. ■

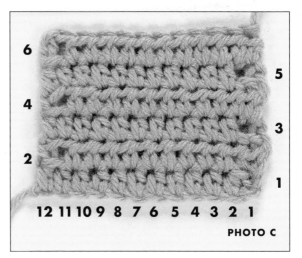

PHOTO C

Treble Crochet (abbreviated tr)

Treble crochet is a tall stitch that works up quickly and is fun to do. To practice, first chain 15 stitches loosely. Then work the first row as follows:

WORKING ROW 1

Step 1: Wrapping from back to front, bring the yarn over the hook twice, skip the first four chains, then insert hook into the fifth chain from the hook (*Fig. 44*).

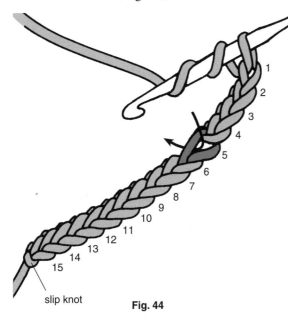

slip knot

Fig. 44

Step 2: Yarn over the hook and draw it through the chain and up onto the working area of the hook; you now have four loops on the hook (*Fig. 45*).

Fig. 45

Step 3: Yarn over the hook and draw it through the first two loops on the hook (*Fig. 46*).

Fig. 46

You now have three loops on the hook (*Fig. 46a*).

Fig. 46a

Step 4: Yarn over the hook again and draw it through the next two loops on the hook (*Fig. 47*).

Fig. 47

Two loops remain on the hook (*Fig. 47a*).

Fig. 47a

Step 5: Yarn over the hook and draw it through both remaining loops on the hook *(Fig 48)*.

Fig. 48

You have now completed one treble crochet; one loop remains on the hook *(Fig. 49)*.

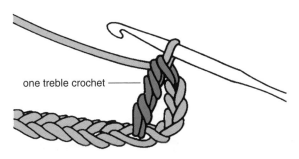

one treble crochet

Fig. 49

In the next chain stitch, work a treble crochet as follows:

Step 1: Wrapping from back to front, bring the yarn over the hook twice; insert hook in the next chain *(Fig. 50)*.

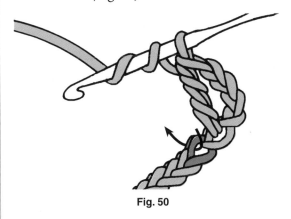

Fig. 50

Step 2: Yarn over the hook and draw it through the chain stitch and up onto the working area of the hook; you now have four loops on the hook.

Step 3: Yarn over the hook again and draw it through the first two loops on the hook; you now have three loops on the hook.

Step 4: Yarn over the hook again and draw it through the next two loops on the hook; two loops remain on the hook.

Step 5: Yarn over the hook again and draw it through both remaining loops on the hook.

Repeat the previous five steps in each remaining chain across.

When you've worked a treble crochet in the last chain, count your stitches: There should be 12 of them, counting the first four chains you skipped at the beginning of the row as a treble crochet *(Fig. 51)*; turn work.

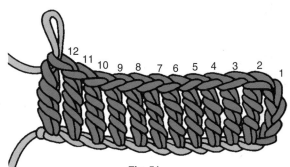

Fig. 51

Hint: In working the first row of treble crochet, the four chains skipped before making the first treble crochet are often counted as a treble crochet stitch.

Here is the way the instructions might be written in a pattern:

Row 1: Ch 15, tr in 5th ch from hook *(beg 4 sk chs count as first tr)* and in each rem ch across, turn. *(12 tr)*

WORKING ROW 2

Chain four to bring your yarn up to the correct height and to count as the first stitch of the row. Skip the first stitch and work a treble crochet in the second stitch *(Fig. 52)*.

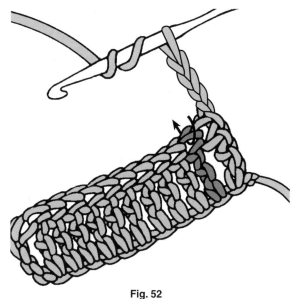

Fig. 52

Work a treble crochet in each remaining stitch across previous row; be sure to work last treble crochet in the top of the beginning chain from the previous row. Count stitches to be sure you still have 12 stitches and turn the work.

Hint: Remember to work last treble crochet of each row in beginning chain of previous row. Missing this stitch in the beginning chain is a common error.

Here is the way the instructions might be written in a pattern:

Row 2: Ch 4, tr in each tr across, turn. *(12 tr)*

WORKING ROW 3

Work row 3 exactly as you worked row 2.

For practice, work three more rows, repeating row 2. At the end of the last row, fasten off the yarn.

Here is the way the instructions might be written in a pattern:

Rows 3–6: Rep row 2. Fasten off at end of last row. *(12 tr)*

Photo D shows a sample of six rows of treble crochet and how to count the stitches and rows. ■

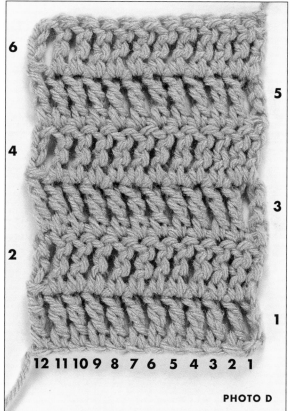

PHOTO D

Slip Stitch (abbreviated sl st)

This is the shortest of all crochet stitches and is really more a technique than a stitch. Slip stitches are usually used to move yarn across a group of stitches without adding height, or they may be used to join work.

MOVING YARN ACROSS STITCHES
WORKING ROW 1

Chain 10, then double crochet in the fourth chain from hook and in each remaining chain across. Turn work.

If you were working an actual pattern, the wording would be as follows:

Row 1: Ch 10, dc in 4th ch from hook and in each rem ch across, turn.

WORKING ROW 2

On the next row, you are going to slip stitch in each of the first four stitches before beginning to work double crochet again. Instead of making three chains for the beginning chain as you would usually do for a second row of double crochet, this time just chain one. The beginning chain-one does not count as a stitch; therefore, insert hook under both loops of first stitch, wrap the yarn over your hook and draw it through both loops of stitch and the loop on the hook (*Fig 53*); one slip stitch made.

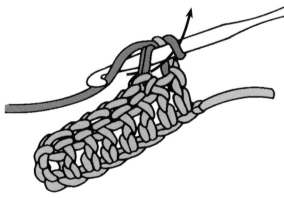

Fig. 53

Work a slip stitch in the same manner in each of the next three stitches. Now we're going to finish the row in double crochet; chain three to get yarn at the right height (the chain-three counts as a double crochet), then work a double crochet in each of the remaining stitches. Look at your work and see how we moved the thread across with slip stitches, adding very little height (*Fig. 54*).

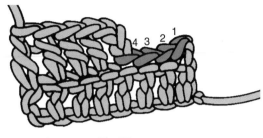

Fig. 54

Fasten off and save the sample.

If written in a pattern, row 2 would be worded as follows:

Row 2: Ch 1, sl st in each of next 4 dc, ch 3 (*counts as first dc*), dc in each rem dc across. (*5 dc*)

Fasten off.

Hint: When working slip stitches across stitches, always work very loosely.

JOINING STITCHES
JOINING A CHAIN INTO A CIRCLE

Chain six, then insert hook through the first chain you made (next to the slip knot—*Fig. 55*).

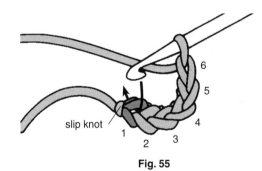

Fig. 55

Wrap the yarn over your hook and draw it through the chain and through the loop on the hook; you have now joined the six chains into a circle or a ring. This is the way many motifs, such as granny squares, are started.

Fasten off and cut the yarn. Keep this practice piece as a sample.

If this instruction appeared in a pattern, it would be worded as follows:

Rnd 1: Ch 6, join in 6th ch from hook to form ring. Fasten off.

JOINING THE END OF A ROUND TO THE BEGINNING OF THE SAME ROUND

Chain six, then join with a slip stitch in first chain you made to form a ring. Chain three, work 11 double crochet in the ring, insert the hook in the third chain of the beginning chain-three *(Fig. 56)*, wrap the yarn over the hook and draw it through the chain and through the loop on the hook. You have now joined the round. Fasten off and cut yarn. Keep this practice piece as a sample.

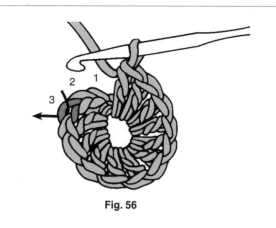

Fig. 56

Here is the way the instructions might be written in a pattern:

Rnd 1: Ch 3, 11 dc in ring, join with sl st in 3rd ch of beg ch-3. Fasten off. ▪

chapter two
weights & measures

Successful crochet depends on knowing which hook size works best with what yarn weight. Sometimes the units of size and measurement given in your patterns don't make sense, so we've got a variety of handy conversion charts to help you understand them.

Standard Yarn Weight System

Weight category	Yarn label symbol	Yarns in category	Recommended hook size(s)	Suggested gauge (ranges in sc to 4")
Lace	0 LACE	Lace	Steel 8/1.50mm to B/1/2.25mm	32–42 sts
Super Fine	1 SUPER FINE	Sock, Fingering, Baby	B/1/2.25mm to E/4/3.5mm	21–32 sts
Fine	2 FINE	Baby, Sport	E/4/3.5mm to 7/4.5mm	16–20 sts
Light	3 LIGHT	DK, Light Worsted	7/4.5mm to I/9/5.5mm	12–17 sts
Medium	4 MEDIUM	Worsted, Afghan, Aran	I/9/5.5mm to K/10½/6.5mm	11–14 sts
Bulky	5 BULKY	Chunky, Craft, Rug, Eyelash	K/10½/6.5mm to M/13/9mm	8–11 sts
Super Bulky	6 SUPER BULKY	Super Chunky, Roving	M/N/13/9mm and larger	5–9 sts

U.S./U.K./Australian Yarn Equivalents

U.S. yarn weight category	U.K./Australia ply category
Lace	2-ply
Super fine, sock, fingering	3-ply
Fine, baby, sport	4-ply
Light, DK, light worsted	6–8-ply
Medium, worsted	10–12-ply
Bulky, chunky	14–16-ply
Super bulky, super chunky	20-ply and up

Metric Chart

INCHES INTO MILLIMETRES & CENTIMETRES (Rounded off slightly)

inches	mm	cm	inches	cm	inches	cm	inches	cm
1/8	3	0.3	5	12.5	21	53.5	38	96.5
1/4	6	0.6	5 1/2	14	22	56	39	99
3/8	10	1	6	15	23	58.5	40	101.5
1/2	13	1.3	7	18	24	61	41	104
5/8	15	1.5	8	20.5	25	63.5	42	106.5
3/4	20	2	9	23	26	66	43	109
7/8	22	2.2	10	25.5	27	68.5	44	112
1	25	2.5	11	28	28	71	45	114.5
1 1/4	32	3.2	12	30.5	29	73.5	46	117
1 1/2	38	3.8	13	33	30	76	47	119.5
1 3/4	45	4.5	14	35.5	31	79	48	122
2	50	5	15	38	32	81.5	49	124.5
2 1/2	65	6.5	16	40.5	33	84	50	127
3	75	7.5	17	43	34	86.5		
3 1/2	90	9	18	46	35	89		
4	100	10	19	48.5	36	91.5		
4 1/2	115	11.5	20	51	37	94		

Measurement Conversions

Unit	Equivalent
1 gram (g)	.035 ounce (oz)
1 kilogram (k)	2.20 pounds (lbs)
50 grams (g)	1.75 ounces (oz)
1 ounce (oz)	28.35 grams (g)
1 pound (lb)	.45 kilogram (k)
1 centimeter (cm)	.39 inch (")
1 meter (m)	39.37 inches (")
1 inch (")	2.54 centimeters (cm)
1 yard (yd)	.9144 meter (m) 36 inches (") 91.44 centimeters (cm)

General Conversions for Generic Yarns

Note: *Yardages given are approximations; weight to length conversions are affected by fiber content.*

Lace (lace) weight: 1 ounce = 232–400 yds

Super fine (sock, fingering, baby) weight: 1 ounce = 170–175 yards

Fine (sport) weight: 1 ounce = 90–100 yards

Light (light worsted) weight: 1 ounce = 70–75 yards

Medium (worsted) weight: 1 ounce = 50 yards

Bulky (chunky) weight: 1 ounce = 30–35 yards

Super bulky (super chunky) weight: 1 ounce = 16–23 yards

Skill Levels

BEGINNER	EASY	INTERMEDIATE	EXPERIENCED
Beginner projects for first-time crocheters using basic stitches. Minimal shaping.	Easy projects using basic stitches, repetitive stitch patterns, simple color changes and simple shaping and finishing.	Intermediate projects with a variety of stitches, mid-level shaping and finishing.	Experienced projects using advanced techniques and stitches, detailed shaping and refined finishing.

chapter three
reading patterns

If you sometimes feel intimidated by the "code" language of crochet, help is at hand! From abbreviations and symbols to special terms and phrases, we'll help you understand the structure and decipher the vernacular of crochet instructions.

Abbreviations & Symbols

Reading a crochet pattern is much like reading a recipe. Both recipes and crochet patterns state the materials needed and give instructions on how to turn the materials into a finished product. Both assume you know certain terms and abbreviations unique to that discipline. So if you can follow a recipe, you can follow a crochet pattern. You just need to learn the lingo.

ABBREVIATIONS

beg .... begin/begins/beginning

bpdc .... back post double crochet

bphdc .... back post half double crochet

bpsc .... back post single crochet

bptr .... back post treble crochet

CC .... contrasting color

ch(s) .... chain(s)

ch- .... refers to chain or space previously made (i.e. ch-1 space)

ch sp(s) .... chain space(s)

cl(s) .... cluster(s)

cm .... centimeter(s)

dc .... double crochet (singular/plural)

dc dec .... double crochet 2 or more stitches together, as indicated

dec .... decrease/decreases/decreasing

dtr .... double treble crochet

ext .... extended

fpdc .... front post double crochet

fphdc .... front post half double crochet

fpsc .... front post single crochet

fptr .... front post treble crochet

g .... gram(s)

hdc .... half double crochet

hdc dec .... half double crochet 2 or more stitches together, as indicated

inc .... increase/increases/increasing

lp(s) .... loops(s)

MC .... main color

mm .... millimeter(s)

oz .... ounce(s)

pc .... popcorn(s)

rem .... remain/remains/remaining

rep(s) .... repeat(s)

rnd(s) .... round(s)

RS .... right side

sc .... single crochet (singular/plural)

sc dec .... single crochet 2 or more stitches together, as indicated

sk .... skip/skipped/skipping

sl st(s) .... slip stitch(es)

sp(s) .... space(s)/spaced

st(s) .... stitch(es)

tog .... together

tr .... treble crochet

trtr .... triple treble

WS .... wrong side

yd(s) .... yard(s)

yo .... yarn over

SPECIAL STITCH ABBREVIATIONS

Ending decrease ....end dec

Ending increase...............................end inc

Large shell.......................................lg shell

Long double crochet.......................lng dc

Long single crochet ....lng sc

Medium shell....................................med shell

Small shell..sm shell

SYMBOLS

( ) **Work instructions within parentheses in place directed; used to indicate collective stitch groups worked as one procedure in the same place; used for additional or clarifying information, indicated in italic text.**

Examples:

(3 dc, ch 2, 3 dc) in next corner sp

(sc, hdc, 3 dc, hdc, sc) in next st

(48 dc)—indicates stitch count at end of row or round

(88 [94, 106, 112]) sc—indicates multiple stitch counts for additional garment sizes or rows/rounds

Row 1 (RS):—indicates front of work

[ ] **Repeat instructions within brackets as directed; also used to indicate additional or clarifying information.**

Examples:

[dc in next dc, cl in next ch-1 sp] 5 times

[dc in each of next 3 dc, shell in next shell] across to next corner

Child's 2 [4, 6, 8]—indicates multiple finished garment sizes

Rows 29–36 [31–38, 31–40]:—indicates additional rows/rounds for multiple sizes

Sc in each of next 4 [5, 6] sts—indicates additional instructions for multiple sizes

{ } **Repeat instructions within braces as directed; used to indicate multiple repeats of stitch patterns that are part of a collective stitch group contained within parentheses only.**

Examples:

({dc, ch 1} 5 times, dc) in next ch-2 sp

({sc, ch 3} 3 times, hdc, ch 2, hdc, ch 3, {sc, ch 3} twice, sc) all in corner sp

* **Repeat instructions following a single asterisk or between two single asterisks as directed.**

Examples:

Ch 1, sc in first sc, *ch 1, sk next ch-1 sp, sc in next sc, rep from * across.

*Sc in each of next 2 sts, 2 sc in next st, rep from * around.

Ch 1, *(sc, dc, tr, dc, sc) in next ch-2 sp, ch 2, sc in next hdc, ch 2, rep from * 6 times.

Ch 1, sc in same st, sc in each of next 22 sc, *[2 sc in next sc, sc in each of next 3 sc] twice, 2 sc in next sc*, sc in each of next 23 sc, rep between * once, join in beg sc.

Dc in each of next 3 sts, [shell in next ch-1 sp] twice, rep between * 4 times.

** **This symbol has two uses, as follows:**

1. Repeat instructions between or from double asterisks as directed, usually in combination with a set of single-asterisk instructions.

Examples:

Ch 1, *(sc, 2 dc, ch 1, 2 dc, sc) in corner sp, (sc, 2 dc, sc) in next ch-3 sp, **ch 1, sk next ch-1, sl st in next ch-1 sp, ch 1, sk next ch-1**, [(sc, dc, ch 1, sc) in next ch-3 sp] 3 times, rep between ** once, (sc, 2 dc, sc) in next ch-3 sp, rep from * 3 times, join.

Sl st in next st, sl st in corner ch sp, ch 3, dc in same sp, *[(picot, 2 dc) 3 times in same sp, **2 dc in next ch sp, (picot, 2 dc) twice in same sp, rep from ** across to next corner ch sp], 2 dc in next ch sp, rep from * twice, rep between [ ] once, join.

2. Work a partial set of repeat instructions as indicated by double asterisks.

Examples:

*Ch 3, (sc, ch 3, sc) in next ch-2 sp, ch 3**, V-st in next dc, rep from * 3 times, ending last rep at **.

2 sc in first st, *ch 2, sk next st, cl in next st, ch 2, sk next st**, 2 sc in next st, rep from * around, ending last rep at **.

◊**Repeat instructions between or from diamonds as directed, usually in combination with single-asterisk instructions.**

Examples:

Ch 1, sc in same sc, *◊sk next ch-2 sp, [sc in next sc, ch 3] 4 times◊, sc in next sc, sk next ch-2 sp, sc in next sc, rep from * 6 times, rep between ◊◊ once, sc in next sc.

({Sl st, ch 3} 3 times, sl st) in corner sp, ch 3, sk next 3 sts, (sl st, ch 3, sl st) in next st, ch 3, sk next 3 sts, (sl st, ch 3, sl st) in next ch-2 sp, ◊ch 3, sk next 3 sts, sl st in next st, ch 3, sk next 3 sts, (sl st, ch 3, sl st) in next ch-2 sp, rep from ◊ across to last 7 sts before corner sp, ch 3, sk next 3 sts, (sl st, ch 3, sl st) in next st, ch 3, sk next 3 sts, rep from * around, join. ■

pretty par

DESIGN BY **JEWDY LAMBERT**

SKILL LEVEL
INTERMEDIATE

FINISHED SIZE
9 inches tall after felting

MATERIALS
- Medium (worsted) weight wool yarn:
  9 oz/450 yds/255g periwinkle
  5 oz/250 yds/142g each yellow-green, leaf green, yellow, rose and purple
- Size I/9/5.5mm crochet hook or size needed to obtain gauge
- Tapestry needle

GAUGE
14 sts = 4 inches; 10 rows = 4 inches

PATTERN NOTES
Avoid superwash or machine-washable wools

Join with slip stitch as indic... otherwise state...

Chain-...
first d...

SPECIA
Popcorn (p
  drop lp f...
  group, pu...

INSTRUC
BAG
FRONT BO
Row 1: With pe...
from hook and...

Rows 2-20: Ch 1,

FRONT SHAPIN
Row 1: Ch 1, sk first...
working in b...

Good Patterns

Pattern-writing style may vary between publications; but as a general rule, good crochet instructions will include the following items:

- The gauge as worked and measured in pattern stitch. If more than one pattern stitch is used, the gauge should state which stitch was used to determine the gauge.

- The complete size information, including schematics, if applicable. Having the finished measurements can help determine which finished size to make, and a schematic can help determine where size adjustments need to be made.

- A complete list of materials, including the complete yarn information, yarn weight category, amount of ounces, yards and grams per unit, suggested size and type of hook (regular, steel, afghan, double-ended), tapestry needle, buttons/trims, etc.

- Easy-to-read type and standard abbreviations. Patterns are easier to work if the stitcher doesn't have to learn new abbreviations or struggle with hard-to-read print. If you come across a pattern that is hard to read, it may be helpful to enlarge the pattern at a copy center.

- A list of abbreviations, especially any special abbreviations/techniques. This may include techniques like cables, post stitches, etc.

- The pattern-stitch multiple, if applicable. If you are going to make size adjustments, knowing the stitch multiple is crucial.

- Special pattern notes for finishing, joining, beginning chains, etc., if applicable— especially if specific pattern elements have to be worked in specific places.

A WORD ABOUT YARNS & THREADS

Patterns generally specify the yarn or thread used for the photographed projects, but you may choose to substitute yarn or thread of the same weight that will work to the same gauge and has a fiber content that is suitable for the project *(see the article, Yarn Substitution Made Easy, beginning on page 89).*

A WORD ABOUT ZEROS

In patterns which include various sizes, zeros are sometimes necessary. For example, "Dc in each of next 0 (0, 2) sts" means if you are making the one of the two smaller sizes, you would do nothing, and if you are making the largest size, you would double crochet in each of the next two stitches.

A WORD ABOUT SWATCHES

Patterns generally don't tell you how to make a swatch before beginning. This is an important step, especially for garments and other items that need to be made to specific measurements. See the article, The Importance of Gauge, on pages 38–41 for great information on making swatches.

A WORD ABOUT MISTAKES

Despite everyone's best efforts, published patterns may contain mistakes. If you think you have found an error in the pattern, contact the publisher with your concern. There may be other people who have found the same error. ▪

felting

bag

...inning of row or round counts as ...rochet unless otherwise stated.

...CH

...as indicated in instructions, ...k, insert hook in first tr of ...ed lp through, ch 1.

...s

..., ch 46, sc in 2nd ch ...ch across, turn. *(45 sc)*

...ach st across, turn.

Special Terms & Phrases

Commonly used terms and phrases are given in bold letters; the meaning of each is given directly below it.

at the same time
You are going to be doing two things at once. For example, the neckline and shoulder shaping often occur at the same time.

Back, Left Front, Right Front, Left Shoulder, etc.
These are the names of garment pieces as they are worn. The left shoulder is the part that will be on the wearer's left shoulder. If you have trouble remembering which piece you are working on, hold it up to your body and see which way it fits. **Hint:** Garment piece names are usually capitalized.

back, front
These terms aren't capitalized as they are general guidelines to refer to which side of the piece you are looking at as you work. The "back" of the stitch is the side away from you. The "front" is the side closest to you.

ball band/yarn band
This is the identification label on each ball, skein or hank of yarn (*see sample label below*). It contains information on fiber content, weight, yardage, care instructions and suggested gauge.

Balls and skeins can generally be used as is, but hanks typically are rewound using a yarn swift.

block
Blocking is a very important step in giving your projects a finished look, and it can solve a multitude of problems. (*See Blocking Basics on page 150.*)

Hank

Ball   Skein

body is worked in one piece to underarm
You start with enough stitches to work the Front and the Back of the garment and work the Front and Back as one piece until you divide for the armhole openings.

continue working in pattern/continue in established pattern
Keep on doing whatever you have been doing: increasing, decreasing, working in stitch pattern, whatever the preceding instructions have said.

draw up lp (loop)/pull up lp (loop)
When given this instruction, wrap the yarn around the hook and pull it through the stitch, chain or space indicated. This term is often preceded by "insert hook in st (stitch)/ ch (chain)/sp (space) and"

ease
This is the difference between the wearer's body measurements and the finished measurements of the garment. Ease is necessary for a good fit, but it varies according to the style of the garment.

ending with WS/RS (wrong-side/ right-side) row

These instructions tell you which side your last row should face.

fasten off

After the last stitch is worked, pull working yarn through last stitch to secure it.

Finished Measurements

These measurements are given at the beginning of the pattern. When your project is finished and blocked, your project's measurements should match those given for the size you made.

front lp (loop) and back lp (loop):

The front loop is the loop toward you at the top of the stitch. The back loop is the loop away from you at the top of the stitch. *(See illustration.)*

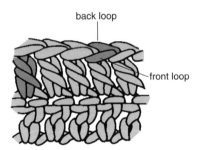

join

You will connect the end of the current round with the beginning of the same round. Joining often uses a slip stitch.

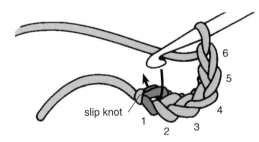

join color

When instructed to "join color," you will join a new color of yarn as instructed, and you will work with this color until otherwise stated. Follow instructions for previous color (i.e., fasten off, drop, etc.) To join a new color,

work the last stitch to be done in the working color until two loops remain on the hook *(Photo A)*. Draw new color through the two loops on hook. Drop working color *(Photo B)* and continue to work in the new color.

PHOTO A

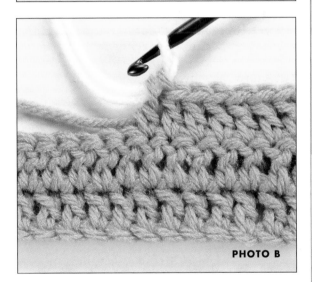

PHOTO B

left-hand side

This means the side nearest your left hand as you are working.

or size needed to obtain gauge

If your first attempt at getting the gauge results in too many stitches or too few stitches, change hook sizes until you get the gauge called for in the pattern. If you have too many stitches, use a larger hook. If you have too few stitches, use a smaller hook.

post

This is the vertical body of the stitch.

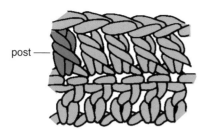

post

pull lp (loop) through/draw lp (loop through

When given this instruction, you will use the loop that you have drawn/pulled up to complete the indicated stitch.

reverse/reversing shaping

When working on a garment, you are often given the instruction to "Make 2." If you are told to, "reverse shaping" or "make 2nd piece reversing shaping," in essence, you are being told to work a mirror image of the first of the two. On the mirrored piece, you will need to work the shaping on the opposite side from the piece you just worked in order for the placement to be correct.

right-hand side

This means the side nearest your right hand as you are working.

RS (right side), WS (wrong side)

These terms refer to the side of the project that will be on the outside or the inside after the project is finished.

schematic

This is a graphic representation of a finished project, such as the drawings shown below for a jacket, showing finished dimensions.

selvage stitch

A selvage stitch is a stitch at the beginning or end of a row that will be used for seaming or other finishing. It is not part of the pattern stitch. Not all patterns contain selvage stitches, and many patterns that do contain selvage stitches do not identify them as such.

stitch multiple

The stitch multiple is the number of stitches used to complete a repeat of a pattern. For example, a stitch multiple of 8 + 3 would mean that the pattern is worked on a multiple of eight stitches, plus three extra/selvage stitches. Thus, it could be worked on 19 sts (16 + 3), 27 sts (24 + 3), 35 sts (32 + 3), etc.

swatch

A swatch is a small piece of stitching worked according to gauge in order to determine whether or not the finished size and finished measurements can be reached with the yarn and hook being used. It is crucial to make a swatch for most projects, garments in particular.

work even

This means to continue to work in the pattern on the same number of established stitches as indicated, without working any increases or decreases.

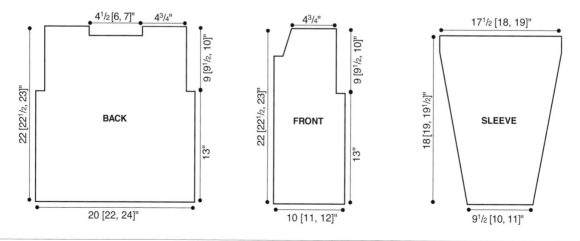

chapter four
special helps

Once you have a good handle on the
fundamentals of crocheting, a few special
helps can take you beyond the basics to
enhance your crochet experience and
improve the quality of your work.

The Importance of Gauge

Gauge is the number of stitches per inch and the number of rows per inch you need to get when stitching with a particular weight of yarn and a specific crochet hook.

Because the hook size stated in the pattern instructions is just a suggestion, and because each crocheter handles the yarn slightly differently, gauge can vary from person to person even when they are using identical hooks and yarns. Making a proper gauge swatch at the beginning of a project saves both time and money. Learning why and how to make a proper swatch is a crucial step toward enhancing a crocheter's confidence and ability to make a successful project every time.

WHAT IS A SWATCH?

A swatch is a small sample of crocheted fabric made in the same yarn and stitch pattern you intend to use for your project. Learning how to make a proper swatch is a crucial step toward enhancing both your confidence as a crocheter and ability to make a successful project every time. If done properly, it can provide a wealth of information and save you time and money. "Swatching" is the verb that describes the process of making the swatch. "Gauge swatch" and "swatch" are often used synonymously, but it is important to think of a swatch as more than just a way to measure gauge. So, this article uses the term "swatch" exclusively to get you in the right frame of mind.

WHY BOTHER?

Why bother doing a swatch at all? Why not just start stitching and see what happens? A swatch can give you a lot of useful information before you start your project. Sometimes the information you get from a swatch will determine whether or not you will continue with the project as written, make adjustments or even abandon the project for something totally different. Learning the pitfalls of a project from a 4- to 6-inch square swatch can save time and money in comparison to finding the same hazards after working a much larger piece.

HERE'S WHAT YOU'LL LEARN

The standard way to write the gauge information is as follows:

20 sts = 4 inches; 20 rows = 4 inches

The part of the gauge statement that is important to you is the measurement of 20 sts and 20 rows over four inches, or five single crochet stitches and five rows per inch. If a pattern calls for more that one hook size, only one of the hooks will be used to get the stated gauge. If this is the case, the gauge will be written as follows:

Size H hook: 20 sts = 4 inches; 20 rows = 4 inches

INCORRECT GAUGE

Let's look at an example of what may happen when you work to a different gauge than that given in the pattern. Let's say that you are using a sweater pattern that calls for a gauge of 12 single crochets = 4 inches, or 3 single crochets per inch, and you want to make a sweater with a finished bust measurement of 44 inches. If you start stitching and you get $3\frac{1}{2}$ single crochets per inch, your finished sweater will be $37\frac{1}{2}$ inches around, or $6\frac{1}{2}$ inches too small! If you worked the same sweater with a gauge of $2\frac{1}{2}$ single crochets per inch, the finished sweater would be $52\frac{3}{4}$ inches around, or $8\frac{3}{4}$ inches too large! You can see that being just half a stitch off per inch can make a huge difference.

Can you see that it makes much more sense to take the time and effort necessary to match the gauge at the beginning of a project than to find out your gauge is off after hundreds of stitches have been worked? See Swatch How-Tos on page 40 for more information on measuring gauge.

CLEANING

If you plan to wash your finished project, it is best to wash your swatch too, as gauge can change dramatically after washing. Some yarns will shrink or stretch out of shape after washing, and some colors will run. Many crocheters have been disappointed to find that their red-and-white striped afghan turned into a red-and-pink striped afghan after its first wash.

YARN CHARACTERISTICS/DURABILITY

Make observations as you stitch and after you wash the swatch. Does the color rub off on your hands? Does the yarn make you sneeze or break out? Does it shed? Does it pill or stretch?

Try abusing the swatch a bit. Put it in the bottom of your pocketbook or your child's backpack. Take it out after a week and examine it. Is the fabric going to stand up to its intended use?

FABRIC

The fabric that is produced when the yarn is stitched to the gauge given in the pattern is what the designer considers to be the perfect tension for that particular yarn for that particular project. The fabric will have a certain "hand" and "drape," which are characteristics that describe how the stitching feels and how it hangs.

For example, a stuffed animal is usually worked to a tighter gauge than a sweater since the animal's fabric needs to be tight enough so that the stuffing will not show through or fall out. A sweater worked with the same yarn at the same gauge would probably be so stiff as to be unwearable.

COMFORT

If you are planning to make a garment that will be worn next to the skin, do the "underwear test." Wear the swatch next to your skin for a day.

STITCH COMPATIBILITY

There is more than one type of stitch compatibility. In this case, stitch compatibility has to do with the relationship between the stitch and the stitcher. When you're trying out a new-to-you stitch pattern, a swatch can help you decide if you want to complete the project. Is the stitch pattern too difficult? Is it too boring? Is it neither, but just annoying to work?

FINISHING TECHNIQUES

Even though you are just beginning a project, you need to begin thinking of finishing. What kind of edging will this project have? Where will the edging be worked? How will the project be put together? What size buttons do I need? Work out bugs and practice seaming and edging on the swatch before moving on to the finished product. Work the button bands on the swatch, then take the swatch with you to purchase the perfect button.

YARN AMOUNTS

If you do not work to the same gauge as the instructions, you may find yourself running out of yarn. Pattern instructions give the amount of yarn used for that project in a certain size in the given gauge, so while you may not be worried about finished size, you should be concerned about having adequate yarn to complete the project.

SOME TIPS

Don't be discouraged if a swatch turns out to be a disaster. Swatching can be a trial-and-error process. If your swatch doesn't turn out well, don't think of it as a mistake. Think of it as a learning experience.

WHEN SWATCHING DOES NOT MATTER

You've read this far, hoping for a hint that swatching really doesn't matter. You're in luck. There actually are a few instances when a swatch won't help. A swatch wouldn't help in the following instances:

- When making small objects with relatively large yarn—a swatch would be as big or bigger than the actual finished project. Examples: Christmas ornaments, small home decor items.

- When you have plenty of yarn, you don't anticipate laundering the item, and when the finished size doesn't matter.

A FINAL WORD OF ADVICE

A swatch is important, but don't make the mistake of relying on it completely. Sometimes stitches will become more relaxed as the stitcher learns the pattern. Measure your work as you progress in case the gauge on a larger piece changes. Also, weight and gravity may do their work on a larger piece, resulting in a different gauge.

SWATCH HOW-TOS
GETTING STARTED

- Swatch in the stitch pattern called for in the gauge information. Don't assume that plain double crochet will yield the same gauge as a double-crochet-based stitch pattern.

- Whether or not you decide to use the yarn suggested in the materials list, you need to swatch using the exact yarn in the same color that you plan to use for your project. Different colors of the same yarn may work up differently. Use all the colors together in the same proportion that the project requires.

- Use the same hook that you plan to use for you project. Hook styles and sizes vary, even within a particular size. Don't assume that your gauge is the same with a size G Susan Bates hook as with a size G Boye hook, as shown in the photos below.

- After you have worked a few rows, measure over at least 2 inches to see if you are in the ballpark. If you realize your gauge is way off, you'll probably need to change hook sizes. Start over with a different size hook and a new swatch—don't change hook sizes mid-swatch.

- Make an adequate-size swatch. The thicker the yarn, the bigger the swatch must be. Your swatch should be a minimum of 4 inches square for any fiber but the thinnest cotton thread. For cotton threads, a 6-inch square is more accurate.

- Work in the same direction required by the project whether you are working in the round or back and forth in rows. Most people get a different gauge when working in the round.

- As you work, make sure to jot down notes of how many stitches were on your beginning chain, how many stitches are in the width of your swatch and how many rows or rounds you have worked. Note yarn name, color and hook size and brand.

- Label your swatch with this information, even if you have a fantastic memory. Small hang tags are great for this purpose.

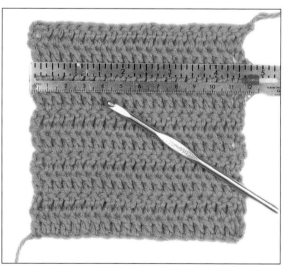

21 double crochet stitches and 10 rows worked with a Susan Bates size G hook.

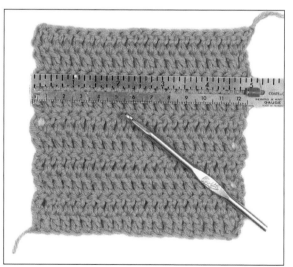

21 double crochet stitches and 10 rows worked with a Boye size G hook.

- Relax! Your gauge may change as you become more comfortable with the stitch pattern. Just stitch at a comfortable tension—don't try to change the tension to match a given gauge.

- Pay attention to your beginning edge. Sometimes you will need to work the foundation chain with a larger hook. Practice on your swatch until you are happy with the result. It is much easier to correct the problem on your swatch than to try to fix a too-tight chain on a finished project.

- Allow the swatch to rest for a half an hour, and then measure and take note of your "before" gauge. Sometimes gauge changes after washing and blocking. Making a note of the gauge right off the hook allows you to compare the "before" and "after" effect of blocking. The "after" gauge is the one that matters for the final fitting, but if it is substantially different from your "working" or "before" gauge, you may be nervous about the finished size of your piece. If you have made note of the changes that will take place, you can reassure yourself as you work that the working gauge is indeed correct.

- Treat the swatch the same way you plan to treat your finished item. If you plan to wash your project, wash your swatch. Use the same washing and drying method on the swatch that you plan to use on the finished product.

- Block the swatch (see Blocking Basics on page 150).

MEASURING
- Use a ruler, yardstick or tape measure.

- Place the blocked swatch on a table and place the ruler on top of the swatch. Allow the swatch to lie as is. Do not rearrange it to make it fit the gauge you want.

- Do not measure edge stitches as they can be distorted.

- Measure at least 4 inches worth of stitches. Some rulers are not accurate between the end and the 1 inch mark, and it's better to be safe than sorry.

- Measure across as many stitches as possible. Count the number of stitches and divide by the number of inches for your "per inch gauge." Round to the nearest hundredth of an inch. For example, if you count 17 stitches over 6 inches, your gauge is approximately 2.83 stitches per inch ($17 \div 6$ = approximately 2.83). If possible, take the same measurement elsewhere on the same swatch and compare the two. If they are different, take an average. Note your findings.

- If a row gauge is given, repeat the above step, measuring in the other direction.

- Now look at your notes. If you have too few stitches per inch, make a swatch using a smaller hook size. If you have too many stitches per inch compared to the instructions, make another swatch using a larger hook size. For example, if the pattern calls for 12 sc = 4 inches (3 sc per inch) and your swatch measures 3½ stitches per inch, increase one hook size and make a second swatch following all the rules outlined above.

- If you have trouble getting the right gauge because it seems to be between two hook sizes, try switching hook brands rather than sizes.

- Once you are satisfied that you have determined the correct hook size to give you the gauge in your yarn, make a note of it. If you need to put down the project for a while or need to use the hook for a different project, you don't want to have to go through this process again! ▪

Beginning Chains

The table below indicates the number of beginning chains needed to bring the work up to the level of a stitch at the beginning of a new row. However, don't feel bound by these rules. You may find you need to adjust the number of chains up or down. Those who crochet tighter may need to add a chain, and those who crochet looser may need to subtract a chain in order to keep a tidy edge. You can also adjust the number of chains to create a smooth curve instead of a stair-step edge when shaping. ▧

Stitch used	No. of chains to make at beginning of row
Slip stitch	1
Single crochet	1
Half double crochet	2
Double crochet	3
Treble crochet	4

EXAMPLES

Number of chains to make at beginning of single crochet row.

Number of chains to make at beginning of half double crochet row.

Number of chains to make at beginning of double crochet row.

Number of chains to make at beginning of treble crochet row.

Joining New Yarn or Thread

Never tie or leave knots! In crochet, yarn ends can be easily worked in and hidden because of the density of the stitches. Always leave at least 6 inches when fastening off yarn just used and when joining new yarn.

Whenever possible, join new yarn at the beginning or end of a row. To do this, work the first stitch or the last stitch with the old yarn until two loops remain on the hook; then complete the stitch with the new yarn. (*Fig. 1*)

When you have to join new yarn in the middle

Fig. 1

of a row, work until you have approximately 12 inches of the old yarn remaining. Hold the end of the new yarn behind the working row and, using the old yarn, work several more stitches over the end of the new yarn (*Fig. 2 shown in double crochet*). After doing so, change yarns in stitch as previously explained.

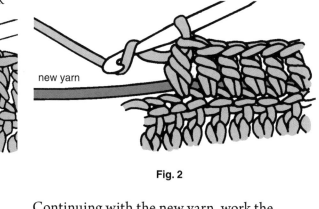

new yarn

Fig. 2

Continuing with the new yarn, work the remaining stitches over the old yarn end. ▧

Increasing & Decreasing

Shaping is done by increasing, which adds stitches to make the crocheted piece wider, or decreasing, which subtracts stitches to make the piece narrower.

Make a practice sample by chaining 15 stitches loosely and working four rows of single crochet with 14 stitches in each row. Turn, and do not fasten off at end of last row. Use this sample swatch to practice the following method of increasing stitches.

INCREASING

To increase one stitch in single, half double, double or treble crochet, simply work two stitches in one stitch. For example, if you are working in single crochet and you need to increase one stitch, you would work one single crochet in the next stitch; then you would work another single crochet in the same stitch.

For practice: On your sample swatch, turn work and chain one. Single crochet in each of the first two stitches; increase in the next stitch by working two single crochet stitches in the next stitch. (*Fig. 1*)

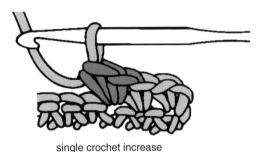

single crochet increase

Fig. 1

Repeat increase in each stitch across row to last two stitches; single crochet in each of next two stitches. Count your stitches: You should have 24 stitches. If you don't have 24 stitches, examine your swatch to see if you have increased in each specified stitch. Rework the row if necessary.

Increases in half double, double and treble crochet are shown in Fig. 2, 3 and 4.

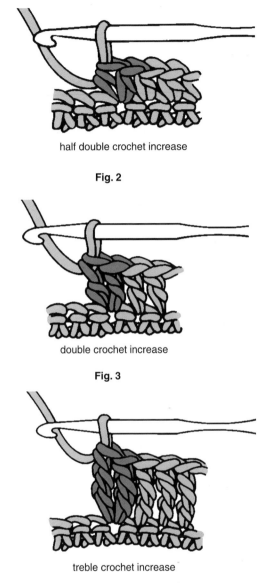

half double crochet increase

Fig. 2

double crochet increase

Fig. 3

treble crochet increase

Fig. 4

Make another practice sample by chaining 15 loosely and working four rows of single crochet. Do not fasten off at end of last row. Use this sample swatch to practice the following methods of decreasing stitches.

DECREASING

With each decrease, you will have one fewer stitch than you had before.

To decrease one stitch in each of the four main crochet stitches, work as follows:

Single crochet decrease (sc dec): [Insert the hook into the next stitch and draw up a loop] twice *(three loops now on hook)*, yarn over hook yarn and draw through all three loops on the hook *(Fig. 5)*, single crochet decrease made. *(Fig. 6)*

Double crochet decrease (dc dec): [Yarn over, insert hook in indicated stitch, yarn over, draw loop through, yarn over, draw through two loops on hook *(Fig. 7)*] twice *(three loops now on hook)*, yarn over, draw through all three loops on hook *(Fig. 8)*, double crochet decrease made *(Fig. 9)*.

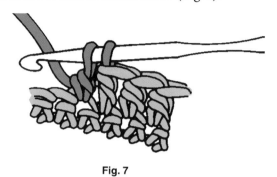

Fig. 7

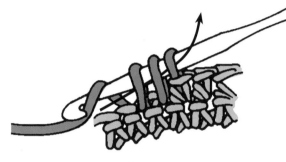

Fig. 5

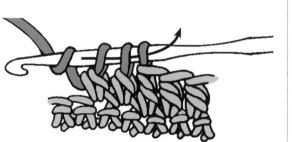

Fig. 8

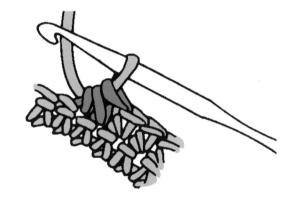

Fig. 6

Fig. 9

Half double crochet decrease (hdc dec):
[Yarn over, insert hook in indicated stitch, yarn over, draw loop through *(Fig. 10)*] twice *(five loops now on hook)*, yarn over, draw through all five loops on hook *(Fig. 11)*, half double crochet decrease made *(Fig. 12)*.

Treble crochet decrease (tr dec): [Yarn over twice, insert hook in indicated stitch, yarn over, draw loop through, (yarn over, draw through two loops on hook) twice *(Fig. 13)*] twice *(three loops now on hook)*, yarn over, draw through all three loops on hook *(Fig. 14)*, treble crochet decrease made *(Fig. 15)*. ■

Fig. 10

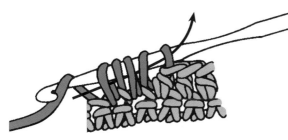

Fig. 11

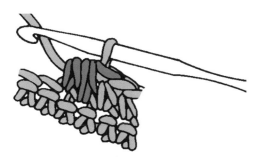

Fig. 12

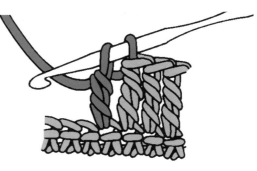

Fig. 13

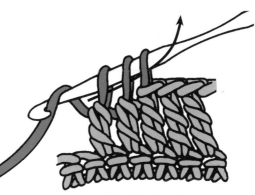

Fig. 14

Fig. 15

Off to a Great Start

Beginning a crochet project successfully is key to ensuring positive results in the finished piece. Here are some helpful tips for getting your crochet projects off to a great start.

If you think about it, a successful crochet project starts even before it actually begins! Preparation and planning are key elements to achieving success in any venture, and crochet is no different.

- Before beginning any new project, it's important to carefully select and purchase all of the necessary materials. It's rather frustrating to get a project nearly finished and then realize you cannot find one or more of the required materials. If you're unsure about any of the materials, read through the pattern to see where and how each material is used. This should clear up any confusion.

- It's also extremely important to make sure you purchase an adequate quantity of each material, as indicated in the pattern. It can be very disheartening to have a partially or nearly completed project and then run out of something, only to discover you can't find the same color or even the same material. It's always a good idea to purchase a little more than the exact quantity the pattern calls for—just to be safe.

- Using a highlighter to mark special stitches and notes in the pattern before beginning is another good way to prevent setbacks. If your pattern uses unfamiliar stitches or stitch patterns, it's a good idea to practice them before starting the actual project so that your work will be picture perfect! It can also be helpful to mark repeat symbols, joining instructions, turns, fasten-offs and color changes.

- To keep your beginning/foundation chain from being too tight (a very common problem in crochet work), try making the beginning/foundation chain with a hook that is one size larger than the hook size called for in the materials. Doing so will help ensure that your beginning edge is the same width as your ending edge.

- Before beginning an intricate motif or stitch pattern while you are working the project, first practice the motif or stitch pattern on its own using yarn and a large hook. This step can often be a big help in helping you familiarize yourself with the motif or stitch pattern, which in turn will prevent you from having to rip out your motif or stitch pattern multiple times.

- Most crocheters have a favorite way of working into the beginning/foundation chain. One way is to insert the hook only through the center of the V. Another way is to insert the hook through the center of the V and under the back bar. Another popular way is to work into the **back bar** *(see illustration)* of each chain.

Back Bar of Chain

These are just a few of the many ways you can ensure a successful journey to the end of your crochet project. ▪

The Countdown

Here is something every crocheter can relate to: crochet distraction. Basically, this refers to the frustration we all experience when we're diligently concentrating on our crochet work, and then we get interrupted. When we come back to our work, we discover that we've lost our place in our stitch work. It's a pain to have to go back and recount stitches, rows or motifs to regain our position.

Checking stitch counts and marking rows and rounds as you go are just a few of the ways that can help eliminate a lot of confusion as well as needless redos. Here are some simple counting tricks that reduce crochet distraction and help you stay on track.

- For intricate patterns, count across the previous row or around the previous round and mark the beginning of each repeat for the next row or round before you work it. That way, if you get interrupted, it won't be hard to pick up right where you left off.

- For projects with lots of pieces, bundle motifs or blocks into stacks of five or 10 for easy, at-a-glance counting.

- Use a "handy adder" (like the kind for adding your groceries while shopping) or handheld tally counter to count rows and rounds. One click for each row or round you complete will help ensure you don't lose your place. A knitting counter also works well for keeping track of rows or rounds.

- The little clips that hold buttons to display cards make great stitch markers when you need to keep a stitch count.

- For long starting chains (for afghans, for example), place a marker every 20 chains or so. If you happen to lose your place, recounting will be so much easier if you've marked groups of chain stitches.

- When working from a stitch chart, it may be easier to convert the information to written instructions first.

- Make a copy of your pattern protector; as you crochet, use a grease pencil to mark on the sheet protector the end of each completed row/round. The pencil wipes right off when you're through!

- Take the time to double-check the stitch count at the end of each row and round throughout the pattern instructions. The time you take to count stitches as you go will be worth it when you think of the time you could spend later pulling out rows of stitches when you discover you were three stitches short 30 rows back!

The next time you're distracted from your crochet, give these ideas a try to help you slip right back into it with ease. Your work will go more smoothly and the time you invest in your projects will really "count"! ▪

Making Sense of Multiples

If, like so many crocheters, you find calculating crochet pattern multiples intimidating, don't despair—there is a way to understand and make sense of it all. Knowing how to read patterns is the answer!

Prior to beginning any crochet project, work a 4 x 4-inch sample swatch in your pattern stitch of choice. Not only will this good habit help to familiarize you with a new pattern—it will also provide you with enough crochet fabric to measure that all-important gauge!

Let's start with the basic pattern for the Multiples Square Pillow *(see page 51)*:

Row 1 (RS): Ch 33, hdc in 3rd ch from hook *(beg 2 sk chs count as first hdc)* and in each ch across, turn. *(32 hdc)*

Row 2 (WS): Ch 1, hdc in first st and each rem st across, turn.

Row 3: Ch 1, hdc in each of first 2 sts, *sk next 2 hdc, **fpdc** *(see Stitch Guide)* around hdc on row below next hdc, hdc in next st, fpdc around hdc on row below first sk st, hdc in each of next 2 hdc, rep from * across, turn.

Row 4: Rep row 2.

Row 5: Ch 1, hdc in each of first 2 sts, *fpdc around next fpdc, **pc** *(instructions for this stitch are in the Special Stitch section on page 51)* in next st, fpdc around next fpdc, hdc in each of next 2 sts, rep from * across, turn.

Row 6: Rep row 2.

This particular pattern is a multiple of **5 + 2**. That means the count of five is the number of stitches required for each **individual** pattern repeat. Rows 1 and 2 of this pattern are calculated to set up the required number of stitches needed for this particular pattern.

THE KEY TO REPEATS

Different publishers use different styles, so—using the example above—let's look at row 3, which not only holds the key, but also is simpler than one might think at first.

Begin by counting the number of stitches you will actually work between the asterisk (*) and the comma (,) that immediately precedes the word "rep." The pattern says to skip the next two *(third and fourth)* half double crochets. Because these two skipped stitches are not worked at the beginning, they are not counted at this point—we are counting stitches only as they are worked. Thus, the next stitch, "fpdc around hdc on row below next hdc" *(counts as the first stitch of the pattern)*, "hdc in next st" *(counts as the second stitch)*, "fpdc around hdc below first sk st" *(counts as the third stitch)* and "hdc in each of next 2 hdc" *(counts as the fourth and fifth stitches)*. We now have a total of five stitches worked between the asterisk and the comma that immediately precedes the word "rep." Thus, our pattern is a multiple of five (stitches) meaning five stitches are required for one full pattern. Repeats are determined by the number of times you wish to work a full pattern.

Now you're thinking, "That was easy enough, but what does the '+ 2' mean?"

The number that follows the plus sign (+) indicates the required number of extra stitches needed to balance the look of a pattern. These stitches are worked at the beginning and/or end of a row. In row 3 of our pattern, notice that the first two stitches before the asterisk—two half double crochet—are included in our single repeat. Two half double crochet stitches are worked between each cable and are also part of the count of five. After finishing the last repeat, you work two more hdc stitches for balance. If you started the pattern at the asterisk, your work would look off-kilter because you would have two half double crochet stitches only on the left side of your work.

Sometimes, you will find there are extra stitches that must be worked **before** you see the asterisk, as well as **after** the comma that immediately precedes the word "rep." Count such stitches one by one and make sure the count is the same as the number following the plus sign.

If you wish to crochet four pattern repeats of this pattern, simply multiply the first number (5) by the number of desired repeats. For example, 4 x 5 = 20 sts, then add the + 2 for the additional stitches needed to balance your work: 20 + 2 = 22 total stitches needed.

UNDERSTANDING PATTERN WORDING

The tricky part of knowing how to understand multiples is in understanding *precisely* what is stated in written instructions. When a pattern states "multiple of 5 + 2" it is referring only to the number of stitches that are worked in one repeat. However, a stitch dictionary for this same pattern is likely to use wording a bit differently and state the following: "chain a multiple of 5 + 3" for the same Popcorn Cable stitch. Why? Because this is the number of chains (not stitches)

needed to set up the first row of the pattern.

If you find a pattern stitch you like that states the multiple number only, how do you know how many beginning chains to make if you simply wish to use the stitch pattern and not the afghan or garment shown in a magazine or book? If the first stitch of the first row is either single crochet or half double crochet, mentally add one chain to the stated multiple. If the first stitch of the first row is double crochet, mentally add two chains, and if the first stitch of the first row is worked in treble crochet, mentally add three chains.

FIGURING OUT LACE OR OPENWORK PATTERNS

Many lace or openwork patterns do not start with a row of plain stitches (sc, dc, hdc, etc.).

Instead, these patterns immediately launch you into the pattern setup. Follow the general rule of counting the number of stitches between the asterisk and the comma that immediately precedes the word repeat (rep) for one repeat, and also count any extra stitches or chains used before and after these indicators.

If you find yourself confused and not quite certain how many chains are required to begin, just use one of my favorite tricks: Make any number of extra chains and jot down the number of those extra chains. Work the first few rows according to instructions. At any time, you can easily unravel the extra chains. After working several rows, to ensure you are now working on the correct number of stitches, gently unravel those extra chains.

If you like the pattern and might entertain the thought of using it again for a different project, make pencil notations such as how many chains you needed to add, gauge using a specific yarn and hook size, etc., in your book, magazine or stitch dictionary for future reference.

WHEN NOT TO COUNT STITCHES

Maybe you've noticed stitch patterns found in stitch dictionaries that include a note telling you to count stitches only on specific rows or not to count on certain rows. Such cautionary words can often cause new crocheters to shy away from such patterns; most likely because they're unsure of what the wording means.

Some fancy patterns call for stitches to be increased on one or more rows, followed by one or more rows that decrease those extra stitches. Counting stitches on rows where the total varies from those stated in the multiple can be confusing. If you just count on the rows stated or avoid the noted rows per the instructions, you'll not have a problem! Those cautionary words are meant to avoid, not cause, confusion.

ADAPTING MULTIPLES

There are many crochet patterns that allow you to increase or decrease stitches in between cables, popcorns or shells. Our stitch example features two half double crochet stitches between the Popcorn Cables, but after becoming familiar with the instructions, you might prefer to add more half double crochet stitches. For example, you might like to use five half double crochet stitches and space the cables farther apart. If you are very comfortable with how the stitches and stitch pattern are made, feel free to make changes to get the look you like the best or to insert a design element such as the following: popcorns, clusters or puff stitches.

When using a multiple pattern for a garment, take a good look at the instructions before beginning. Sometimes those extra stitches, half shells, V-stitches, etc., at the beginning and end of a row are meant to create a balanced look for an afghan or other flat item.

If you have already worked the multiple pattern and you feel comfortable with it, you may decide that you want to use it to make a jacket instead. If this is the case, you may need to make changes in the number of stitches at the beginning and end of a row so the individual pieces maintain the pattern when they are seamed at the sides. Better yet, if you are so familiar with the pattern that you are getting bored, you can try avoiding side seams by working the lower body to the underarms in one piece, thus cutting down on finishing time, as well as reducing bulk. Another plus is that those end stitches (as given in the pattern) almost always look good when they meet at the center front of the jacket.

If you can count, you can conquer multiples with ease! ▪

MULTIPLES SQUARE PILLOW

SKILL LEVEL
INTERMEDIATE

FINISHED SIZE
18 inches square

MATERIALS
- Red Heart Eco-Ways medium (worsted) weight yarn (4 oz/186 yds/113g per skein):
    2 skeins #1615 lichen
    1 skein #1821 blue cloud
    50 yds #3313 oyster
- Size I/9/5.5mm crochet hook or size needed to obtain gauge
- 18-inch square pillow form

GAUGE
4 sts = 1½ inches

SPECIAL STITCH
Popcorn (pc): 4 hdc in place indicated, drop lp from hook, insert hook in first hdc of group, pull dropped lp through.

PILLOW
BODY
Multiple of 5 + 2

Row 1 (RS): With lichen, ch 33, hdc in 3rd ch from hook *(beg 2 sk chs count as first hdc)* and in each ch across, turn. *(32 hdc)*

Row 2 (WS): Ch 1, hdc in first st and in each st across, turn.

Row 3: Ch 1, hdc in each of first 2 sts, *sk next 2 hdc 2 rows below, **fpdc** *(see Stitch Guide)* around next st 2 rows below, sk next st on this row behind fpdc, hdc in next st, working behind first fpdc, fpdc around first sk st 2 rows below, sk next st on this row, hdc in each of next 2 sts, rep from * across, turn.

Row 4: Ch 1, hdc in first st and in each st across, turn.

Row 5: Ch 1, hdc in each of first 2 sts, *fpdc around next fpdc, **pc** *(see Special Stitch)* in next st, fpdc around next fpdc, hdc in each of next 2 sts, rep from * across, turn.

Row 6: Ch 1, hdc in first st and in each rem st across, turn.

Rows 7–78: [Rep rows 3–6 consecutively] 19 times, ending last rep with row 3. At end of last row, fasten off.

SIDE PANEL

Row 1: With RS facing, working in ends of rows, join oyster with sc in end of last row, evenly sp 96 sc across, turn. *(97 sc)*

Row 2: Ch 1, **fpsc** *(see Stitch Guide)* around first st and each st across, turn. Fasten off.

Row 3: With RS facing, join blue cloud with sl st in first st, ch 1, hdc in same st, hdc in each rem st across, turn.

Row 4: Ch 1, hdc in first st and in each rem st across, turn.

Row 5: Ch 1, hdc in each of first 2 sts, *sk next 2 sts 2 rows below, fpdc around next st 2 rows below, sk st behind fpdc, hdc in next st, fpdc around first sk st 2 rows below, sk st behind fpdc, hdc in each of next 2 sts, rep from * across, turn.

Row 6: Ch 1, hdc in first st and in each rem st across, turn.

Row 7: Ch 1, hdc in each of first 2 sts, *fpdc around next fpdc, pc in next st, fpdc around next fpdc, hdc in each of next 2 sts, rep from * across, turn.

Row 8: Ch 1, hdc in first st and in each rem st across, turn.

Rows 9–12: Rep rows 5–8.

Row 13: Rep row 5. Fasten off.

FINISHING

Fold Body and Side Panel in half. Sew tog, inserting pillow form before closing.

MULTIPLES BOLSTER PILLOW

SKILL LEVEL

EASY

FINISHED SIZE

6 x 14 inches

MATERIALS

- Red Heart Eco-Ways medium (worsted) weight yarn (4 oz/186 yds/113g per skein):
    2 skeins #1821 blue cloud
- Size I/9/5.5mm crochet hook or size needed to obtain gauge
- 6 x 14-inch bolster pillow form
- Stitch marker

GAUGE

6 sts = 2 inches

PATTERN NOTES

Work in continuous rounds, do not turn or join.

Mark first stitch of each round.

SPECIAL STITCH

Front post double crochet decrease (fpdc dec): Holding back last lp of each st on hook, fpdc around same st as last fpdc, sk next 2 sts 2 rows below, fpdc around next st, yo, pull through all lps on hook.

PILLOW
END
MAKE 2.

Rnd 1: Ch 2, 8 sc in 2nd ch from hook, **do not join** *(see Pattern* Notes), **place marker** *(see Pattern Notes)*. *(8 sc)*

Rnd 2: 2 sc in each st around. *(16 sc)*

Rnd 3: *Sc in next sc, 2 sc in next sc, rep from * around. *(24 sc)*

Rnd 4: *Sc in each of next 2 sc, 2 sc in next sc, rep from * around. *(32 sc)*

Rnd 5: *Sc in each of next 3 sc, 2 sc in next sc, rep from * around. *(40 sc)*

Rnd 6: *Sc in each of next 4 sc, 2 sc in next sc, rep from * around. *(48 sc)*

Rnd 7: *Sc in each of next 5 sc, 2 sc in next sc, rep from * around. *(56 sc)*

Rnd 8: *Sc in each of next 6 sc, 2 sc in next sc, rep from * around. *(64 sc)*

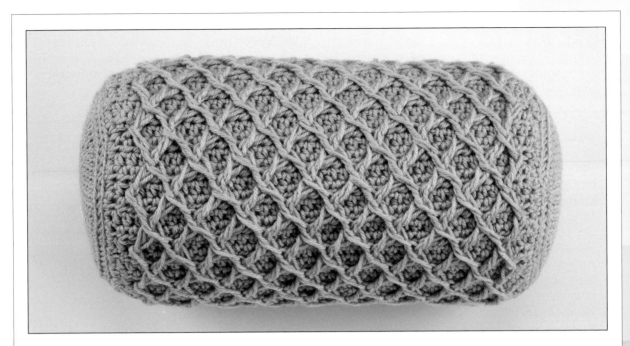

Rnd 9: *Sc in each of next 7 sc, 2 sc in next sc, rep from * around, join with sl st in beg sc. Fasten off. (72 sc)

BODY
Multiple of 4 + 1

Row 1 (RS): Ch 42, working in **back bar of chs** (see illustration), hdc in 3rd ch from hook (beg 2 sk chs count as first hdc) and in each rem ch across, turn. (41 hdc)

Back Bar of Chain

Row 2: Ch 1, hdc in first st and in each rem st, turn.

Row 3: Ch 1, hdc in first st, sk next 2 sts 2 rows below, **fpdc** (see Stitch Guide) around next st 2 rows below, sk st on this row behind fpdc, *hdc in each of next 3 sts, **fpdc dec** (see Special Stitch), sk next st on this row behind fpdc dec, rep from * 8 times, hdc in each of next 3 sts, fpdc around same st as last leg of fpdc dec, sk next st on this row behind fpdc, hdc in last st, turn.

Row 4: Ch 1, hdc in first st and in each rem st, turn.

Row 5: Ch 1, hdc in each of first 3 sts, *fpdc dec around next 2 fpdc dec, sk next st on this row behind fpdc dec, hdc in each of next 3 sts, rep from * across, turn.

Rows 6–53: [Rep rows 2–5 consecutively] 12 times. At end of last row, fasten off.

FINISHING
Join with sc in end of first row. Working in ends of rows, evenly sp 71 sc across. Rep on other edge. Fasten off. (72 sc)

Sew rows 1 and 53 of Body tog.

Sew 1 End to end of Body.

Insert pillow form.

Sew rem End to rem end of Body. ▪

Taming the Curl

If your crochet work becomes frilled, fluted or formed—and it's not supposed to—here are some things you can do when your flat motif gets bent out of shape.

When you're working any crochet, but especially thread crochet, there is nothing more exasperating than beginning the pattern with the correct hook and the correct thread and then noticing after a few rounds in that your piece that should be flat is having a hard time lying flat. Usually the first thought is, "What have I done wrong? Did I misread the pattern?" Now begins the double-check process—beginning at the center, you carefully begin checking each round. When you have reached the point where you stopped crocheting because your project is shape-shifting, and there doesn't appear to be anything you misread or omitted, your enthusiasm takes a dive.

You begin to think of other reasons. Maybe you picked up a thicker (or finer) weight of thread, or perhaps you accidentally misread the hook size. However, when you find these are also correct, both your joy and your confidence begin to fade. So what can you do to perfectly produce that delightful pattern you really wanted to make?

After being unable to find any place in the pattern where you might have made an error and not being able to see where to go next, you could be tempted to rip it out and find something else to make. While there may not always be an immediate solution to producing the exact article you set out to make, there are ways to adapt what you have already created into something beautiful. So, instead of ripping it out and wasting all the time and effort spent on it so far, think about the ideas given here—one of these may be just right for you.

If time is at a premium, look at the Be Creative section that follows to change what you have started into a different article. However, if you do have the time to start again to produce your original project, take the time to read the How Were the Stitches Worked?

section on the facing page before you begin. The solution of what you need to do in order to make your piece lie flat is probably there.

BE CREATIVE

The following photos show a small ecru doily (*Photo A*) worked as the pattern instructs and using the traditional method of working basic stitches. The yellow doily pattern (*Photo B*) was worked the same way but on a hook that was too small, leading to the result shown—a doily forming a cup shape. From round 9, to make the cup shape more pronounced, you can reduce the number of chains, creating the chain spaces as given in the original pattern.

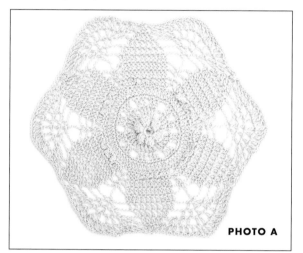

PHOTO A

PHOTO B

Once you notice your motif is curving inward or upward (*often after a whole night's work*), curb any impulse to rip it out immediately

PHOTO C

containers, which are particularly useful for keeping the flies out in summer. It may not be necessary to stiffen the crochet if using it as a lid. Instead, you may wish to thread ribbon through one of the last few rounds and tie the ribbon around the neck of the container to prevent its contents from falling out of the jelly jar or pot.

When working with a hook that is too large, you may find the doily is not lying flat and is beginning to flute (Photo D). Be creative and keep the fullness that has started to emerge

for it is always worth spending a moment or two to think about what it can be turned into. Finding an idea you like and making it happen—even if it's in a different way than you originally planned—can give you a wonderful feeling, and, as a bonus, you know your end result is an original.

Obviously, there will be some things that will limit what the motif can be made into, since the modification will have to be based on the size and design of the original. One modification suggestion would be to convert a circular motif into a bonnet. Depending on the size of the original, this can range from a bonnet for a tiny doll in a doll's house to a bonnet for an infant or full-size baby doll.

If the original did not contain any heavily textured stitches, the crochet could be lined with silk and used as a christening bonnet. The small doily pattern would not be suitable for a baby because of its embossed center. However, for a small bag design, it might be perfect. With the addition of a pretty edging, ribbon and/or other embellishments, a failed flat motif can become a successfully formed project!

Alternatively, if the motif is not too open and lacy, it can be immersed in a stiffening solution and then draped over a bowl to dry (Photo C). When it's completely dry, turn it upright to use as a wonderful container for candy, cookies or even fruit. Bowl shapes can be turned upside down and made into decorative covers for jars and other

PHOTO D

and "play" with the pattern, allowing the fullness to form frills or pleats.

Accentuate the frilling in the last row by working two stitches in each stitch and then nipping the edges to form regular flutes —as you would when making a pie. You can, of course, add more rounds to form a much bigger frill, but in that instance you would not necessarily need to continue increasing the number of stitches.

HOW WERE THE STITCHES WORKED?

Working with thread is much different from working with yarn. Most threads are made of cotton, linen or bamboo, and therefore, do not have the characteristic "give" that wool, acrylics and other fibers and fiber mixes have. This means the gauge needs to be accurate and the stitches worked evenly. If these criteria aren't met, the differences in the way it has been crocheted will be obvious to the eye of even a non-crocheter.

Remember it is the top of the stitch that gives the correct circumference to a round because the base of the stitch can be squashed together without the shape being distorted. Keep your eye on the top of the round being worked, checking the gauge after completing each round, especially at the beginning and for the first few rounds, as that often is where the distortion starts. Watch the gauge for a minimum of six rounds, preferably 10, to be sure your work is going to turn out as you hope it will.

One point to remember is that the pattern being followed may have been designed in a different country where those learning to crochet are taught to make the stitches in a different way. An obvious example is the American double crochet, which is worked exactly like the British treble crochet. Sometimes the name is the only thing that is different. However, in some cases, it is not only the stitch name that may differ; it can also be the way the stitch is formed. Using the double crochet as our example, it is normally accepted that when you insert the hook into the fabric being made, the loop on the hook, the yarn over and the loop being pulled through the fabric should all be the same size, and the hook should be on a diagonal (*Photo E*).

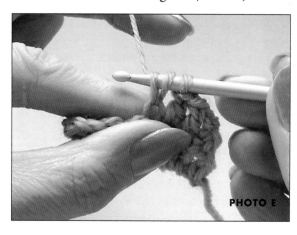

PHOTO E

In Europe (not including the U.K.), however, they would work this stitch by lifting the loop being pulled through to the front of the work, so the hook is either horizontal or just a little bit tilted (*Photo F*).

PHOTO F

Sometimes a double crochet has been worked in the same way as an extended double crochet. This begins as a double crochet, but once the loop has been pulled through and there are three loops on the hook, the yarn is placed over the hook and pulled through only one loop (*Photo G*). The double crochet is then completed in the normal way.

PHOTO G

So, as you crochet the pattern in front of you in the traditional American way, if the pattern has been produced by a designer trained to crochet using either of the other two methods, your motif probably will not lie flat. Using a magnifying glass and placing it over the stitches photographed in the commercial pattern can give you a clue. Alternatively, try both of the other methods over three or four rounds to see if that helps to keep your project flat.

THE HOOK

There are two main ways to hold a crochet hook. One is to hold it like a pencil; the other is to hold it like a knife. In both cases it is necessary for one of the fingers of the hand holding the hook to be used as a stop to prevent the thread loop from sliding further up the shaped part of the crochet hook. It is this finger that will regulate the size of the loop and keep the stitches consistent (*Photo H*).

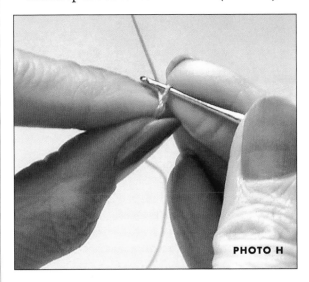

PHOTO H

HOW ARE YOU FEELING?

There is one other point to keep in mind when working with thread. If you are feeling stressed, your crochet may reflect your added tension, especially in the gauge. If it does, however, start another project that is smaller, keeping it for only those moments when you are tense or "uptight." Leave your larger projects for more relaxed moments such as watching TV, listening to the radio, sitting outside on a beautiful day, or whenever and wherever you can have some quiet, restful time. It just might help make your flatwork crochet piece a "no frills" project! ▪

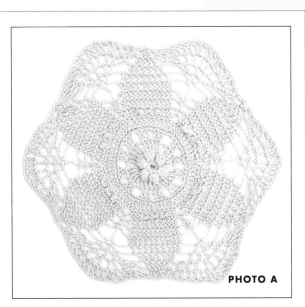

PHOTO A

SMALL ECRU DOILY
(*Photo A*)

SKILL LEVEL

EASY

FINISHED SIZE
7 inches in diameter between straight edges

MATERIALS
- DMC Traditions size 10 crochet cotton (400 yds per ball):
  1 ball ecru
- Size B/1/2.25mm crochet hook or size needed to obtain gauge

GAUGE
Rnds 1–4 = 1¾ inches

PATTERN NOTES
Join with slip stitch unless otherwise stated.

Chain-3 at beginning of row or round counts as first double crochet unless otherwise stated.

SPECIAL STITCHES
Beginning popcorn (beg pc): Ch 3 (*counts as first dc*), 5 dc in same st as beg ch-3, drop lp from hook, insert hook in 3rd ch of beg ch-3, pull dropped lp through.

57
Everything Crochet

Popcorn (pc): 6 dc in indicated st or ch sp, drop lp from hook, insert hook in first dc of group, pull dropped lp through.

MOTIF

Rnd 1: Ch 5, sl st in first ch to form ring, ch 1, 12 sc in ring, **join** (see Pattern Notes) in beg sc. (12 sc)

Rnd 2: Ch 1, sc in next st, **beg pc** (see Special Stitches) in next st, [sc in next st, **pc** (see Special Stitches) in next st] around, join in top of beg pc. (6 pc, 6 sc)

Rnd 3: Ch 1, sc in first st, ch 2, [sc in next sc, ch 2] around, join in beg sc. (6 ch-2 sps)

Rnd 4: Sl st in first ch-2 sp, ch 4 (counts as first tr), 4 tr in same ch sp as beg ch-4, ch 1, [5 tr in next ch-2 sp, ch 1] around, join in 4th ch of beg ch-4. (30 tr)

Rnd 5: Sl st in next st, **ch 3** (see Pattern Notes), dc in same st as beg ch-3, dc in next st, ch 2, dc in next st, 2 dc in next st, ch 2, [sk next st, 2 dc in next st, dc in next st, ch 2, dc in next st, 2 dc in next st, ch 2] around, join in 3rd ch of beg ch-3. (36 dc, 12 ch-2 sps)

Rnd 6: Ch 1, sc in each st and in each ch around, join in beg sc. (60 sc)

Rnd 7: Ch 3, dc in each of next 8 sts, 2 dc in next st, [dc in each of next 9 sts, 2 dc in next st] around, join in 3rd ch of beg ch-3. (66 dc)

Rnd 8: Ch 1, sc in each of first 3 sts, *[ch 3, sc in each of next 2 sts] 3 times, sc in next st, ch 4, sk next st**, sc in each of next 3 sts, rep from * around, ending last rep at **, join in beg sc. (60 sc, 18 ch-3 sps, 6 ch-4 sps)

Rnd 9: Ch 3, dc in each of next 2 sts, working behind ch-3 sps, *ch 1, dc in next st on rnd 7 beside sc of last rnd, [ch 1, sk next st on last rnd and on rnd 7, dc in next st on rnd 7 beside sc of last rnd] twice, dc in each of next 3 sts, ch 1, sc in next ch-4 sp, ch 1**, dc in each of next 3 sts, rep from * around, ending last rep at **, join in 3rd ch of beg ch-3. (54 dc, 6 sc, 30 ch-1 sps)

Rnd 10: Ch 3, [dc in each st and in each ch sp across to ch sp before next sc, ch 2, sk next ch sp, sc in next sc, ch 2, sk next ch sp] around, join in 3rd ch of beg ch-3. (72 dc, 6 sc, 12 ch-2 sps)

Rnd 11: Ch 3, [dc in each st across to next ch sp, ch 3, sc in next sc, ch 3] around, join in 3rd ch of beg ch-3.

Rnd 12: Ch 3, *dc dec (see Stitch Guide) in next 2 sts, dc in each of next 6 sts, dc dec in next 2 sts, dc in next st, ch 4, dtr (see Stitch Guide) in next sc, ch 4**, dc in next st, rep from * around, ending last rep at **, join in 3rd ch of beg ch-3. (60 dc, 6 dtr, 12 dc dec)

Rnd 13: Sl st in next st, ch 3, *dc in each of next 6 sts, dc dec in next 2 sts, ch 3 (dc, {ch 1, dc} twice) in next dtr, ch 3**, sk next st, dc in next st, rep from * around, ending last rep at **, join in 3rd ch of beg ch-3. (66 dc, 12 ch-1 sps)

Rnd 14: Sl st in next st, ch 3, *dc in each of next 4 sts, dc dec in next 2 sts, ch 3, [dc in next st, ch 1, dc in next ch sp, ch 1] twice, dc in next st, ch 3**, sk next ch sp, dc in next st, rep from * around, ending last rep at **, join in 3rd ch of beg ch-3. (66 dc, 24 ch-1 sps)

Rnd 15: Sl st in next st, ch 3, *dc in each of next 2 sts, dc dec in next 2 sts, ch 3, [dc in next st, ch 1, dc in next ch sp, ch 1] 4 times, dc in next st, ch 3**, sk next st, dc in next st, rep from * around, ending last rep at **, join in 3rd ch of beg ch-3. (78 dc, 48 ch-1 sps)

Rnd 16: Sl st in next st, ch 3, *dc dec in next 2 sts, ch 3, [dc in next st, ch 1, dc in next ch sp, ch 1] 8 times, dc in next st, ch 1, rep from * around, ending last rep at **, join in top of dc dec.

Rnd 17: Ch 1, sc in first st, sc in each st and in each ch around, join in beg sc. Fasten off. ■

The Finish Line

Earlier in the chapter we talked about ways to get your crochet projects off to a great start to help ensure a successful journey to your project's end. Now, let's look at some suggestions for achieving a great finish to your project.

- Never work over yarn ends. While this might be the easiest and quickest way to hide the ends, it doesn't really anchor them as securely as weaving them in does.

- Always leave an end at least 6–8 inches in length. Using a tapestry or yarn needle (depending on the thickness of the yarn), weave the end through the back of the stitches for at least 1½ inches, and then turn and weave in the opposite direction. Pull the end gently and clip, allowing the yarn to ease back into the stitches.

- If working with multiple colors, if possible, weave yarn ends through same-color stitches to keep them invisible. If weaving ends into a very open, lacy design that doesn't offer much in the way of solid fabric to work through, weave the ends through the tops of the stitches.

- When working with two or more strands held together, don't weave the ends in together. Always weave them in separately, and in different directions, to avoid unsightly lumps and bumps in your crochet. This also makes them more secure.

- Weave in ends as you go. It is worth taking the time to weave the ends in as your work progresses to make the task much less tedious and to help you do a better job.

- When cutting yarn for fringe, use the yarn from the outside of the skein or ball rather than the yarn pulled from the inside, so that the yarn will be smooth and not crinkly. If you're toward the end of your ball or skein and must use the crinkly yarn, wrap it around a large piece of cardboard, and then steam lightly to remove the wrinkles. You can also wrap fringe around a plastic food container lid (or other similar-type piece of plastic), wet it and let it dry naturally.

- For straight, even fringe, cut uniform lengths more quickly by using a stiff piece of cardboard that is cut to the size you want the fringe length to be. For example, for 6-inch fringe, cut a 6-inch piece of cardboard. Wrap the yarn around the cardboard using an even tension (not too tightly), and then cut the strands free across one edge.

- If desired, trim the bottom edge of the fringe using a rotary cutter and a plastic or metal straightedge like the kind used in quilting. A large ruler can be substituted for a straightedge.

- For motifs and other pieces that will be sewn together later, leave the ends long enough to use for sewing. This saves yarn and reduces the number of ends you have to conceal.

- When sewing light- and dark-color motifs together, use the light-color yarn. It will usually blend better and make the seam less visible.

- If crocheting pieces together, use the next-size-larger hook to avoid seams that pucker.

- If you are working on a project comprised of numerous pieces that need to be the same size, such as a strip or block afghan, be sure to measure each piece as you make it and compare each finished piece to the previously completed ones. This step ensures that your finished pieces will be the correct size, as well as helps you avoid having to remake pieces.

- If the last round on your project's border starts to ruffle, use a smaller size of hook to help tame it down.

- If you must use hot glue to attach finishing decorative accents to your crochet project (not generally recommended), use a blow dryer on leftover "spiderwebs" of hot glue to remove them.

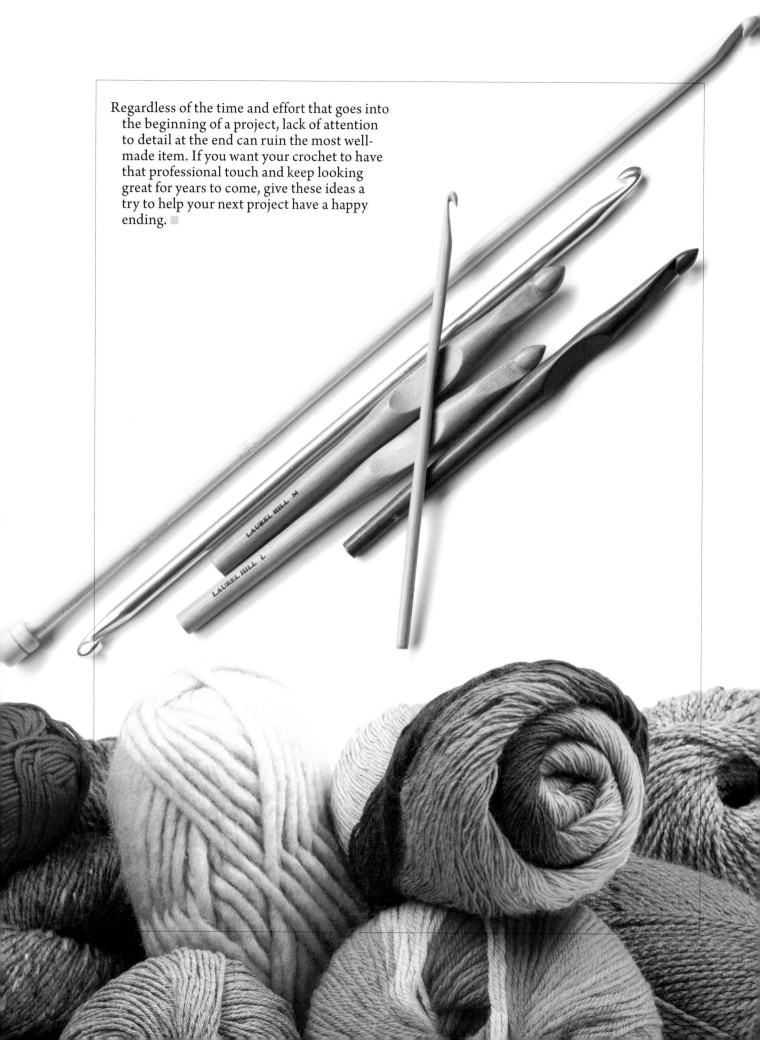

Regardless of the time and effort that goes into the beginning of a project, lack of attention to detail at the end can ruin the most well-made item. If you want your crochet to have that professional touch and keep looking great for years to come, give these ideas a try to help your next project have a happy ending.

Help for the Left-Hander

For left-handed people in a predominantly right-handed world, crocheting can be a very frustrating experience! Why would a left-handed person consider themselves to be living in a right-handed world? First of all, only approximately 10 percent of people in the world are left-handed, and the majority of people within that 10 percent are males. Since more crocheters are women, left-handed crocheters really can be in the minority! One would think that we could safely assume, then, that 10 percent of all crocheters are left-handed, but perhaps this is not the case as it can be so difficult for left-handed people to learn to crochet.

Finding information to help left-handed crocheters is nearly impossible, mostly because not a lot of things have been written specifically for left-handed people. Even though there are some helpful articles, some of the most prominent how-to books written on crochet actually suggest that you would be better off learning to crochet right-handed! It's no wonder that those of us who are left-handed have trouble finding help with our crochet questions!

One of the most popular methods for teaching a left-handed person to crochet is for the left-hander to sit directly across from a right-hander or to watch a right-hander in a mirror. Learning to crochet when you are left-handed can be as simple as anything else you are trying to learn, as long as you have the correct instructions. As with any new skill you are trying to learn and be successful at, practice makes perfect. And we do mean, PRACTICE, PRACTICE, PRACTICE! Expect that, as with anything new, it might feel awkward at first to try and manipulate the hook and the yarn. Whether you are left-handed or right-handed, practicing your newly learned skill can be the most important thing to the success of crocheting.

GETTING STARTED

How you will hold your crochet hook is the first thing you will want to determine. Your hook will be held in your left hand and the yarn or crochet thread will be held in, and manipulated by, your right hand. There are two most commonly used ways to hold the crochet hook. The first is called the pencil hold, where you will hold the crochet hook between your thumb and index finger. The second is called the knife hold, where you grip the crochet hook in much the same manner as you would hold a knife. (See the photos of these two types of hook holds on page 69).

It is up to you to determine which hold feels more comfortable as there is no correct or incorrect way to hold the hook.

Just as there are different ways to hold your hook, there are also different ways to hold the crochet yarn or thread. The most widely accepted way, though, is to loop the yarn over the middle or index finger of your right hand, holding it loosely across the hand. With your yarn, make a slip knot on your hook.

Hold the slip knot in your right hand between your thumb and middle finger. The yarn will come out between the hook and your index finger. Use your index finger to keep the yarn tight to create an even tension, which is very important if you want to maintain even stitches.

The phrase used to loop the yarn over the hook is called "yarn over." That is the way you will be pulling the yarn through the stitches to create chains and/or stitches. Nearly every crochet project begins with a beginning/foundation chain, abbreviated "beg/foundation ch."

With the hook in front, yarn over and bring the hook up and over to catch the yarn and bring it through the loop (which directly follows the slip knot). This is your first chain. Never count the loop on the hook as a chain. Continue in this manner until you have the required amount of chain stitches for the pattern you want to make. It will be necessary for you to practice the chain stitch until you are able to make nice uniform chains, as this chain will be the foundation for your first row of crochet.

DIFFERENCES BETWEEN LEFT- AND RIGHT-HANDED CROCHETERS

Here are some very important differences to remember about left-handed crochet. When working back and forth in rows, left-handed crocheters work their stitches from left to right, and right-handed crocheters work from right to left.

When working in rounds, left-handed crocheters work to the right (clockwise) and right-handed crocheters work to the left (counterclockwise).

When working back and forth in rows, the finished crochet project will look exactly the same for both right- and left-handed crocheters, except for where the work was started and fastened off (ended).

When working in rounds, the finished crochet project will look different for left- and right-handed crocheters because the stitches will be worked in opposite directions.

Some people actually prefer the look of crocheting-in-the-round done by left-handed crocheters, while others think it looks backwards!

The majority of adjustments that left-handed crocheters will have to make will be in reading and interpreting the written patterns and the charts used in crochet.

There are several types of charts that are used in crochet. Of these, there are two types in particular that could be problematic for left-handed crocheters—color-specific charts and filet crochet charts.

At first glance, color-specific charts would not seem to be that much of an issue, however if the chart is not modified for a left-handed crocheter, the finished project will be a mirror image of what it should be. In most cases, this would not be an issue, but sometimes, color placement makes a big difference.

Reading filet crochet charts can be a bit challenging for anyone at first. The "filled-in" squares of the graph are called blocks. The open squares are the "mesh" or spaces.

The charts are generally numbered by rows, and sometimes stitches, and are automatically written for right-handed crocheters. It will be necessary for left-handed crocheters to amend the chart slightly before beginning to work with it. If you do not amend the chart, you would still be able to complete your project, but the finished crochet piece would be reversed or backward from the chart and crochet project pictured in your pattern! As with color-specific charts, for some projects, this would not be a problem, but if you are using a filet crochet chart for a design that has wording, the words in your finished project would be backward!

It is necessary for the left-handed crocheter to read the first row of the graph from left to right; (right-handed crocheters read the first row of the graph from right to left).

Using the color-specific charts for the Botanica Pillows on pages 146 and 148 as examples, the stitches will be the same, but you will need to amend the charts as follows for left-handed crochet: All odd-numbered rows will be read from left to right, and all even-numbered rows will be read from right to left.

Filet crochet charts will be worked according to the text instructions and the stitch key, but the charts will be read in the same way. The first row (and all odd-numbered rows), usually the right side (front) of the project, will be read from left to right. The second row (and all even-numbered rows), usually the wrong side (back) of the project, will be read from right to left.

Fortunately, most crochet instructions written today are suitable for both right- and left-handed crocheters. The majority of patterns that will need to be amended will be clothing. But occasionally, you will need to reverse instructions for other crochet patterns as well. An example of an adjustment for a non-clothing item might read "join yarn in upper right-hand corner." In this case, you would be joining the yarn in the upper left-hand corner.

When crocheting garments, most of the directional instructions need to be reversed. We can illustrate this by using the following pattern that was written for a right-handed crocheter. It is a simple vest pattern that is suitable for a doll or toy bear.

As with most things, it will seem less intimidating if you begin your project and follow along with the instructions as you are crocheting it.

Note: This pattern is a standard-type pattern written for right-handed crocheters. Any changes left-handed crocheters will need to make, will be in bold italic type (for example, ***"Right Front Shaping"****).*

VEST

MATERIALS

- 50 yds medium (worsted) weight yarn
- Size G/6/4mm crochet hook or size needed to obtain gauge
- Tapestry needle

GAUGE

4 sc = 1 inch

VEST
BODY

Row 1: Starting at bottom of vest, ch 45, sc in 2nd ch from hook and in each rem ch across, turn. *(44 sc)*

Rows 2–7: Ch 1, sc in each sc across, turn.

Divide for fronts

Left Front Shaping (*Right Front Shaping*)

Row 8: Ch 1, sc in each of first 7 sc, leaving rem sts unworked, turn.

Rows 9–15: Ch 1, sc in each sc across, turn.

Row 16: Ch 1, **sc dec** (*see Stitch Guide*) in first 2 sc, sc in each rem sc across, turn. (*6 sc*)

Row 17: Ch 1, sc in each of next 4 sc, sc dec in last 2 sc, turn. (*5 sc*)

Row 18: Ch 1, sc dec in first 2 sc, sc in each rem sc across, turn. (*4 sc*)

Rows 19–22: Ch 1, sc in each sc across, turn. At end of last row, fasten off.

Right Front Shaping (*Left Front Shaping*)

Row 8: With WS (*RS*) facing, join yarn with sc in first (*7th*) unworked st in row 7, sc in each of next 6 sc, turn. (*7 sc*)

Rows 9–15: Ch 1, sc in each sc across, turn.

Row 16: Ch 1, sc in each of first 5 sc, sc dec in next 2 sc, turn. (*6 sc*)

Row 17: Ch 1, sc dec in first 2 sc, sc in each rem sc across, turn. (*5 sc*)

Row 18: Ch 1, sc in each of first 3 sc, sc dec in next 2 sc, turn. (*4 sc*)

Rows 19–22: Ch 1, sc in each sc across. Fasten off.

BACK

Row 8: With WS (*RS*) facing, sk 4 (*25*) sts on row 7, join yarn with sc in next st, sc in each of next 21 sc, leaving last 4 sc unworked, turn. (*22 sc*) (***next to right front shaping; this is actually the 2nd side you shaped***)

Rows 8–18: Ch 1, sc in each sc across, turn.

Right Back Shoulder (*Left Back Shoulder*)

Row 19: Ch 1, sc in each of next 4 sc, turn. (*4 sc*)

Rows 20–22: Ch 1, sc in each sc across, Fasten off.

Left Back Shoulder (*Right Back Shoulder*)

Row 19: With WS (*RS*) facing, sk next 14 (*17*) sc on row 18, join yarn with sc in next st, sc in each of next 3 sc, turn.

Rows 20–22: Ch 1, sc in each sc across, turn. Fasten off.

FINISHING
Sew shoulder seams.

BORDER
Join yarn with sc in any st on Back of Vest, working in ends of rows and in each sc, sc evenly sp around outer edge of Vest, join with sl st in first sc. Fasten off.

This reversed-shaping example can be applied to many crochet clothing patterns that you might come across. Fortunately, many crochet patterns are written to make them easily understood by both right- and left-handed crocheters. The terms "Left Front" and "Right Front" have been replaced with "First Front" and "2nd Front," which can be very helpful to a left-handed crocheter. Try not to shy away from patterns that are not written for a left-handed crocheter. As with anything, pattern conversion will become easier as you do it more often. ■

chapter five
crochet hooks & tools

All crochet hooks are not created equal. In this chapter we'll show you the standard styles of crochet hooks as well as special hooks that create specific types of crochet fabric. We'll also tell you how to care for your hooks, plus we'll give you an overview of the basic tools important for the crocheter's tool bag.

The Evolution of the Crochet Hook

With today's wide variety of lovely crochet hooks crafted in a plethora of fabulous materials, styles and colors, it's hard to imagine the rather crude, unappealing tools some of our earliest crochet forbearers had to use. It helps us appreciate all the more the wonderful tools we have available today and admire anew the incredible stitch work created by our ancestors with their limited and rudimentary implements.

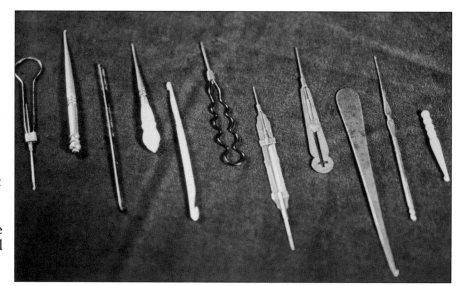

Beautiful antique crochet hooks in a variety of materials, including sterling silver, tortoiseshell, bone and ivory. From the private collection of Annie Potter.

Most of us give little thought to our crochet hooks other than to check the instructions for the suggested size for the project at hand. If we don't have the appropriate size at home, we can always run out to the nearest craft or yarn store and pick one up.

The earliest crocheters, however, didn't have chain stores or mail-order catalogs to fulfill their needs for crochet implements. They fashioned their own, usually of wood, bone or metal. In Ireland, exquisite Irish crochet laces were worked with hooks made from stiff wire inserted into a piece of wood or cork. The end of the wire was filed down and a hook turned at the end. Poor farmers often carved wooden hooks for their wives out of whatever was readily available, like the rough-hewn hook shown at right that was created from a chair leg.

Looking back through history, it's amazing that these early crocheters could turn out such lovely pieces of needlework with the crude tools with which they had to work.

As crochet grew in popularity and technology flourished, crocheters enjoyed a renaissance in the production of crochet hooks. Crocheters in the upper classes could take their pick of beautiful hooks hand-carved from wood, bone or ivory, or made of mother-of-pearl, tortoiseshell, abalone, horn, agate or sterling silver, and sometimes inlaid with gemstones.

In the early 1920s, sets of interchangeable crochet hooks became popular. Each set consisted of a single handle, perhaps of bone or amber, with an assortment of short steel hooks generally ranging in sizes from 1 to 14. The crocheter simply selected the size hook she needed for her project and screwed it into the tip of the handle.

In America, the Boye Needle Co. produced the first complete line of American-made steel crochet hooks in 1917. Each hook sold for a nickel. Aluminum crochet hooks appeared in 1923, and hooks for hairpin crochet were introduced in 1935.

World War II forced the government to order the cessation of nickel plating for crochet hooks in 1942, and Boye began a special black plating process known as "hoto" black process, or hot oxide black process, in order to prevent corrosion. Nickel plating was not reinstated until the latter part of May 1945.

Today, we enjoy the convenience and availability of crochet hooks in an almost limitless variety of eye-catching styles and colors.

From exotic woods and sparkling glass, to dazzling beaded and hand-painted creations, we can revel in the pleasure of using beautiful, finely crafted crochet hooks that look as good as they work! ▮

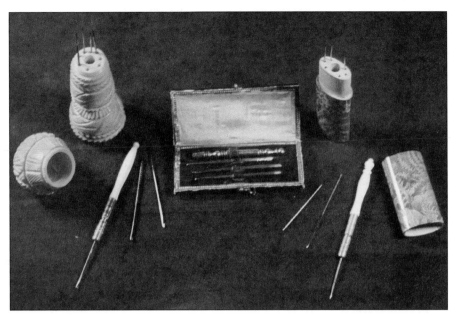

Vintage sets of interchangeable crochet hooks from the early 1900s. From the private collection of Annie Potter.

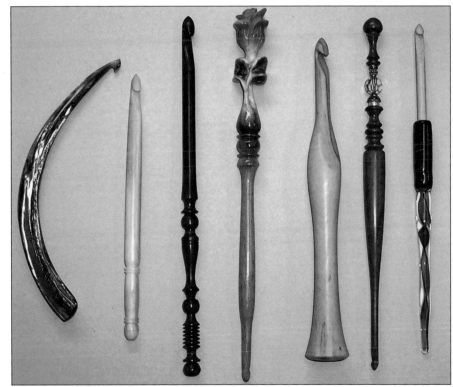

Today's crochet hooks are made from many different materials—including abalone, glass, bamboo and exotic woods such as rosewood and ebony— and feature a wide variety of styles and embellishments.

Crochet Hook Sizes

Crochet hooks come in many sizes, from very fine steel hooks used with threads to make intricate doilies and other fine lace designs, to very large hooks made of plastic or wood used to create bulky yarn projects such as sweaters, afghans and rugs.

Although hooks for working with yarn can be made in a variety of materials, the hooks generally used most often for yarn are made of aluminum, are about 6 inches long and are sized by letter and number from B/1/2.25mm (*the smallest*) to N/P/15/10mm (*the largest*). Here is a chart showing these sizes, plus larger sizes that are usually made of wood or plastic. Also included in the chart are the metric and U.K. equivalents.

YARN HOOKS

U.S.	Metric	U.K.
B-1	2.25mm	13
C-2	2.75mm	12
D-3	3.25mm	10
E-4	3.5mm	9
F-5	3.75mm	8
G-6	4mm	7
H-8	5mm	6
I-9	5.5mm	5
J-10	6mm	4
K-10½	6.5mm	3
L-11	8mm	0
M/N-13	9mm	00
N/P-15	10mm	000
P/Q	15mm	
Q	16mm	
S	19mm	

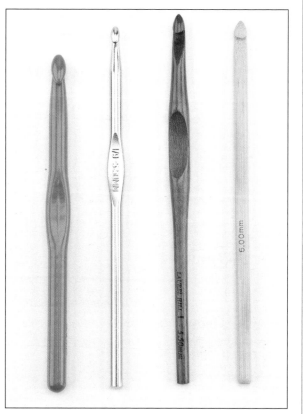

Some of the most popular types of yarn hooks are (left to right) plastic, aluminum, exotic wood and bamboo.

The aluminum crochet hook looks like this:

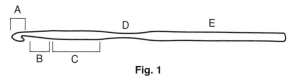

Fig. 1

In Fig. 1, (A) is the hook end, which is used to hook the yarn and draw it through other loops of yarn (called stitches). (B) is the throat, a shaped area that helps you slide the stitch up onto (C), the working area. (D) is the fingerhold, a flattened area that helps you grip the hook comfortably. (E) is the handle, which helps provide balance for easy, smooth work.

It is important that every stitch is made on the working area, never on the throat (which would make the stitch too tight) and never on the fingerhold (which would stretch the stitch).

Generally, the hook can be held one of two ways: the "pencil" hold (*Photo A*) or the "knife" hold (*Photo B*).

PHOTO A

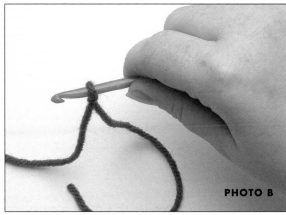

PHOTO B

Here is a chart showing the sizes for steel hooks, including the metric and U.K. equivalents.

STEEL THREAD HOOKS

U.S.	Metric	U.K.
16	0.60mm	
14	0.75mm	7
13	0.85mm	6½
12	1.00mm	6
11	1.10mm	5½
10	1.15mm	5
9	1.25mm	4
8	1.50mm	3
7	1.65mm	2½
6	1.80mm	2
5	1.90mm	1½
4	2.00mm	1
3	2.10mm	1/0
2	2.20mm	2/0
1	2.25mm	3/0
0	2.50mm	00
00	2.70mm	

However, there is no "right" or "wrong" way to hold a hook. The way a hook feels most comfortable and works best in your hand is the correct way for you. Whichever way you prefer to hold your hook, it should be held firmly, but not tightly. Holding a hook too tightly can cause discomfort and cramping in your hand. The hook end should be turned slightly toward you, not facing up or down.

Steel crochet hooks, used for crocheting with threads, can also be held either way and should be worked with in the same manner. Steel hooks are not sized by letters, only numbers. However, the difference between sizing in yarn and thread hooks is that for yarn hooks, the smaller the number is, the smaller the hook size. For thread hooks, however, the higher the number means the smaller the size.

Crocheters often develop a preference for a favored style and size of crochet hook, whether it's for thread or yarn crochet. Working with hooks that are the most comfortable and functional for you will help ensure enjoyment and happy results in your projects! ■

Crocheting With Special Hooks

Crochet is the most versatile of all the lace-making techniques. It becomes even more versatile when you use crochet hooks that are specially designed to produce new looks.

Hooks have been made in nearly every material available. Early hooks were made of bone, ivory or wood. These hooks were short—only 6 to 10 inches long. This may have been because the natural raw materials were only available in short lengths. Less common materials included horn, tortoiseshell, vulcanite (hard rubber) and celluloid. After World War I, hooks made of wood, plastic, steel and aluminum measured up to 14 inches long. In the 1970s, afghan hooks with a flexible plastic cord for part of the shank could have been 22 inches or more in length.

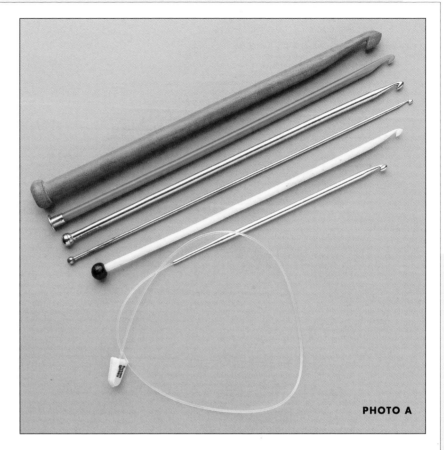

PHOTO A

The short length of the early hooks made it necessary to work large pieces such as blankets in smaller squares or strips. This is still the most popular way to work the afghan stitch today. Full-width blankets are cumbersome to work even if the hook is sufficiently long.

Special crochet hooks have been used ever since crochet became popular in the mid-1800s. Three of these long-ago-developed hooks are currently undergoing a popular revival: the afghan hook, the double-ended hook and the crochet-tatting hook.

THE AFGHAN HOOK

The afghan hook (*see Photo A*), is a crochet hook with a long shank that provides room for many stitches. The shank is the same diameter throughout, and it looks similar to a standard crochet hook, except for the length and the absence of a finger grip. Also, the end opposite the hook has a knob to keep the stitches from sliding off.

The afghan stitch was introduced in England around 1859. In *The Lady's Manual of Fancy Work*, Mrs. Pullan called it the Princess Frederick William Stitch. "A new stitch in crochet has recently been given to the world, which I call, in compliment to our English royal bride, the Princess Frederick William crochet. It is done with a hook having a knot at the end, and somewhat larger than those usually employed, in proportion to the material to be worked."

The stitch is formed by first picking up one loop through each stitch in the previous row. These loops are all stored on the hook shank much as in knitting. Then, when the end of the row is reached, the loops are

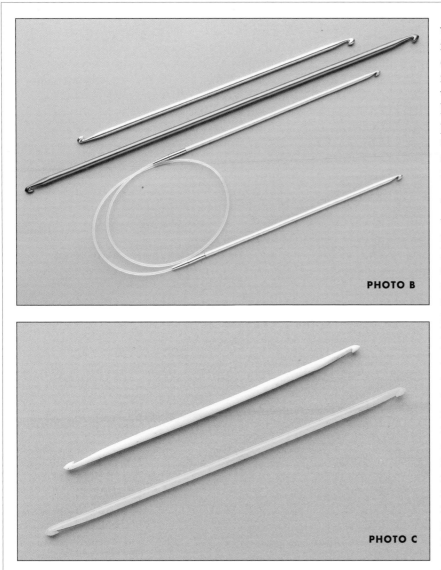

with a single head. The first identical-end double-ended hooks produced for a special crochet style were cellulose acetate hooks, and these were produced between 1935 and 1950. These came in a variety of lengths from 5 to 15 inches.

The technique is a variation of afghan stitch using two colors of yarn. Loops are picked up like afghan stitch in the first color. The work is turned and the loops worked off in the second color. New loops are picked up with the second color. Then the work is turned and these loops worked off in the first color. A striped fabric with a ribbed effect is produced. It is thicker and more flexible than fabric produced with regular afghan stitch. The flexibility makes it ideal for clothing. The fabric is reversible, but the pattern is different on each side. One side will highlight the first color and the second side the other color. In the 1960s, the double-ended technique was called Cro-Hook by Boye. Currently, it is called Crochet on the Double by Annie's Attic.

worked off two at a time just as one finishes a single crochet stitch.

By the 1880s, most pattern books carried afghan stitch patterns under such names as Tunisian crochet, tricot crochet, idiot's knitting and railway knitting.

DOUBLE-ENDED HOOK

The double-ended crochet hook (see Photos B and C), is a more recent invention. It has two identically sized heads and a long, smooth center shank without a grip. Double-ended hooks were made in the mid-1800s but they usually had two different-size hooks. Each end would be used independently like a hook

Most of the post-World War II double-ended hooks are made of aluminum. They range in length from 10 to 14 inches. Like afghan stitch, wide projects are usually in squares or strips. One of the longest hooks of this type is a 34-inch double-ended hook with a flexible plastic cable running between the shafts of the hooks and a swivel connector on the end of each hook. The length of this hook makes it possible to work wide pieces without joins.

CROCHET-TATTING

Crochet-tatting (or cro-tat) has a strong appeal to most crocheters who make lace, but using this method makes the lace-making process much slower. Therefore, it's no wonder someone found a way to incorporate tatted rosettes into crochet. The technique was first described by Sophia Caulfield and Blanche Saward in 1882 in their *Dictionary of Needlework*.

A cro-tat hook *(see Photo D)* needs to have a long shank with a consistent diameter throughout and no finger grip. This did not require a special hook in 1882. Common steel hooks were made from a wire mounted in a bone or wood handle. The finger grip that is so common on hooks today wasn't patented until 1896.

Our modern steel hooks with grips are not suitable for crochet-tatting. The grip does not allow enough knots to be placed on the shank. A cro-tat hook is currently available for use with size 10 thread. For smaller thread sizes, you will have to acquire an antique hook. For yarn, you can use an afghan hook.

Why not expand your crochet repertoire and try one of these "special" crochet techniques today!

REFERENCES

Pullan, Mrs., *The Lady's Manual of Fancy Work*, Dick and Fitzgerald Publishers, New York, 1859, page 43.

Caulfield, Sophia, and Saward, Blanche, *The Dictionary of Needlework*, Facsimile of the 1882 Edition, Arno Press, New York, 1972, pages 116–118.

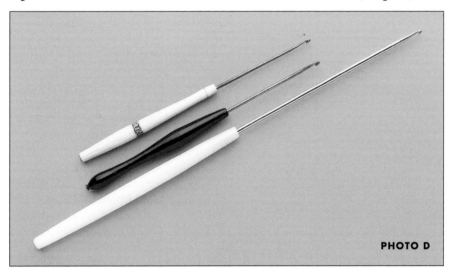

PHOTO D

HOOKS (SHOWN IN PHOTOS)

Afghan—bone with black wood knob 1860–1950, wood 1860–1950, green cellulose acetate plastic 1935–1950, Boye steel (size C) about 1950, Boye aluminum (size G) about 1950, Susan Bates flexible 1970–1990.

Cro-hook (double-ended)—bone 1910–1950, yellow cellulose acetate plastic 1935–1950, blue Boye aluminum 1935–1980, mint green Susan Bates aluminum 2000–present, swivel hook 2001–present.

Cro-tat—black wood handle Penelope hook 1880–1915, bone handle Milward hook 1880–1915, Cro-tat 2001–present.

Rosettes are composed of a series of double-hitch knots worked on the shank of the hook just as you would form rosettes in needle tatting today. But, unlike needle tatting, where the rosette is closed by pulling a threaded needle through the knots, the hook is used to pull the thread back through the knots followed by a slip stitch to close the rosette. The rosettes are placed as desired among chain stitches or in a single crochet ground as needed. Early patterns included edgings, grounds for counterpanes and blankets.

Caring for Your Crochet Tools

Crocheters are usually pretty conscientious when it comes to taking care of their crochet materials, such as yarns, threads, books and magazines, but often don't give much thought to their crochet tools. Here is some helpful information about hooks and needles as well as some suggestions for which tools to use when and how to care for them.

ALUMINUM VS. PLASTIC HOOKS

Aluminum and plastic hooks are by far the most economical options in crochet hooks, but which is really the better purchase?

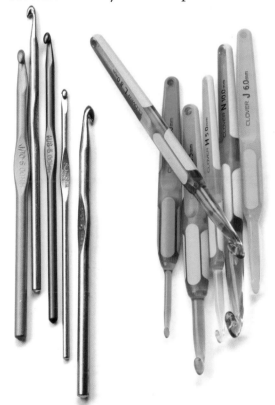

Aluminum hooks are strong, lightweight and smooth. They don't bend or snag the yarn. Plastic hooks are often brittle, and the surface of the hook isn't as smooth as aluminum. Plastic hooks can bend and even break and easily become pitted, which can cause snags that slow you down, resulting in nonuniform stitches. The jumbo plastic hooks are the exception to the rule—they are made differently, are excellent for large or bulky projects, and their design is satisfactory to their purpose.

Aluminum hooks can also become pitted over time from being dropped or stored carelessly. A snag on the hook will cause your yarn to pull and separate as you crochet. If your hook begins to snag your yarn, but you can't see or feel any surface damage on your aluminum hook, try passing a piece of nylon stocking or another silky fabric over the hook; the slightest imperfection will snag the fabric.

Never try to correct the problem by sanding the aluminum hook. Discard it and get a new one.

Overall, even though they cost a little more, aluminum hooks are the better choice. You'll find that in the long run, they are by far the most economical choice between the two. Being thrifty is wonderful, but most times, you get what you pay for. Always try to use the finest materials and tools your crafting budget will allow.

CLEANING HOOKS

A great way to clean steel crochet hooks is to soak them in rubbing alcohol from time to time and dry them with a soft cloth. They'll sparkle and give you a smoother stitching experience.

Beeswax, available at sewing-notion counters nationwide, is a great tool for keeping your hooks stitching smoothly. Try buffing your newly cleaned crochet hooks with beeswax, and they'll zip through your crochet work!

Treat your wooden hooks as you would any fine furniture: Don't use water! Clean them with wood oil and buff them with beeswax to keep the wood well-protected. Over time, wooden hooks will take on a satiny patina if they are cared for properly. This also will improve their performance and preserve them.

Due to the nature of a wooden hook, if it's not made correctly or cared for properly, a wooden hook will sometimes split or snag your yarn. In this case, sand the hook carefully with superfine sandpaper, steel wool or the fine side of an emery board until it is smooth. Then, apply a coat of paste wax and polish, or you might apply one or two coats of clear varnish, sanding lightly between coats.

Care for bone hooks as you would plastic hooks, but never soak them in a soapy solution. Just clean them gently with a wet cloth, dry them thoroughly and then give them a good buffing with beeswax to keep them from drying out.

Keeping your crochet hooks cleaned and preserved is important, and so is storing them safely. Never throw your unprotected hooks in with the rest of your supplies. Keep hooks protected in a case made specifically for this purpose, or wrap them in felt.

TAPESTRY NEEDLE VS. YARN NEEDLE

Some pattern instructions call for a tapestry needle and some call for a yarn needle or even an embroidery needle. Each one serves a specific purpose and is shaped to best do its job.

An embroidery needle has a sharp point designed for finer needlework and is not suggested for projects crocheted with yarn as it tends to split the yarn plies. A tapestry needle, with a point that is slightly less sharp, is used for tapestries, larger embroidery designs, finishing garments and some crocheted items. It has a large enough eye to accommodate fine and lightweight yarns.

Yarn needles, either plastic or steel, are a bit more blunted on the end, usually have a larger eye than tapestry needles and are perfect for conveying medium and bulky weight yarns. Yarn needles glide right through the stitches for perfect alignment and ease in working. Using a yarn needle ensures the best results for your heavier crochet projects.

When not in use, it's best to keep needles in an appropriate storage case. While it might be tempting to stick your yarn or tapestry needle into a piece of furniture while working on a project, this can ultimately dull the tips of steel needles and might break plastic needles. ■

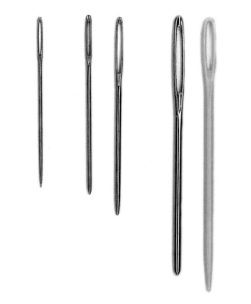

Left to right: embroidery needle, tapestry needles (second and third) and yarn needles (fourth and fifth)

The Crocheter's Toolbox

In crochet, as in many other trades, having the right tool for the job can make a big difference. Every crochet project requires certain commonly used tools, and it is helpful to have these together at all times in a small bag or box.

Some of the following tools are popular basics, and others are less well-known but valuable additions to the crocheter's tool bag.

box or a specially purchased container that holds your most-needed items in a way that suits you. Slip the tool case or bag into your larger project bag.

Scissors. Choose the style that fits your needs; scissors come in a variety of styles: compact, foldable, decorative, snips.

Project bag. There are as many varieties of project bags as there are crocheters. Bags should be smooth on the inside, have comfortable straps and be large enough to carry your project, your tool bag and extra yarn. Some bags open to sit flat on the floor. Be careful about bags that close with a zipper or hook-and-loop tape—both are yarn-grabbing hazards!

Tool case or bag. This can be a small cosmetics bag, a zippered bank bag, a plastic pencil

Tapestry or Yarn needles. These come in several sizes, each appropriate for a different-size yarn, and with either blunt or sharp tips. Some larger blunt-tip needles have a bent tip which is particularly helpful for seaming. Keep one of each kind available in your bag.

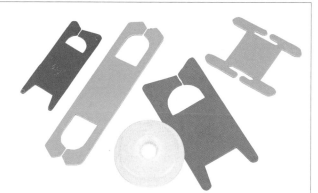

Tape measure. It should be long enough to measure the entire length of the pieces you are working on, marked in both inches and centimeters, and should be made of a material that does not stretch. It may be the familiar fiberglass tape or a retractable tape in a small case.

Bobbins. These are useful but not crucial for intarsia work. Several styles are available— the newer clam-type bobbin is a popular favorite.

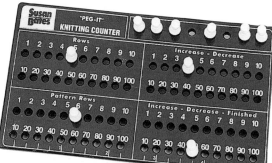

Hook/needle gauge for checking hook size. This is a vital tool since some hooks do not have the size permanently marked.

Split stitch markers. These are available in a variety of styles.

Safety pins. Coilless safety pins are a particular help—they can be used to mark buttonhole spaces, keep track of increases and/or decreases, hold pieces together to be sewn or mark even intervals for stitch pick-up, and to hold stitches.

Straight pins. Non-rust pins with large heads are used for blocking. Several styles are available: T-pins, lollipop pins and plastic pins.

Row counters. This tool may be useful for intricate pattern work.

Hand lotion/lip balm/nail file/adhesive bandage. These items aren't necessary, but they are personal comforts to make your stitching time comfortable and stress-free.

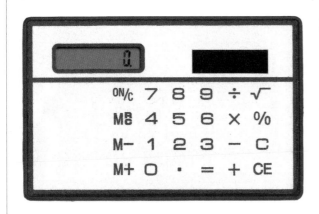

Calculator. This is a helpful tool for making pattern adjustments or designing your own item.

Extra crochet hook. Keep one in the size you are using for your current project in case the one your are using becomes damaged, or you are sitting on a hook-eating sofa.

Pompom makers. Pompoms are a fun accessory for hats and children's wear.

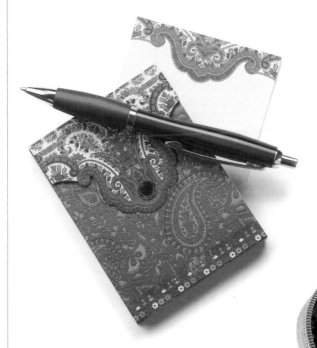

Hook cases. Manufacturers offer many styles to suit your needs: zip cases, plastic cases, roll-up cloth cases, etc.

Pen/pencil and notepaper. These tools are necessary for making notes on the pattern, reminding yourself where you left off or changes you have made, or for jotting down a phone number or recipe while chatting with other crocheters.

Hang tags. Use these handy tags instead of notepaper to keep track of hook size and other information as you work.

Cushion grips. These come in a variety of sizes to make your stitching more comfortable.

Therapeutic gloves. Fingerless spandex gloves offer support and massage for the wrist and hand. These gloves may help those with arthritis or repetitive stress injury.

YarnBras®. This is a plastic-mesh slipcover for center-pull balls or skeins, allowing the yarn to be pulled from the center without coming unwrapped from the outside. Particularly useful for very slippery yarns.

Magnifying tools. These are useful for those of us who have reached a "certain age." Use a regular magnifying glass, magnifying lamp, line magnifier, or try the magnifying glasses sold in drugstores and yarn shops. ▪

chapter six
yarns 101

In today's market, there are a multitude of yarns available with a wide variety of characteristics. Understanding how yarns are manufactured and the differences in their fundamental qualities will help you make enlightened decisions in choosing the best yarns for your projects.

Understanding Yarn Characteristics

Years ago, yarn choices were pretty limited. Times have changed! Today, yarns are manufactured from a wide variety of fiber sources and offer a wonderful array of characteristics that enhance the crochet and knitting experience. Having a basic understanding of how yarns are manufactured and the key differences in their attributes will help ensure success in your crochet projects.

FIBERS

Many different plant, animal (protein) and synthetic fibers are used to make yarn. Cotton, linen, ramie, bamboo and corn are examples of plant fibers. Protein fibers include wool, mohair, angora, silk, cashmere, camel, llama, alpaca and qiviut (pronounced "kiv-ee-ute"). Acrylic, nylon, polyester, metallic and microfiber are synthetic.

Each fiber has its own characteristics, and different fibers are often blended to take advantage of the best properties of each. Fiber characteristics include how it feels to the touch (the hand), how much elasticity it has (resilience), how well it absorbs moisture (absorbency), how fluffy or fuzzy it is (loft) and how well it accepts dye.

The helpful charts on pages 82 and 83 show show the origin and characteristics of a variety of yarn fibers.

MANUFACTURING

Natural fibers other than silk come in short strands rather like locks of hair, called staples. While silk comes in one continuous strand, it is often cut into manageable lengths for processing. Most man-made fibers are produced in single, long filaments.

Before being spun, these fibers must be prepared by a carding, or combing, process (*see photo above*). This process aligns the staples so they are parallel to one another.

Fibers are spun, or twisted together, in either an S twist or a Z twist. An S-twist yarn is spun so that the fibers look like the center curve of an S. A Z-twist yarn resembles the center slant of a Z, or /.

The twisted strand, or ply, may then be twisted together with other plies in the opposite

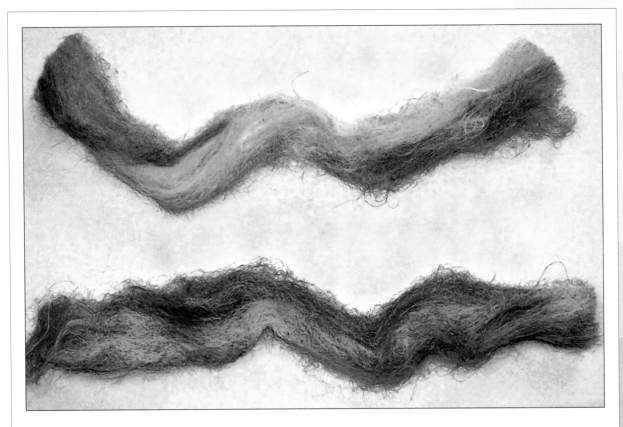

direction to make a multi-ply yarn, which adds strength and balance to the yarn. An unbalanced yarn may pull to one side or the other (bias) when stitched. A tight twist will produce a strong yarn with good stitch definition. These yarns will resist pilling and may be used for garments that will get a lot of heavy wear, like socks or work sweaters.

Sometimes fibers are left unspun (*see photo above*). Unspun fiber, called "roving," is weak and breaks easily during crocheting or knitting. However, it creates a very warm garment for its weight because the air between the fibers traps heat.

FINISHING

Certain fibers may be specially treated after spinning to change their characteristics. Mercerized cotton is cotton that has gone through a finishing process that makes the fiber stronger, more lustrous and more accepting of dyes than regular cotton. Superwash wool fibers have been coated with a resin to prevent the fibers from felting, thus making the yarn machine-washable and dryable.

Knowing and understanding the specific traits of various yarn fibers is an important factor in the yarn choices we make for our projects. The old saying "forewarned is forearmed" is certainly true when it comes to making sure we select the right yarn for those special patterns we want to make. ▪

YARN CHARACTERISTICS CHART

Fiber	Where it comes from	Fiber characteristics
Acrylic	Synthetic fiber produced from propylene, a derivative of natural gas	Exceptionally durable, washable and dryable, nonallergenic, moth-resistant, reasonably inexpensive, has a lower melting point than cotton or wool so it should not be exposed to high heat
Alpaca	Hair of an alpaca	Comes in several natural colors, lustrous, strong fibers, nonresilient
Angora	Hair of an angora rabbit	Silky, soft fiber, expensive, lofty/fluffy, can be dyed, extremely warm for its weight
Bamboo	Manufactured as a cellulose fiber produced from the starchy pulp of bamboo plants processed with bamboo culms	Strong, flexible, absorbent, cool and breathable, soft hand, excellent drape, shiny luxurious look, naturally antibacterial, UV protective
Camel	Down from a Bactrian camel (two humps)	Available in "camel" color only, does not accept dye, very warm, fragile
Cashmere	Undercoat hair from a cashmere goat	Expensive, very soft, fragile and delicate
Corn	Produced from fermented starch from a corn plant	Strong, lustrous look, breathable, elastic, comfortable to wear, soft hand, excellent drape, UV protective
Cotton	Inside the pod of a cotton plant	Heavy, nonelastic, accepts dye well, stretches, absorbent, noninsulating, stronger wet than dry, machine washable
Linen	Inside stalk of a flax plant	Extremely strong, takes dye well, but is often left natural, becomes smoother and softer with age, absorbent, quick-drying, nonelastic, nonpilling, stronger wet than dry
Milk	Produced from milk protein fibers	Strong, lustrous look and silky feel, environmentally friendly, good for the skin, comfortable to wear, antibacterial and antifungal, absorbent, dyes well, colorfast, blends well with other natural fibers

Fiber	Where it comes from	Fiber characteristics
Mohair	Hair from an angora goat	Accepts dye well, soil-resistant, durable, strong, resilient, very warm for its weight, long lustrous staple
Qiviut	Down of a musk ox	Extremely soft, accepts dye well, very expensive
Ramie	Nettle plant	Similar to linen—often used as a substitute for linen, absorbent, accepts dye well
Rayon	Manufactured from cellulose in wood pulp or cotton	Absorbent, accepts dye well, quick-drying, heavy, stretches—but will recover in dryer, weak fiber, most common type of rayon is viscose, may shrink if not laundered properly
Silk	Filament unreeled from the cocoon of a silkworm (tussah silk comes from the wild silkworm)	Smooth, shiny, strong fiber; thinnest of all the natural fibers; accepts dye well; resists pilling; drapes well; stronger dry than wet
Soy	Produced from soybean proteins	Strong, absorbent, soft hand, silky luster, excellent drape, comfortable to wear, exceptional dyeing property, colorfast, heat-resistant
Wool	Fleece (hair) of a sheep	Comes in natural colors: gray, brown, white; accepts dye well; contains lanolin, a natural oil that is water-repellent; breathable—keeps the wearer warm and dry; water- and soil-resistant; good insulator—lots of warmth for its weight; resilient; will felt if subjected to heat and friction; naturally flame-retardant; staple lengths and properties vary with different breeds of sheep
Wool (merino)	Hair of a merino sheep	Has the same characteristics as hair from other breeds of sheep but is much softer, finer and less abrasive; excellent for blending with other fibers such as silk and cashmere; draws moisture away from skin (known as wicking)

Yarn Classification

It is important to understand not only fiber characteristics but also the size, and/or diameter of yarns. Yarn sizes can range from the finest gossamer silk thread to super bulky wool yarn. They are often classified by weight or ply. Unfortunately, these terms are deceptive and might not provide the actual information you need.

In older patterns, yarn was often described simply by ply: 2-ply, 3-ply, 4-ply and so on. This was not a problem because crocheters at the time understood a 2-ply yarn to be much thinner than a 4-ply. Things are different today. Don't be fooled into thinking that a 2-ply yarn is thin and 12-ply yarn is thick.

The diameter of the plies is what determines the size of the yarn. The first three photos below illustrate some of the differences among classic yarns. All of the yarns are 3-ply yarns, but you can tell that there is a definite difference in the thicknesses.

3-ply fingering weight wool yarn

3-ply sport weight wool yarn

3-ply worsted weight wool yarn

In the following photos, the top two show that a 1-ply yarn can be quite thick indeed. Each of the 12-plies in the bottom photo is actually two smaller plies.

1-ply worsted weight wool yarn

1-ply bulky weight wool/mohair yarn

12-ply light worsted weight cotton/wool yarn

In the United States, yarns are categorized from smallest to largest as lace, super-fine, fine, light, medium, bulky and super bulky. The Standard Yarn Weight System chart on page 26 shows the various yarn classifications in each of these categories.

As seen in the U.S./U.K./Australian Yarn Equivalents Chart on page 26, yarns in the U.K. and Australia are often classified according to ply number to describe the size. The British may classify a heavy worsted weight yarn simply as "Aran."

Not all yarns fall neatly into a particular size category—there is some overlap. For example, some yarns work equally well as a sport or DK weight yarn. Worsted weight yarns can sometimes actually be more of a light worsted or heavy worsted weight or even somewhere in between. Super bulky yarns can vary widely in size.

It's not always possible to determine a yarn's size just by looking at it. Some yarns that have apparently small diameters are actually categorized as bulky and are meant to be worked at a larger-than-expected gauge because their loftiness fills in the empty spaces. Mohair is a good example of this principle.

DETERMINING YARN WEIGHTS

Fortunately, there are guidelines for weight classification. The easiest way to determine a yarn's weight is to check the label (*see example on next page*).

Yarn labels provide a wealth of information. The label will generally state the fiber content, washing instructions, color number/name and dye-lot number. It will also usually state a suggested needle/hook size and a suggested gauge.

Weavers and spinners use a classification system of "wraps per inch" (WPI) which is an effective way of categorizing a yarn while taking into account its unique characteristics.

To figure WPI, hold one end of the yarn and wrap it evenly around a ruler for 2 inches, taking care to place the strands of yarn next to one another without crowding or overlapping them, and making sure not to pull the yarn too tightly. Count the number of wraps and then divide by two to get the number of wraps per inch. For extra bulky yarn, measure over a longer distance and divide accordingly.

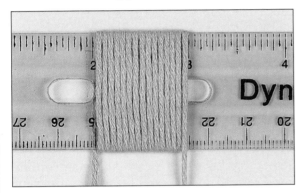

YARDAGE

A common mistake crocheters and knitters make when purchasing yarns is to buy by weight (ounces and grams), not by yardage. Cotton yarn weighs much more per yard than wool does, some wools weigh more per yard than others and some acrylics are very light in weight. If the yardage is not listed on the yarn label, check the yarn company's website for the information. Some companies list their yarn in meters, as opposed to yards. If this is the case, multiply the number of meters by 39 to get an approximate number of yards per ball/skein/hank. Having adequate yardage is the key to having sufficient yarn to complete your project.

THREADS

Most crochet threads are made of cotton. Thread sizes are classified by numbers, such as 10, 20, 30 and so on. The larger the number, the smaller the thread and finer the weight *(see chart below)*. Threads may be packaged as balls, skeins or cones. ■

THREADS

Size	Weight	Recommended hook size(s)
50	Very Fine	12–13/1.00–0.85mm
40	Fine	11–13/1.10–0.85mm
30	Fine	10–12/1.15–1.00mm
20	Light/Bedspread	8–11/1.50–1.10mm
10	Bedspread	5–8/1.90–1.50mm
8	Fingering	5/1.90mm
5	Baby	0–5/2.50–1.90mm
3	Sport	00–0/2.70–2.50mm

Facts About Cotton

Crocheters often ask, "Is cotton yarn better to use for certain items? Can it successfully be substituted for yarns of other fiber content?" The answer to the first question is, "Yes." The answer to the second is, "Not always." The more you know about the characteristics of cotton, the better you'll be able to decide when to use cotton yarn for satisfactory results in your crochet projects.

NATURAL CHARACTERISTICS
Cotton is the most-used fiber in the world today, whether woven into fabric or spun into yarn. It has the following natural characteristics:
- Comfortable
- Soft hand
- Absorbent
- Good strength
- Drapes well
- Easy to care for
- Durable
- Dyes well

Yarn spun of 100 percent cotton tends to have similar qualities to woven fabric and little, if any, natural elasticity. For example, you've probably noticed that the more you wash a

pair of 100 percent cotton pants or flannel pajamas, the shorter they become. Cotton T-shirts tend to not only shrink in length but also grow in width.

Unlike mohair and silk yarns that grow in length with wearing over time, cotton gradually shortens and widens. Keep this characteristic in mind when selecting patterns and determining both body and sleeve lengths.

Cotton has durability and absorbency up to 27 times its own weight. A longtime favorite for warm weather, cotton breathes, making it comfortable to wear in any climate. While many man-made fibers hold heat closer to the body, cotton naturally conducts heat away from the body, making it more comfortable to wear in warmer climates. This quality makes cotton especially good to use for spring or summer throws, baby items, jackets, camisoles, wraps, hats, beachwear and other warm-weather garments, accessories and home accent pieces.

MERCERIZED COTTON
Sometimes known as "pearl" or "perle" cotton, mercerized cotton is put through a treatment process of alkali that alters the cotton and increases both its luster and absorbency. The

process of mercerization leaves yarn both softer and shinier. Cotton is introduced to the mercerization process while under a state of tension.

Originally, this process was found to be a way to improve the finish/sheen of cotton, but it also resulted in an added bonus: greater absorbency when the cotton is exposed to water or dye. Mercerized cotton undergoes certain changes in characteristics and is generally more desirable than non-mercerized cotton.

BLENDED COTTON

Cotton is often blended with other fibers, most often polyester, to enhance performance and to improve the overall appearance of the finished product. Yarn manufacturers select and blend certain proportions so the best qualities and characteristics are retained. You'll find that combinations of fibers and percentages vary from yarn to yarn.

If you're looking for minimal-care yarns, check labels for cotton-blend yarns that are 50 to 60 percent polyester. Most blends within these percentage ranges are both machine washable and dryable. You'll still have the best qualities and the look of cotton with the blend, while the polyester adds durability and resistance to wrinkles.

TIPS FOR CROCHETING WITH COTTON

Always make a swatch before beginning any project. This is especially true for cotton, as working with it is different than with most other yarns due to the lack of elasticity. Cotton stitches stand alone, unlike acrylic, microfiber and most other yarns where the stitches snuggle next to one another. The gaps created while forming stitches with cotton remain gaps and do not fill in.

Fancy stitches worked with cotton yarns tend to be more distinct and stable than those worked with other fibers because of the "stand alone" factor. Cables take on more depth, relief stitches stand out more, popcorns are more stable and other fancy patterns are enhanced when crocheted in cotton.

Soft and pleasant to work with, cotton yarn feels good running between your fingers as you crochet, and feels equally good worn next to the body. A great choice for children, it readily releases soil when washed. Because of its easy-care factor, it's also the ideal fiber for kitchen items like pot holders, dishcloths and towels.

Like many other wonderful things in life, you have to experience cotton yarn to understand and appreciate its advantages. Having the facts about cotton and cotton-blend yarns will help you make informed decisions about when to use them for your crochet projects. ■

How Acrylic Yarn Is Made

There are many things in life we take for granted and still other things that we simply have never thought about. For instance, have you ever wondered where acrylic yarn comes from?

Acrylic yarn is made from synthetic, man-made fibers. The basic building block of acrylic fiber is propylene, a derivative of natural gas. It begins as a clear, watery liquid which is transformed into a flourlike powder through the process of polymerization (a chemical reaction in which two or more molecules combine to form larger molecules that contain repeating structural units). This powder is then mixed with a solvent, and the resulting concoction is a viscous liquid that resembles honey.

Now comes the amazing part. This amber-color goo is forced through a spinneret, a small metal strainer that looks like a showerhead and contains a hundred thousand microscopic holes. As the viscous liquid is pumped through these tiny holes into a vat of warm water and solvent, the actual fibers are created. They can now be dyed, carded and spun like wool or any other natural fiber.

Some acrylic yarns advertise "bounce-back fibers." What exactly does that mean? Regular acrylic yarns are made with only one component and must be crimped by machines. Once this crimp wears out, it won't come back. Who of us hasn't worn or washed a beautifully crafted sweater, only to have it grow twice its original size?

Acrylic yarns with bounce-back fibers, however, have a built-in crimp that is rejuvenated by the laundering process.

When a bounce-back fiber gets wet, one side relaxes and the other side doesn't. During the tumble-dry cycle, the heat reverts the fibers to their original shape. The resiliency is inherent in the fiber, giving the yarn the ability to "remember" its shape.

Because acrylic yarn is manufactured for exceptional durability, is washable and dryable, and is reasonably inexpensive, it's ideal for many different types of charity projects such as hats, mittens, baby blankets, afghans, slippers and pet blankets. And, because it contains no animal fibers, it's nonallergenic and moth-resistant. Keep in mind, however, that acrylic yarn has a lower melting point than cotton or wool so don't iron it or use it for projects that will be exposed to high heat such as pot holders or hot mats. ■

Yarn Substitution Made Easy

Before you substitute one yarn for another, there are several important factors to take into consideration. How does the yarn feel to the hand and on the body? Do you want to crochet fabric for a garment that drapes well or a garment that is firm? Do you want the garment to keep you warm or cool? Do you want the garment to be machine washable and dryable?

The Yarn Characteristics Chart on pages 82 and 83 gives important basic information about various yarn fibers and their characteristics. Understanding the natural characteristics of yarns helps you make more informed yarn choices. For example, if you intend to make a baby garment, silk or mohair yarns are not the most appropriate choices. In case you are concerned about allergies to wool, you'll be glad to know that most wool yarns are treated to avoid such problems. In addition, there are many "superwash" wools on the market that can be machine washed and dried.

If you've fallen in love with a pullover sweater pattern that calls for a soft microfiber yarn with good drape but you decide to use a cotton yarn instead, you probably will not get the same results in either the completed look or feel. A quick glance at the Yarn Characteristics Chart shows you that cotton lacks elasticity and will not drape well. If you want the body and sleeves to have a soft, pliant feeling, you cannot achieve that look and feel using a firm cotton yarn.

TWO YARNS THAT CHANGE THE MOST

The natural yarn fibers that tend to change the most after a garment is finished are mohair and silk. Garments of either fiber tend to grow a significant amount in length. Unfortunately, it is impossible to calculate how much either silk or mohair will grow in length, but knowing about this tendency helps in making yarn choices.

BLENDS

Natural fibers are often blended with synthetic fibers, resulting in yarn choices that give us the best of both worlds. For example, a cotton yarn that is blended with acrylic tends to keep its shape better than 100 percent cotton, yet it still has the same feel of all cotton when worn. In addition, stains are more likely to dissolve during laundering. Always check the yarn label for fiber content information.

LAUNDERING

Yarn labels are often tossed aside, but an educated crocheter reads all the pertinent information the manufacturer provides, including critical information about laundering. When you begin a project, make a habit of setting aside the first label or keep a crochet project notebook, noting laundering information or other pertinent information that can be referred to in the future. Also, note the number of skeins used in case you may want to duplicate a project at a later time. Short on time? Just staple the label next to a description of your project for future reference.

Acrylic yarns are known as "memory" yarns because of their "bounce-back" fibers. Easy to care for, and especially good for children's garments, they can simply be tossed in the washer and dryer. However, due to the fact that acrylic yarns expand when wet, acrylic yarns should not be used for swimsuits. It is the drying cycle that brings these yarns back to their original state.

Many of the new microfiber yarns also include acrylic fibers, but, unlike true memory yarns, their labels are likely to state they must be hand-washed and laid flat to dry. Always follow label instructions for laundering. Never substitute information about laundering yarn with information about laundering woven fabrics because there are often distinct differences between knit/crochet yarns and the thin threads used in woven fabrics.

The finish and appearance of the yarn also should be a determining factor when choosing a substitute yarn, especially if you are hoping to crochet a garment similar to your pattern. Before making a yarn choice, consider the following: Does your substitute yarn have a flat or shiny appearance? Is the original yarn textured, twisted, thick-and-thin, fuzzy, fluffy, bouclé or smooth? Does the pattern call for a yarn in a solid color, a tweed, a variegated or a self-striping pattern? Does it have some other distinctive look such as a metallic thread, or perhaps one color wrapped with a strand of another color or type of yarn? There are often various factors that have to be taken into account before making a wise yarn substitution.

DOES GAUGE REALLY MATTER?

If you want your finished project to match the size given in your pattern, you need to match the gauge given for the specified hook size. This is an important factor to keep in mind when substituting yarn. Most yarn labels tell you the recommended gauge and hook size. Read the label and purchase a yarn that not only is a suitable replacement based on fiber content, but also comes closest to the specified gauge in your pattern.

The best and most definitive way to make sure your chosen yarn will work in your particular pattern is to work up a small test swatch, about 4 or 5 inches square, and measure to see if it matches the pattern gauge. As previously discussed in this chapter, yarns in the same weight category are not all created equal and have variances in both weight and thickness.

In the photos at right, all three swatches were crocheted in half double crochet using three different worsted weight yarns and a size H hook. You can see they vary slightly in size to each other. This is attributable to the true diameter of each yarn as well as the fiber content. The difference in gauge seen in these three small swatches would be greatly increased over the size of a large project, resulting in a very different finished size.

When making a test swatch with your substitute yarn, if the gauge is very close but not exact, sometimes a simple change to the next size smaller or next size larger hook will take care of it without compromising the look or feel of the item.

Making successful yarn substitutions is easy when you can make informed decisions based on some basic, important information. It will help ensure the best possible crochet results for your crochet projects. ■

chapter seven
getting it together

Whether it's knowing which joining technique to use to create the desired seaming in your projects or understanding which adhesive will work best for gluing certain crocheted items, the information in this chapter will help you pull it all together successfully!

Secrets of Seaming Success

Whether joining afghan blocks or strips, or seaming a garment, the various pieces can be joined using one or more of several methods. Crocheting pieces together generally results in a stronger, more stable seam, while sewing often produces a lighter, less bulky seam.

Let's look at some of the most common joining methods using afghan pieces as an example. You can choose a specific type of joining method that best suits your project, depending on the look you want or the strength that your design needs. Note that in photos, a contrasting color yarn was used for seaming for better visibility; for your project, use a matching color to help your seams blend in.

WHIPSTITCH IN ONE LOOP

One of the most common sewing methods for joining crocheted pieces is an overhand stitch, or whipstitch. Hold the pieces with right sides together and sew through the **back loops** (see Stitch Guide) only (see Photo A). Sewing through the back loops only gives a pretty result with the remaining loops, forming a subtle outline ridge on the right side of the work that defines each block or strip.

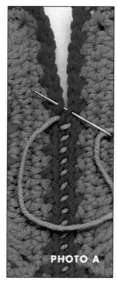

PHOTO A

SINGLE CROCHET

For a raised ridge on the right side of your project, use a single crochet joining, holding the pieces with wrong sides together. The photo example is worked in the back loops only (see Photo C). This type of joining can also be worked on the wrong side if a decorative raised ridge on the front side of the project isn't desired.

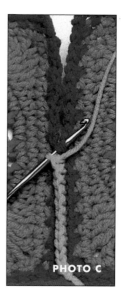

PHOTO C

WHIPSTITCH IN BOTH LOOPS

If you prefer not to have a ridged outline around the pieces visible on the front side, sew through both loops of the stitches as shown here (see Photo B).

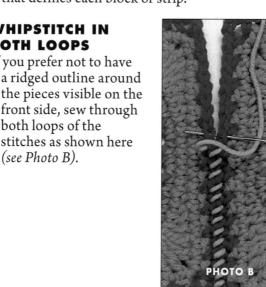

PHOTO B

REVERSE SINGLE CROCHET

Joining pieces using reverse single crochet stitches produces a braided cord effect (see Photo D). As the name implies, you are working your single crochet stitches in reverse, or from left to right (right-handed) or right to left (left-handed).

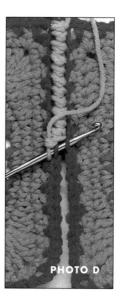

PHOTO D

SLIP STITCH ON FRONT SIDE

This joining creates an attractive chain stitch on the right side of the work. Place the pieces with right sides facing up and edges overlapping. Keeping the yarn behind the pieces, insert the hook through the back loop of each stitch to the back of the work and draw the yarn through all loops to the front of the work *(see Photo E)*.

PHOTO E

SLIP STITCH & CHAIN

Using this seaming method gives a pretty lattice-type insert between the joined pieces. Holding the pieces with wrong sides together, simply slip stitch back and forth between the pieces, chaining two or three between and skipping one or two stitches on the motifs *(see Photo G)*.

PHOTO G

SLIP STITCH ON BACK SIDE

Slip stitching the pieces together from the wrong side will produce an almost invisible joining. This method is faster and easier than sewing and will keep the seams flatter and the stitches more even. Place the pieces together with right sides facing and slip stitch either through the back loops only *(see Photo F)* or through all loops, depending on whether or not you want an outline stitch to be visible on the right side of the work.

PHOTO F

Have fun experimenting with different joining techniques to give your project the right finished look and necessary stability. Knowing which technique works best for your project will help produce successful results time after time. To get you started, turn the page to find two bold and beautiful afghan projects that incorporate two of the seaming techniques discussed in this article. ▪

Aztec Medallions

SKILL LEVEL

INTERMEDIATE

FINISHED SIZES
Afghan: 45 x 45 inches
Square: 14 x 14 inches

MATERIALS
- Medium (worsted) weight yarn:
  14 oz/728 yds/396g black
  150 yds each 11 scrap colors
- Size H/8/5mm crochet hook or size
  needed to obtain gauge
- Tapestry needle

GAUGE
3 sc = 1 inch; 3 sc rnds = 1 inch

Check gauge to save time.

PATTERN NOTES
Weave in loose ends as work progresses.

Join with a slip stitch unless otherwise stated.

SQUARE
MAKE 9.
Rnd 1 (RS): With first scrap color, ch 2, 6 sc in 2nd ch from hook, **join** (*see Pattern Notes*) in beg sc. (*6 sc*)

Rnd 2: Ch 1, 2 sc in each sc around, join in beg sc. (*12 sc*)

Rnd 3: Ch 1, [sc in next sc, 2 sc in next sc] around, join in beg sc. (*18 sc*)

Rnd 4: Ch 1, working in **back lps** (*see Stitch Guide*) only, [sc in each of next 2 sc, 2 sc in next sc] around, join in beg sc. (*24 sc*)

Rnd 5: Ch 1, working in back lps only, [sc in next sc, 2 sc in next sc] around, join in beg sc, fasten off. (*36 sc*)

Rnd 6: Join 2nd scrap in first st of rnd 5, ch 1, [sc in each of next 2 sc, sk next rem lp on rnd 4, dc in next rem lp, sk next 2 rem lps of rnd 3, 2 tr in next rem lp, sk next rem lp of rnd 4,

dc in next rem lp, sk next 4 sc of rnd 5] 6 times, join in beg sc.

Rnd 7: Ch 1, [sc in each of next 5 sc, 2 sc in next sc] around, join in beg sc. (*42 sc*)

Rnd 8: Ch 1, [sc in each of next 6 sc, 2 sc in next sc] around, join in beg sc. (*48 sc*)

Rnd 9: Ch 1, working in back lps only, [sc in each of next 3 sc, 2 sc in next sc] around, join in beg sc. (*60 sc*)

Rnd 10: Ch 1, working in back lps only, [sc in each of next 4 sc, 2 sc in next sc] around, join in beg sc, fasten off. (*72 sc*)

Rnd 11: Join 3rd scrap color in first st of rnd 10, ch 1, [sc in each of next 2 sc, sk next 2 rem lps of rnd 9, dc in next rem lp, sk next 2 rem lps of rnd 8, tr in each of next 2 rem lps, sk next rem lp of rnd 9, dc in next rem lp, sk next 4 sc of rnd 10] 12 times, join in beg sc.

Rnd 12: Ch 1, sc in each st around, join in beg sc.

Rnd 13: Ch 1, [sc in each of next 5 sc, 2 sc in next sc] rep around, join in beg sc, fasten off. (*84 sc*)

Rnd 14: Join 4th scrap color in any back lp of rnd 13, ch 1, working in back lps only, [sc in each of next 7 sts, hdc in each of next 3 sts, dc in each of next 2 sts, tr in each of next 2 sts, ch 2, tr in each of next 2 sts, dc in each of next 2 sts, hdc in each of next 3 sts] 4 times, join in beg sc.

Rnd 15: Ch 1, *sc in each of next 7 sts, hdc in each of next 3 sts, dc in each of next 4 sts, (2 dc, ch 2, 2 dc) in next ch-2 sp (*corner*), dc in each of next 4 sts, hdc in each of next 3 sts, rep from * 3 times, join in beg sc, fasten off. (*100 sts*)

Rnd 16: Join 5th scrap color in first st of rnd 15, ch 3 (*counts as first dc*), dc in each st around, working (3 dc, ch 2, 3 dc) in each corner ch-2 sp, join in 3rd ch of beg ch-3. (*124 dc*)

Rnd 17: Ch 1, working in back lps only, sc in each st around, working (2 sc, ch 2, 2 sc) in each corner ch-2 sp, join in beg sc, fasten off. *(140 sc)*

Rnd 18: Working in back lps only, join 6th scrap color in first st of rnd 17, ch 1, sc in back lp of each st around, working (sc, ch 2, sc) in each corner ch-2 sp, join in beg sc. *(148 sc)*

Rnd 19: Ch 1, *(sc, ch 2, sc) in corner ch-2 sp, sc in each of next 2 sts, sk next rem lp of rnd 17, dc in next rem lp, tr in first rem lp of rnd 16, sk next rem lp of rnd 17, dc in next rem lp, [sk next 3 sts of rnd 18, sc in each of next 2 sts, sk next 2 rem lps of rnd 17, dc in next rem lp, sk next 4 rem lps of rnd 16, tr in next rem lp, sk next rem lp of rnd 17, dc in next rem lp] 6 times, sk next 3 sts of rnd 18, sc in each of next 2 sts, rep from * 3 times, join in beg sc. *(156 sts)*

Rnd 20: Ch 1, sc in each st around, working 3 sc in each corner ch-2 sp, join in beg sc, fasten off. *(168 sc)*

JOINING

Arrange squares in 3 rows of 3 squares each. With desired color, matching sts and working in back lps only, sl st squares tog.

BORDER

Rnd 1: Attach same color as used in joining in back lp of any st on outer edge, ch 1, sc in each st around, join in beg sc.

Rnd 2: Ch 1, hdc in each st around, join in beg hdc, fasten off. ■

Joyous Squares

SKILL LEVEL

▰▰▰▱
INTERMEDIATE

FINISHED SIZE

Approximately 48 x 56 inches

MATERIALS

- Red Heart Soft Yarn medium (worsted) weight yarn (5 oz/256 yds/140g per skein):
  3 skeins each #9518 teal (A), #9779 berry (B) and #9522 leaf (C)
  2 skeins #3720 lavender (D)
- Size I/9/5.5mm crochet hook or size needed to obtain gauge
- Tapestry needle

GAUGE

Rnds 1 and 2 = 3 inches in diameter

PATTERN NOTES

Join with slip stitch unless otherwise stated.

Chain-3 at beginning of rounds counts as first double crochet unless otherwise stated.

SPECIAL STITCHES

Double crochet corner (dc corner): (4 dc, ch 3, 4 dc) in indicated sp.

Single crochet-double crochet corner (sc-dc corner): (Sc, ch 1, 3 dc, ch 1, sc) in indicated sp.

Round 9 corner (rnd 9 corner): [Dc in next ch, ch 1] 3 times.

3-single crochet corner (3-sc corner): 3 sc in indicated st.

SQUARE A
MAKE 5.

Rnd 1: With B, ch 5, **join** (see Pattern Notes) in 5th ch from hook to form ring, **ch 3** (see Pattern Notes), 3 dc in ring, [ch 3, 4 dc in ring] 3 times, join with hdc in 3rd ch of beg ch-3.

Rnd 2: Ch 3, 3 dc in sp formed by joining hdc, ch 1, *dc corner (see Special Stitches) in next ch-3 sp, ch 1, rep from * twice, 4 dc in same sp as beg ch-3, join with hdc in 3rd ch of beg ch-3.

Rnd 3: Ch 3, 3 dc in sp formed by joining hdc, ch 1, *4 dc next ch-1 sp, ch 1, dc corner in next ch-3 sp, ch 1, rep from * twice, 4 dc in same sp as beg ch-3, ch 1, join with hdc in 3rd ch of beg ch-3.

Rnd 4: Ch 3, 3 dc in sp formed by joining hdc, *[ch 1, 4 dc next ch-1 sp] twice, ch 1, dc corner in next dc corner ch-3 sp, rep from * twice, [ch 1, 4 dc next ch-1 sp] twice, ch 1, 4 dc in same sp as beg ch-3, ch 3, join in 3rd ch of beg ch-3. Fasten off.

Rnd 5: Join A with sc in 3rd dc of any corner, work rem rnd as follows:

A. *Ch 1, **sc-dc corner** (see Special Stitches) in next corner ch-3 sp, ch 1, sk next dc, sc in next dc, ch 3, sk next 2 dc on rnd 3, sc in next dc on rnd 3, ch 3, sk next 2 dc on rnd 2, sc in next dc on rnd 2;

B. ch 3, sk next 2 dc on rnd 1, sc in next dc on rnd 1, ch 3, sk next 2 dc of next corner on rnd 2, sc in next dc on rnd 2, ch 3, sk next 2 dc of corner on rnd 3, sc in next dc on rnd 3, ch 3, sk next 2 dc of corner on rnd 4**, sc in next dc;

C. rep from * 3 times, ending last rep at **;

D. join in joining sc. Fasten off.

Rnd 6: Join D with sc in 2nd ch-1 sp between any 2 corners on rnd 4, work rem rnd as follows:

A. Ch 1, (3 dc, ch 1, sc) in same sp as beg ch-1;

B. *ch 4, sc in 2nd ch-3 sp of next 3 ch-3 sps on rnd 5, ch 4, sk next sc-dc corner on rnd 5, sc in 2nd ch-3 sp of next 3 ch-3 sps on same rnd, ch 4**, (sc, ch 1, 3 dc, ch 1, sc) in next ch-1 sp on rnd 4;

C. rep from * 3 times, ending last rep at **, join in joining sc. Fasten off.

Rnd 7: Join C in first ch-1 sp to left of any corner on rnd 4, work rem rnd as follows:

A. Ch 3, 2 dc in same sp as beg ch-3, *ch 2, sc in next ch-4 sp on rnd 6, ch 3, working behind next 5-st group on rnd 6, sc in 3rd dc of next 4-dc group on rnd 3, ch 3;

B. working on front side, sc in next ch-4 sp on rnd 6, ch 2, 3 dc in next ch-1 sp on rnd 4, ch 2, sc in next ch-1 sp on rnd 5;

C. working behind next corner, ch 35;

D. working on front side, sc in next ch-1 sp on rnd 5, ch 2**, 3 dc in next ch-1 sp;

E. rep from * 3 times, ending last rep at **, join in 3rd ch of beg ch-3. **Do not fasten off.**

F. Pull 1 ch-35 lp from back to front through ch-1 sp of corresponding corner on rnd 3, over ch-4 sp made on rnd 6 and from front to back through same sp on rnd 3, draw lp to front in ch-1 sp on corresponding corner on rnd 2. Rep with rem lps.

Rnd 8: Sl st in next dc, ch 1, sc in same dc, *ch 5, sc in 2nd dc of next 3-dc group on rnd 6, ch 5, sc in 2nd dc of next 3-dc group on rnd 7, ch 5, sk next sc, sc in next dc on rnd 5, ch 5, sk next dc, sc in next dc, ch 5**, sc in 2nd dc of next 3-dc group on rnd 7, rep from * 3 times, ending last rep at **, join in first sc.

Rnd 9: Ch 4 (*counts as first dc and ch-1 sp*), sk next ch, dc in next st, *[ch 1, sk next ch, dc in next ch] twice, ch 1, sk next ch, dc in next st*, rep between * twice, ***rnd 9 corner* (*see Special Stitches*), dc in next st, rep between * 4 times, rep from ** twice, rnd 9 corner, dc in next st, rep between * twice, join in 3rd ch of beg ch-4. Fasten off.

Rnd 10: Join B with sl st in 2nd dc of any rnd 9 corner, ch 1, **3-sc corner** (*see Special Stitches*) in same dc as beg ch-1, *sc in each dc and in each ch around to 2nd dc of next rnd 9 corner, 3-sc corner in 2nd dc of next rnd 9 corner, rep from * twice, sc in each dc and in each ch around to first sc, join in first sc.

Rnd 11: Ch 1, sc in same sc, 3-sc corner in next sc, *sc in each sc to 2nd sc of next 3-sc corner, 3-sc corner in 2nd sc, rep from * twice, sc in each sc around to first sc, join in first sc.

Fasten off and weave in all ends.

CENTER KNOT
Join D in any ch-35 sp, ch 1, sc in same lp and in each rem ch-35 sp, join in first sc.

Fasten off and weave in ends.

SQUARE B
MAKE 5.
Rnds 1–4: Rep rnds 1–4 of Square A.

Rnd 5: With D, rep rnd 5 of Square A.

Rnd 6: With A, rep rnd 6 of Square A.

Rnds 7–11: Rep rnds 7–11 of Square A.

CENTER KNOT
Join A in any ch-35 sp, ch 1, sc in same sp as beg ch-1 and in each rem ch-35 sp, join in first sc.

Fasten off and weave in ends.

SQUARE C
MAKE 5.
Rnds 1–4: With A, rep rnds 1–4 of Square A.

Rnd 5: With B, rep rnd 5 of Square A.

Rnd 6: With D, rep rnd 6 of Square A.

Rnds 7–11: Rep rnds 7–11 of Square A.

CENTER KNOT
Join D in any ch-35 sp, ch 1, sc in same sp as beg ch-1 and in each rem ch-35 sp, join in first sc. Fasten off and weave in ends.

SQUARE D
MAKE 5.

Rnds 1–4: With A, rep rnds 1–4 of Square A.

Rnd 5: With D, rep rnd 5 of Square A.

Rnd 6: With B, rep rnd 6 of Square A.

Rnds 7–11: Rep rnds 7–11 of Square A.

CENTER KNOT
Join B in any ch-35 sp, ch 1, sc in same sp as beg ch-1 and in each rem ch-35 sp, join in first sc. Fasten off and weave in ends.

SQUARE E
MAKE 5.

Rnds 1–4: With D, rep rnds 1–4 of Square A.

Rnd 5: With B, rep rnd 5 of Square A.

Rnd 6: With A, rep rnd 6 of Square A.

Rnds 7–11: Rep rnds 7–11 of Square A.

CENTER KNOT
Join A in any ch-35 sp, ch 1, sc in same sp as beg ch-1 and in each rem ch-35 sp, join in first sc. Fasten off and weave in ends.

SQUARE F
MAKE 5.

Rnds 1–4: With D, rep rnds 1–4 of Square A.

Rnd 5: With A, rep rnd 5 of Square A.

Rnd 6: With B, rep rnd 6 of Square A.

Rnds 7–11: Rep rnds 7–11 of Square A.

CENTER KNOT
Join B in any ch-35 sp, ch 1, sc in same sp as beg ch-1 and in each rem ch-35 sp, join in first sc. Fasten off and weave in ends.

ASSEMBLY
Referring to photo for placement, join Squares in 6 rows of 5 Squares each. To join Squares, hold 2 Squares with WS tog, join A in 2nd sc of right-hand corner, ch 1, sc in same sc and in each sc to 2nd sc of next corner. Join Squares in rows, and then join rows in same manner.

OUTER BORDER
Rnd 1 (RS): Hold piece with RS facing you and 1 short end at top, join A in 2nd sc in upper right-hand corner, ch 1, 3-sc corner in same sc as beg ch-1, *sc in each sc around to 2nd sc of next 3-sc corner, 3-sc corner in 2nd sc, rep from * twice, sc in each rem sc around to first sc, join in first sc.

Rnd 2: Ch 1, sc in same sc as beg ch-1, 3-sc corner in next sc, *sc in each sc to 2nd sc of next 3-sc corner, 3-sc corner in 2nd sc, rep from * twice, sc in each rem sc around to first sc, join in first sc.

Rnd 3: Ch 1, sc in same or sc as beg ch-1 and in next sc, 3-sc corner in next sc, *sc in each sc around to 2nd sc of next 3-sc corner, 3-sc corner in 2nd sc, rep from * twice, sc in each rem sc around to first sc, join in first sc.

Rnd 4: Ch 1, sc in same sc as beg ch-1 and in each of next 2 sc, 3-sc corner in next sc, *sc in each sc to 2nd sc of next 3-sc corner, 3-sc corner in 2nd sc, rep from * twice, sc in each rem sc around to first sc, join in first sc.

Rnd 5: Ch 1, sc in same sc as beg ch-1 and in each of next 3 sc, 3-sc corner in next sc, *sc in each sc around to 2nd sc of next 3-sc corner, 3-sc corner in 2nd sc, rep from * twice, sc in each rem sc around to first sc, join in first sc, turn.

Rnd 6 (WS): Ch 1, sc in next sc, *ch 2, sl st in top of sc just made, sc in each of next 3 sc, rep from * around with 3 sc in 2nd sc of each 3-sc corner, join in first sc.

Fasten off and weave in ends. ▪

Tunisian Joining: From Bulky to Beautiful

If you would like to create smoother seams for a more professional-looking finish in your crochet projects, here are a few questions which may let you know you if need to learn a new, and perhaps better, way to finish your crochet work:

• Does your whipstitch look whipped?

• Do your crochet joins add so much bulk that your garment is bursting at the seams?

• Do you struggle to join your crochet pieces one to another and when your hard work is completed your joins cause your crochet work to appear as though it is a botched, homemade garment?

• Have you ever snagged your beautiful crochet stitches and tangled your sewing thread while trying to sew two crochet pieces together with a needle?

• Have you never learned to join your crochet with a crochet hook?

If you answered "Yes" to even one of the questions, chances are you are looking for a better and faster way to join two pieces of crochet. Your crochet seams and joinings need to look as though they fit together like a long-married couple.

One of the key reasons most crocheters avoid multipiece projects or certain complicated fashions is that the crocheter is not satisfied with the way the projects look after they have been joined.

Tunisian join is created over two rows just like regular Tunisian crochet. It is best to work the Tunisian joining technique using a cro-hook/afghan hook which is one or two sizes smaller than the crochet hook used for the project. After a while, the only method I used to join fashions at the seams, or to join motifs, was the Tunisian join.

The remainder of this article is a workshop. Find three different colors of yarn so that you can easily follow along while you learn.

You need the following materials for this exercise:

MATERIALS

• Same-weight and/or class yarn: 3 colors (A, B, C)
• Size H/8/5mm crochet hook or size appropriate for yarn
• Size G/6/4mm cro-hook/afghan hook or size appropriate for yarn
• Size E/4/3.5mm or F/5/3.75mm crochet hook for weaving in ends
• Safety pins or stitch markers to hold pieces together

Let's get started.

INSTRUCTIONS
SAMPLES
MAKE 1 EACH COLOR A & COLOR B.

Notes: The reason you crochet into back bar of chain is because your pieces will fit together and join better. Mark right side of each sample with a safety pin.

Step 1 (RS): With size H hook and indicated color, ch 26 *(see Photo A).*

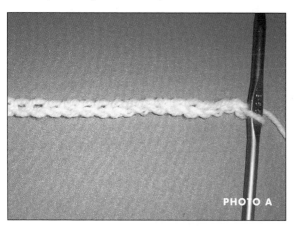

PHOTO A

Step 2: Working in the **back bar** *(see illustration)* of each ch, sc in each ch across, turn *(see Photo B on page 102). (25 sc)*

Back Bar of Chain

PHOTO B

Step 3: Ch 1, sc in each st across, turn.

Rep step 3 for 9 more rows for a total of 12 rows.

Mark front side of each sample with a safety pin.

Step 4: After creating 1 sample each A and B (see Photo C), you are now ready to practice joining the samples.

PHOTO C

JOINING

Step 5: Pin the samples tog so the RS is facing. With joining yarn, make a slip knot on the cro-hook (afghan hook), working with the first group of sts from both swatches, and leaving all lps on hook, insert the cro-hook (afghan hook) into the front lp of the first st on the sample closest to you AND under the back lp of first st on the sample farthest from you, yo, pull through both lps (see Photo D).

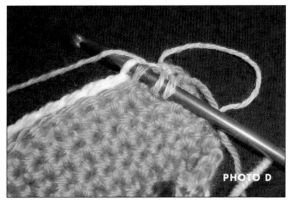

PHOTO D

Step 6: *Insert the cro-hook into next front lp on the sample nearest you AND under the next back lp of the sample farthest from you, yo, pull through both lps.* Rep from * to * until all lps are on the cro-hook (see Photo E).

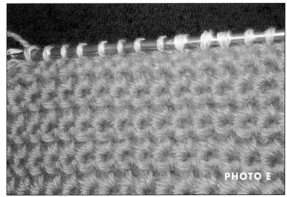

PHOTO E

Step 7: After all lps are on the hook, you will work the lps off the hook as follows: Yo, pull through 1 lp, then *yo and pull through 2 lps* *(see Photo F)*. Rep from * to * to end of row. There will be 1 lp on hook.

Leaving an approximately 5-inch-long tail, cut working yarn. Fasten off. After your work is completed, turn crochet work to the RS.

Step 8: Weave in ends with smaller hook.

The Tunisian join will make your work look much smoother, especially on the front *(see Photo G Front and Back)*.

You can use this method to join motifs, fashion crochet pieces or any two items you need to join. ■

PHOTO F

PHOTO G FRONT

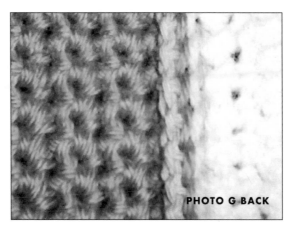

PHOTO G BACK

Using Adhesives: The Right Way to "Stick It!"

Crocheters often face the dilemma of deciding which type of glue is best to use on their crochet projects.

Actually, there is not just a single type of adhesive that is appropriate to use on all crochet projects. It depends on the item and its intended use.

With so many choices available today, crafters have access to a variety of adhesives that can be used effectively on a wide range of surfaces. Because the surface of crochet is porous, certain types of glue work better than others. The texture of the crochet thread or yarn will affect how the adhesive will work. The tighter the twist, the stronger the hold of the adhesive will be.

Worsted yarns have a tendency to soak up liquid glue. A thick, tacky glue works better (in lieu of purchasing a tacky glue, you can apply liquid glue to another surface, such as a piece of waxed paper, for example, and allow it to thicken to a tacky consistency before applying it to the crochet surface).

Hot glue provides one of the strongest bonds on crocheted surfaces, but it must be used carefully and sparingly, applying just enough to invisibly secure the item. If too much hot glue is applied and it squeezes out around the piece being glued, it quickly creates an ugly, hard ridge on the fabric as it sets. Used minimally so that no excess is visible, hot glue is a great choice for crocheted items with pieces that really need some extra strength. Just be sure to carefully clean off any glue strings that are left behind. Using a hair dryer on the "hot" setting and moving it back and forth over the glue strings makes them disappear.

I would suggest testing this on a small practice piece of crochet fabric to which something has been adhered with hot glue.

If you have a crocheted piece with glued-on accents, and it will be washed, be sure to use washable fabric glue, or your embellishments will likely come loose when the piece is laundered.

A spray adhesive that provides a temporary hold is a great choice when you're trying to get the placement just right for pieces that will be permanently glued. Once everything is positioned where you want it, then you can apply your permanent adhesive.

A word of advice: Gluing decorative embellishments on a crocheted project is generally recommended if the item is being used for display purposes only. If it's going to receive a lot of wear and tear (especially if it's for children), the best adhesive is still a good, secure stitching with needle and thread. If it's for a child, and you want it to stay on, sew it on. ◼

chapter eight
the right fit

It's no secret that we all come in different sizes and shapes. We'll show you how to adapt clothing patterns for a perfect fit and share shaping secrets for creating more flattering, comfortable garments. We even have easy steps for creating your own crochet skirt template!

Enlarging Patterns for a Perfect Fit

It's no secret that women come in all sizes and shapes, yet, due to editorial space constraints, most crochet garment patterns are only given for specific sizes and measurements. If you are one of many who want to know how to enlarge a pattern size, help is at hand.

How many times have you wanted to make a beautiful crochet jacket, top or sweater pattern you have seen in a book or magazine, only to discover that the sizes given in the instructions do not include yours? By following the four steps outlined in this article, you can successfully enlarge patterns that result in a perfect, professional look and fit regardless of your size or shape. The Classic Chanel Jacket featured with this article *(page 110)* is the perfect type of garment for your first attempt at enlarging pattern sizing.

Unless you are adept at pattern drafting and the mathematical formulas required, avoid cap or raglan sleeves when enlarging pattern sizes. The sleeves on the Classic Chanel Jacket appear to be cap sleeves, but they are actually straight across the top sleeve and the length of the sleeve is simply extended to fit into the armhole opening.

STEP 1: TAKING MEASUREMENTS

Most women know their bust size and sleeve length, and all too often use those measurements when determining the size of pattern to make. Start by taking a jacket from your own closet which is similar to our pattern in structure and appearance, and most importantly, has a comfortable fit.

The amount of ease allowed *(the difference between the actual and finished measurements)* is rarely given consideration when you decide which size to crochet, yet it is a critical component when it comes to how a garment fits. It is not unusual to discover that the most comfortable fit for a jacket or other outer garment has more ease than one expects. To ensure a comfortable fit, you may

prefer 6 to 8 inches of ease which will allow enough room for comfortable, unrestricted movement.

Measure your jacket *(see Fig. 1)* and write down the following:

1. Bust *(around the fullest part of the chest)*

2. Sleeve length *(underarm to wrist)*

3. Armhole depth *(underarm to shoulder seam on flat garment)*

4. Shoulder to shoulder *(sharp bone on each side of body)*

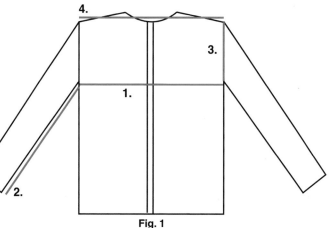

Fig. 1

STEP 2: MAKING SWATCHES

Before making any changes to the basic pattern you wish to enlarge, crochet a swatch at least 4 inches square using the yarn and hook size required to obtain the stated gauge in your pattern. Our pattern calls for a size J hook to get a gauge of five stitches and four rows each to equal 2 inches. To begin, chain 26, half-double crochet in third chain from hook *(beginning 2 skipped chains count as first half double crochet)* and in each remaining chain across, turn. *(25 hdc)*

Work even in half double crochet until swatch measures 4 inches in length.

Remember, when crocheting, you are creating fabric. You need this first swatch to determine the feel and look of the fabric in the original pattern. Your swatch will reveal whether the fabric created is firm or soft, does or doesn't have drape, and how close or far apart stitches are placed.

STEP 3: MEASURING GAUGE ACCURATELY

Gauge is the most critical element of any garment because it determines not only the garment's measurements, but also the ultimate outcome. After completing a swatch, smooth it out gently, and lay it flat. Do not touch or adjust the swatch again before measuring.

Use a slotted gauge and lay it flat against the swatch (*see Photo A*), counting and writing down the number of stitches, including partial stitches, that show within the 2-inch horizontal slot. Then, measure and record the number of rows shown in the 2-inch vertical slot. As you can see, our swatch exactly matches our pattern gauge of five stitches and four rows each to equal 2 inches.

If the stitches that show within the slot are not full stitches, then use the 6-inch side of the gauge to measure over 4 inches or more until you have isolated only a specific number of full stitches. Measuring a second time, over a greater number of inches, also serves to ensure that your first 2-inch measurement is accurate.

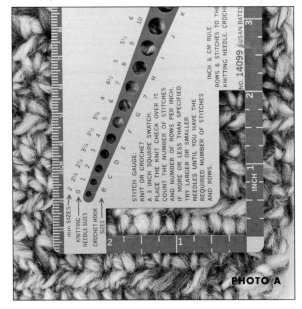

PHOTO A

STEP 4: DOING THE MATH

After comparing your own measurements to those given in our schematic, you may be able to enlarge the pattern simply by using a larger hook. For example, try making another swatch with a hook one size larger (K) than the size called for in the pattern using the same number of stitches specified for the first swatch. Compare the two swatches, writing down the differences.

When it comes to measuring gauge, the number of stitches per inch is more important than the number of rows per inch, as it is the number of stitches per inch that determines the width of the fabric you crochet. If your row count is a bit off, you can crochet to the lengths given on the schematic or to the desired length. A ¼- or ½-inch difference in total length doesn't make a big difference in how a garment fits, but a difference of ¼- or ½-stitch per inch makes a great difference in the width of a garment.

Required Gauge 2.5 sts per inch: 2.5 x 20" = 50 sts (50 divided by 2.25 = 20")	Finished Width of Back: 20"	Double Back for Total Measurement: 40"
If true gauge is 2.25: 50 sts divided by 2.25	22⅛"	44¼"
If true gauge is 2.75: 50 sts divided by 2.75	18⅛"	36¼"
If true gauge is 3: 50 sts divided by 3	16⅝"	33¼"

Fig. 2

Shown above (*see Fig. 2*) are examples of how gauge affects the width of the back of a jacket back with a required 20-inch width and 50 stitches.

As you can see, when you smooth out a swatch and alter the true gauge by as little as ¼ inch, the true difference in width makes a significant and usually unexpected alteration!

I do not recommend increasing the hook size by more than one or two sizes because doing so causes distinct changes in the fabric itself. The larger the hook size, the looser and more stretchy the fabric becomes, resulting in the loss of the integrity of the fabric itself. Changing hook sizes by more than one size works best for lacy fabrics, granny squares or motifs. This technique is best used for items other than garments such as afghans, handbags, pillows or other items where specific measurements are not as critical as those needed for well-fitting garments.

Using your swatch and gauge, you can now calculate the number of stitches required for the width of the finished size you desire. The following examples explain this process. Our examples use the gauge of 2½ stitches per inch as in our instructions. However, if your swatch has a different gauge, you will use that number to determine how many stitches are required for each piece of the jacket.

BACK

If you want to enlarge our pattern by one size, or 4 inches, you will need a total width of 52 inches. The back will be half that amount, or 26 inches; 26 x 2.5 (*our gauge and number of stitches per inch*) to get a total of 65 stitches, or simply use your own gauge (*number of stitches per inch*) if different than our gauge. Write this number down at the bottom of the schematic for the back. Remember to add 1 to your number of 65 for the beginning number of chains, for a total of 66 chains. Work the back to the desired length or number of rows to armhole. Fasten off and follow instructions below.

Before deducting stitches for the armhole opening, check the width of the upper sleeve, which must equal the total of the front and back armhole depths. If you have slim arms,

you may wish to make your sleeves narrower. If you have full arms, you may wish to widen the upper sleeve, remembering to alter the armhole depth accordingly. For example, if you need an upper arm width of 22 inches (*half this number results in an armhole depth of 11 inches*), multiply 22 by 2.5 (*our gauge, or substitute your own gauge*) to get a total of 55 stitches across upper sleeve.

Next, deduct your shoulder-to-shoulder measurement from the total back width. Multiply this number by 2.5 stitches per inch. If this number is an odd number, either add or subtract one stitch so you are working with even numbers. Divide that number in half to determine the number of stitches that must be skipped at both the beginning and end of the next row of the back to shape the armhole. Skipping the required stitches at both the beginning and end of the next row, work even in hdc to within two rows less than desired length. As you can see on the schematic, six (seven–nine) stitches are skipped for each armhole.

To determine the number of stitches for each shoulder, you must first determine the back neck width times the gauge. For example, if you wish a back neck width of 8 inches, multiply 8 x 2.5 (*our gauge, or substitute your own gauge*), which equals 20 stitches. ***Note:*** *However, if the total number of stitches required for the width of your jacket is an uneven number, then you must add one stitch to, or subtract one stitch from, the back neck so each shoulder has the same number of stitches.*

Subtract 20 back neck stitches from the number of stitches needed for the shoulder-to-shoulder measurement and divide that answer in half. The answer is the number of stitches needed for each shoulder. Work across this same number of stitches for first shoulder; turn and work second row. Fasten off. Skip the 20 back neck stitches. Attach yarn to next stitch, chain two (*counts as first half double crochet*), and work the same total number of stitches (*beginning chain-two counts as one stitch*) as were worked for the first shoulder. Fasten off.

FRONTS

Each front requires half the number of stitches of the total back. Should the number of stitches for the back be an uneven number, subtract one stitch from that number and divide the answer in half to determine the number of stitches required for the lower width of the jacket. No changes are required for the armhole depth or for the shoulders as they will remain the same as the back.

The only other change left to make is to calculate the front neck shaping and drop. The drop is measured from the first row of the neckline shaping to the shoulder. Use your garment to determine this measurement. Let's say you want a 5-inch drop and two rows equal 1 inch. Multiply the drop of 5 inches by two rows (per inch), and you will then have 10 rows in which to shape the front neckline.

Begin by dividing the back neck stitches in half to determine the total number of stitches to be deducted. Simply divide the back number of stitches (20) in half for a total of 10 stitches that need to be deducted over 10 rows. Neckline shaping is created by skipping an initial number of stitches and then gradual decreases. In our pattern, one stitch is decreased (by working two stitches together) every other row, three times, for a total of three stitches. Subtract those three stitches from the total number of stitches required for the neck (10), or seven stitches. Then skip the first seven stitches to start the initial neck shaping. Attach yarn to next stitch and work to end of the row. *Work the next row even. Begin the next row by working half double crochet decrease in next two half double crochet stitches. Repeat from * two more times for a total deduction of three stitches at the neck edge, resulting in the same number of stitches remaining for the shoulder as for the back. Simply work even until the front length and number of rows equals that of the back.

SLEEVES

Begin by determining the length desired for sleeves. Deduct 1 inch for the edging. Write this length on the schematic. Write down (across upper sleeve on schematic) the total number of stitches required to fit armhole (as previously described). Using a tape measure held in a circle, determine what width is required to comfortably insert one hand. Use this measurement and multiply it by your gauge to determine the number of stitches needed for the first row of a sleeve. Deduct the number of stitches in the first row (wrist) from the number required for the last row (upper sleeve). Divide this number by two—this is the number of stitches that must be increased, at each edge of the sleeve, to achieve the total needed number of stitches at upper sleeve. For example, for size large, 28 stitches are required for the first row, ending with 48 stitches across the top of the sleeve; 48 minus 28 equals 20 stitches. Divide 20 in half which means 10 stitches must be increased on each edge of sleeve. Multiply row gauge (two rows equals 1 inch, or substitute your own gauge) by desired sleeve length. Size large has a sleeve length of 16½ inches, as the 1 inch has already been deducted from the total length; 16½ inches times two rows equals 33 rows. Divide 33 rows by 10 (number of stitches to be increased) to determine how often to work the increases. Using our example, you would increase one stitch at each end of every third row, 10 times, to equal the needed total of 20 stitches to be increased and then work the remaining three rows even.

The sleeve extension (beyond desired sleeve length) is required to fit into the armhole and must match the measurement of the skipped stitches as closely as possible. Divide the number of stitches skipped for one armhole and divide this number by stitch-per-inch gauge. For size large, five stitches were skipped; five stitches x 2½ equals 2 inches. Thus, work even for 2 inches and fasten off.

The four steps detailed above can be used for any garment using single crochet, half double crochet or double crochet.

Regardless of your size or shape, you, too, can now have comfortable, perfect-fitting crocheted garments. ■

Classic Chanel Jacket

SKILL LEVEL

INTERMEDIATE

FINISHED SIZES

Instructions given fit size small; changes for medium and large are in [ ].

FINISHED GARMENT MEASUREMENT

Bust: 40 inches *(small)* [44 inches *(medium)*, 48 inches *(large)*]

MATERIALS

- Berroco Campus bulky (chunky) weight yarn (3½ oz/130 yds/100g per hank):
  8 [10, 11] hanks #2451 latte
- Berroco Vintage medium (worsted) weight yarn (3½ oz/217 yds/100g per hank):
  2 hanks #5103 mocha
- Sizes I/9/5.5mm and J/10/6mm crochet hooks or size needed to obtain gauge
- Tapestry needle
- ¾-inch buttons: 2

GAUGE

Size J hook: 5 hdc = 2 inches; 4 hdc rows = 2 inches

Take time to check gauge.

BACK

Row 1: With size J hook and latte, ch 51 [55, 61], hdc in 3rd ch from hook *(beg 2 sk chs count as first hdc)* and in each ch across, turn. *(50 [54, 60] hdc)*

Rows 2–26: Ch 2 *(counts as first hdc)*, hdc in each st across, turn. At end of last row, fasten off.

ARMHOLE SHAPING

Row 1: Sk first 5 [6, 7] sts, join with sl st in next st, ch 2, hdc in each st across, leaving last 5 [6, 7] sts unworked, turn. *(40 [42, 46] hdc)*

Rows 2–8 [2–9, 2–10]: Ch 2, hdc in each st across, turn.

SHOULDER SHAPING
FIRST SIDE

Row 1: Ch 2, hdc in each of next 11 sts, leaving rem sts unworked, turn. *(12 hdc)*

Rows 2 & 3: Ch 2, hdc in each st across, turn. At end of last row, fasten off.

Total number of rows 44 [45, 46].

2ND SIDE

Row 1: Sk center 16 [18, 22] sts on last row of Armhole Shaping, join with sl st in next st, ch 2, hdc in each st across, turn. *(12 hdc)*

Rows 2 & 3: Ch 2, hdc in each st across, turn. At end of last row, fasten off.

RIGHT FRONT

Row 1: With size J hook and latte, ch 26 [28, 31], hdc in 3rd ch from hook *(beg 2 sk chs count as first hdc)* and in each ch across, turn. *(25 [27, 30] hdc)*

Rows 2–26: Ch 2, hdc in each st across, turn. At end of last row, fasten off.

ARMHOLE SHAPING

Row 1: Sk first 5 [6, 7] sts, join with sl st in next st, ch 2, hdc in each st across, turn. *(20 [21, 23] hdc)*

Rows 2–15 [2–16, 2–17]: Ch 2, hdc in each st across, turn.

SHOULDER & NECK SHAPING
SMALL & LARGE SIZES ONLY

Row 1: Ch 2, hdc in each st across, leaving last 5 [8] sts unworked, turn. *(15 [15] hdc)*

Row 2: **Hdc dec** *(see Stitch Guide)* in first 2 sts, hdc in each st across, turn. *(14 [14] hdc)*

Row 3: Ch 2, hdc in each st across, turn.

Row 4: Hdc dec in first 2 sts, hdc in each st across, turn. *(13 [13] hdc)*

Row 5: Ch 2, hdc in each st across, turn.

Row 6: Hdc dec in first 2 sts, hdc in each st across, turn. *(12 [12] hdc)*

Rows 7–9 [7–12]: Ch 2, hdc in each st across, turn. At end of last row, fasten off.

MEDIUM SIZE ONLY

Row [1]: Sk first 6 sts, join latte with sl st in next st, ch 2, hdc in each st across, turn. *([15] hdc)*

Row [2]: Ch 2, hdc in each st across, turn.

Row [3]: Hdc dec *(see Stitch Guide)* in first 2 sts, hdc in each st across, turn. *([14] hdc)*

Row [4]: Ch 2, hdc in each st across, turn.

Row [5]: Hdc dec in first 2 sts, hdc in each st across, turn. *([13] hdc)*

Row [6]: Ch 2, hdc in each st across, turn.

Row [7]: Hdc dec in first 2 sts, hdc in each st across, turn. *([12] hdc)*

Rows [8–10]: Ch 2, hdc in each st across, turn. At end of last row, fasten off.

LEFT FRONT
Work same as Right Front, reversing all shaping.

SLEEVE
MAKE 2.
Row 1: With size J hook and latte, ch 25 [27, 29], hdc in 3rd ch from hook and in each ch across, turn. *(24 [26, 28] hdc)*

Row 2: Ch 2, hdc in each st across, turn.

Row 3: Ch 2, hdc in same st, hdc in each st across with 2 hdc in last st, turn. *(26 [28, 30] hdc)*

Row 4: Rep row 2.

Rows 5–31: [Rep rows 2–4 consecutively] 9 times. *(44 [46, 48] hdc at end of last row)*

Rows 32–36 [32–38, 32–39]: Ch 2, hdc in each st across, turn. At end of last row, fasten off.

FLAP
MAKE 2.
Row 1: With size J hook and latte, ch 15, hdc in 3rd ch from hook and in each ch across, turn. *(14 hdc)*

Rows 2 & 3: Ch 2, hdc in each st across, turn. At end of last row, fasten off.

FLAP EDGING
Row 1: With size I hook, join mocha with sc at upper corner, evenly sp 6 sc in ends of rows across to lower corner, 3 sc in corner, working in starting ch on opposite side of row 1, sc in each of next 13 chs, 3 sc in last ch, evenly sp 6 sc in ends of rows across to next corner, turn.

Rows 2 & 3: Ch 1, sc in each st across with 3 sc in center corner st, turn. At end of last row. Fasten off.

ASSEMBLY
Referring to photo, sew Flaps to Fronts and sew 1 button on each Flap. Sew shoulder seams.

Fold 1 Sleeve in half lengthwise, place fold at Shoulder seam, sew in place.

Rep with rem Sleeve.

Sew side and Sleeve seams.

SLEEVE EDGING
Rnd 1: Working in starting ch on opposite side of row 1, with size I hook, join mocha with sc at seam, sc in each ch around, join with sl st in beg sc.

Rnds 2 & 3: Ch 1, sc in each st around, join with sl st in beg sc. At end of last rnd, fasten off.

TRIM
Rnd 1: Working around outer edge of Jacket in ends of rows and in sts, with size I hook, join mocha with sc at corner, 2 sc in same corner, evenly sp 97 [106, 108] sc across Right Front, Back and Left Front to corner, 3 sc in corner, evenly sp 54 [56, 58] sc across to neck shaping, 3 sc in corner, evenly sp 4 sc across to shoulder shaping, evenly sp 14 [16, 18] sc across to shoulder seam, evenly sp 3 [3, 3] in ends of rows across to Back neck edge, evenly sp 16 [18, 22] sc across Back neck edge, evenly sp 3 [3, 3] in ends of rows across to neck edge, evenly sp 14 [16, 18] sc across to neck edge, evenly sp 4 sc across neck edge, 3 sc in corner, evenly sp 54 [56, 58] sc across, join with sl st in beg sc.

Rnds 2 & 3: Ch 1, sc in each st around with 3 sc in each center corner st, join with sl st in beg sc. At end of last rnd, fasten off. ■

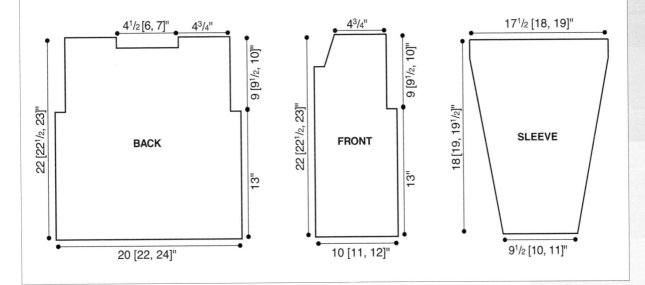

BACK — 4¹/₂ [6, 7]" · 4³/₄" · 9 [9¹/₂, 10]" · 22 [22¹/₂, 23]" · 13" · 20 [22, 24]"

FRONT — 4³/₄" · 9 [9¹/₂, 10]" · 22 [22¹/₂, 23]" · 13" · 10 [11, 12]"

SLEEVE — 17¹/₂ [18, 19]" · 18 [19, 19¹/₂]" · 9¹/₂ [10, 11]"

Understanding Garment Schematics

Garment schematics provide a visual, simplistic outline and various finished measurements for a crochet clothing item. Simplistic and straightforward, the information provided in a schematic is the roadmap for a crocheter to travel from the beginning (*yarn and a pattern*) to the end (*a well-fitting garment*).

Taking the time to review and understand the schematic for a crochet garment allows the crocheter time to double-check actual finished measurements in order to make any adjustments needed for a personalized fit and to avoid unpleasant surprise endings.

Before beginning any crochet garment, scan through the pattern to ensure you have a general idea of the pattern stitch used, sizing and shaping of pieces. Check the gauge, noting weight of yarn and suggested crochet hook size. Make a gauge swatch! This is the most essential step and should never be overlooked because your gauge determines the final measurements of each piece of a garment, and in turn, affects the finished measurements as well. If your gauge is off as little as one-half stitch per inch, your finished pieces probably will not be accurate, resulting in an ill-fitting garment. Make sure your gauge is the gauge required for your pattern.

FIRST THINGS FIRST

Checking a garment schematic quickly answers initial questions such as:

- Is the body worked in one piece to underarm?

- Are body pieces fitted rather than straight?

- Is the sleeve a true cap sleeve or an extended sleeve, or a raglan?

- What is the length from the bottom of the garment to the armhole?

- How is the armhole shaped?

BASIC DROP-SLEEVE PULLOVER

The simplest of all sweaters, the basic drop-sleeve pullover consists of a front and back,

both of which are rectangles, and two simple-shaped sleeves.

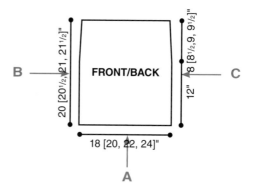

Line A at the bottom shows the width of the finished back.

Line B on the left side shows the total length from bottom to shoulder.

Line C on the right side shows the length to the underarm and the armhole depth which added together, equal the total length or Line B.

WIDTH

Let's say your gauge is 16 stitches = 4 inches, which boils down to four stitches per inch. The schematic shows a width (*Line A*) of 18 [20, 22, 24] inches. If you multiply the width times your gauge (18 [20, 22, 24] x 4), you will need 72 [80, 88, 96] stitches for the back.

Now refer to the first row of the pattern for the back piece. The number of stitches at the end of row 1 should correspond to the necessary number of stitches if the sweater is worked in a plain stitch: single crochet, half double crochet or double crochet. However, if the body of the sweater is worked in a pattern stitch, the count of each pattern multiple may make it mathematically impossible to be exactly 80 stitches. Therefore, if the number of stitches at the end of row 1 is 81 stitches, that is not a problem.

You can widen or narrow the back width by multiplying your gauge of four stitches per inch times the desired finished back width. Make pencil notes of your changes on your pattern.

TOTAL LENGTH

It's easy to lengthen or shorten your front and back pieces; however, if you work the pieces so they are longer, you will need more yarn than listed in a pattern.

ARMHOLE DEPTH

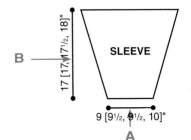

Unless you have unusually thin or thick arms, stay with the given measurements for the best fit. If changes are made to armhole depth, changes also have to be made to the top of the sleeve as both measurements must be the same to fit properly. For example, if the armhole depth is changed from an 8-inch opening to a 7-inch opening, the upper sleeve must be 14 inches across to fit around the opening on both front and back pieces.

In the schematic above, Line A for the lower sleeve provides the number of inches for the wrist measurement, plus ease. Line B is the measurement from wrist to armhole. If you need to make adjustments in length, be sure to refer to the pattern. Increases from wrist to top of sleeve are made at specific intervals. If you wish to lengthen the sleeve, no calculations are required, other than how many extra rows to work, as all increases have been made when the sleeve is worked to the length on Line B. Check the pattern if you plan to shorten sleeves to determine whether adjustments need to be made to increases to accommodate a shorter length.

FRONT PIECES

Sometimes front-piece schematics omit the neck and shoulder measurements. No figure is shown for the front of a drop-sleeve pullover, which generally has either a V-neck or a crew neck. Adapting the width and/or shaping of a neckline can be complicated and is best left as written in pattern instructions.

CAP-SLEEVE PULLOVER

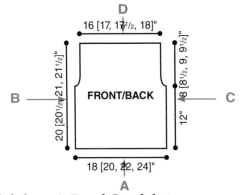

While lines A, B and C and their measurements are exactly the same as for the drop-sleeve pullover, the armholes curve to accommodate a cap sleeve. Again, the outer edges of a sleeve must fit properly around the armhole shaping of the front and back. In addition, note the 2-inch measurement at the bottom of the sleeve which designates the length added to the usual sleeve length for a turn-up cuff. While the shoulder-to-shoulder width *(Line D)* for sweaters is standardized for various sizes, different designers use different formulas to calculate the shaping of the cap part of the sleeve.

While the total length of a cap-sleeve pullover can be lengthened or shortened fairly easily, trying to reshape and recalculate the upper/ cap sleeve of a pullover is not recommended.

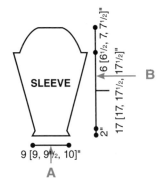

Before beginning your next crochet project, take a moment to look over the schematic. Analyze the schematic and note any adjustments you wish to make in pencil to ensure your project turns out as expected. ■

Make Your Own Crochet Skirt Template

If you have a favorite purchased skirt or skirt sewing pattern, it's easy to use either one as a template to make a fabulous crochet version.

There are so many benefits to working with crochet! There's the sheer pleasure of crocheting and the delight of unlimited creative possibilities. Crocheting your skirt will allow you to actually "build" the fabric of the skirt. Regardless of yarn weight, thickness, color or texture, you can choose just about any yarn or combination of yarns that appeal to you. Then, you can add texture and visual complexity to those yarns by choosing stitches and patterning. You can create a skirt that is a one-of-a-kind masterpiece!

There is no limit to the ways that you can combine yarn and stitches in the creation of your totally unique garment, but you do have to consider a few things.

Crocheted fabric can be very mobile and can behave in erratic and unexpected ways if you haven't done your homework. You will need to do some exploration before you embark on the construction of your crocheted skirt.

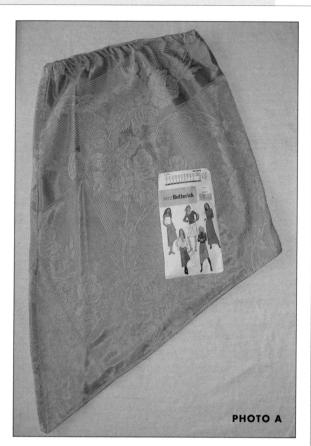

PHOTO A

WHAT DO YOU NEED?
You'll need to have a skirt that fits you comfortably. The skirt in our project was made with an A-line asymmetrical skirt pattern (*see Photo A*). If you are not a sewer, you can use this technique by working with a purchased skirt.

YOU WILL ALSO NEED
Crochet hooks, yarn, scissors, a tape measure, safety pins, a tapestry needle, a notebook and pen or pencil, a straightedge and elastic for the waistband of the skirt. For beginners, choose a pattern or skirt that doesn't need buttons or a zipper.

WHERE TO BEGIN?
Start with a swatch, using the hook size and number of rows and kind of stitches that the yarn label recommends. Measure your swatch. Make notes recording the hook size, the number of rows, the number of stitches, the crochet stitches used and the finished dimensions.

Pull at your swatch in several different directions:

How flexible is the swatch? What kind of memory does it have, i.e. does it return to its original dimensions and shape quickly, or does it distort?

Which way does it drape best? For example, would it be better to work the rows of crochet across the skirt, from side to side, or from top to bottom?

Does it feel too stiff? (*You'll need to switch to a larger hook.*)

Does it look too holey? (*You'll need to switch to a smaller hook.*)

How will the structure of the crochet work visually in the different sections of the skirt?

For example, Tunisian crochet was chosen for the skirt in our project because of the strong lines it gave to the finished skirt and for the close, dense stitches used for this crochet technique. Also, the area across the tummy was worked with the wrong side of the fabric on the outside so that the vertical lines were emphasized, rather than the horizontal ones.

Now, make more swatches with different-size crochet hooks and different stitches.

Measure the swatches and write down all the information.

What stitch did you use? What size hook? How many stitches? How many rows? What size did your swatch turn out to be? Test these swatches the way you did your first one.

Did you want to work some stitch patterning into your skirt?

The swatch will give you all kinds of valuable information.

Some stitch patterns work better with certain kinds of yarn than others. Working a small swatch is going to show you fairly quickly which stitch combinations and patterns will work for your skirt and which ones are better used elsewhere.

Are you happy with the look and feel of your swatch? If you have purchased enough yarn to save your swatches, then you might want to try washing one according to the directions on the label. It's a great idea to abuse your swatch heartlessly so that you know your skirt is going to stand up to years of use.

If you do wash your swatch, ask the following questions and record your answers. How did it stand up to laundering? Did it shrink, pull off in wild directions, fade or behave in an otherwise unacceptable and undesirable manner? If it came out of the wash and was able to be encouraged into the same dimensions as when it went into the wash,

then that's good. If it didn't distort, shrink, stretch or otherwise misbehave, then you've got a winner.

MORE FOOD FOR THOUGHT

How are you going to put your skirt together? Sew it? Crochet it?

Are you going to make the seams into decorative accents? If so, you could choose a contrasting color of yarn. Or you could add texture at the seams with scallops or shells or fringe.

Do you want to have open lacy sections in your skirt? If so, are you planning on wearing an underskirt or slip? Would that work in a contrasting color?

What about the hem? Do you want it to be straight, scalloped, fringed, beaded, filet, flowered or zigzagged? With your crochet hook, you can create any hem you want!

THE NITTY-GRITTY

You'll be working with templates. What's a template?

It's a piece of paper or fabric that is the exact shape of the finished piece that you want to make. Your skirt can be your template if you wish.

If you are working with a sewing pattern, you can either cut fabric or sturdy paper pieces out, following the pattern, or you can use the tissue-paper pattern itself.

Remember to draw the seam allowance (⅝-inch) around each edge and trim it off. You are going to be butting the edges of each section of the skirt up against the others, so you don't need to crochet overlapping seam allowances.

Cut one template for each section of the skirt. Remember that the front and back may be reversed by the type of stitch patterning that you use, so you may wish to cut separate templates.

It is also possible to simply use the front and back of the same template for both the front and back sections of the skirt.

Label your templates with important information such as where the template fits into the skirt, the lines that indicate crosswise, lengthwise or bias grain of the fabric, which edge connects to what edge on other pattern pieces and anything else that seems relevant.

If you don't like the "piecemeal approach," or are working from a purchased skirt that is already sewn together, not to worry. It will work great as your template. One advantage to working with a premade skirt is that you can more accurately adjust the crocheted skirt to the "fit" of the template skirt. For example, by shaping the crocheted pieces over gathers at the waistline, you can reduce bulk. Just be very careful to keep smoothing out the skirt to its full measurements, as there is a tendency for a premade garment to pull in while being used as a template.

The crocheted skirt shown in the photos was made over a premade skirt.

COVERING YOUR TEMPLATE WITH CROCHET

Note: It is easiest to work at a table, with the skirt laid out in front of you.

You may need to adjust the height of the chair you are sitting in to avoid muscle strain while crocheting.

Always work from the widest point of the section to the narrowest. You will decide the length of the starting chain by measuring the section of the skirt that you want as the beginning point *(see Photo B)*. Using your favorite swatch, calculate how many stitches you'll need per inch, and chain that number plus one *(or however many chain stitches you need as your beginning chain—see Beginning Chains on page 42)*. You do need to make your calculations based on your swatch! Your chain is not going to be the same length as the template!

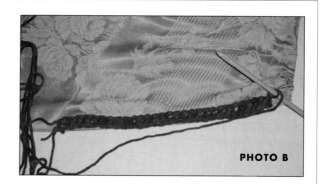

PHOTO B

You will build the crocheted piece up row by row, shaping it by increasing and/or decreasing stitches. Or you can make many smaller elements and attach them to each other by stitching or crocheting them together to end up with a piece that fits the template exactly.

You will "grow" your crocheted skirt by pinning it to the original skirt or the template as you work it. Lay the crocheted piece down on the template or skirt, and smooth it out after each row. This will tell you when you need to increase, decrease or work other shaping such as short "flaring" rows. As the crocheted piece gets larger, pinning the sections to the template skirt will ensure that you are working to the full dimensions of the skirt *(see Photo C)*.

PHOTO C

The crocheted piece will sometimes pull in somewhat after resting for awhile if you have set it aside overnight. Release the pins, re-pin the skirt, and add more rows if necessary.

The skirt in the photos was made by picking up stitches along an edge of a finished section. The picked-up stitches then became the first row of the next section (see Photo D).

PHOTO D

One side of the skirt was worked, and then the skirt was turned over and the second side was worked by picking up the stitches along the wide end of the top section of the skirt.

The second side was worked in the same order as the first one, and the ends of the rows were joined to adjoining edges on the first side as each section was worked.

If you prefer, you can work each section individually and wait until the skirt is completed to join the sections. If this is your choice, then it's a good idea to pin your finished crocheted sections to the skirt or the individual templates as they are completed; this will help to avoid errors such as repeated sections or lost pieces. (Use large safety pins.) If you don't want to pin the finished sections to the skirt, then label them clearly.

Crocheting a skirt using this template technique is a fun way to create a truly unique garment that you will treasure for years!

SKIRT

SKILL LEVEL

◼◼◼▢
INTERMEDIATE

FINISHED SIZE
Sized to individual

MATERIALS

- Bulky (chunky) weight yarn: 732 yds in color of choice
- Sizes J/10/6mm and K/10½/6.5mm crochet hooks
- Size L/11/8mm Tunisian crochet hook or size needed to obtain gauge
- Tapestry needle
- Sewing needle
- Sewing thread
- Safety pins
- A-line skirt pattern (optional)
- 1½ yds fabric for templates or to construct a sewn version of the skirt, OR your favorite premade skirt
- 1-inch-wide elastic to fit around waist

GAUGE
Size L Tunisian hook: 2 TSS = 1 inch

Take time to check gauge.

PATTERN NOTE
Join with slip stitch unless otherwise stated.

SPECIAL STITCHES
Tunisian simple stitch (TSS):
Row 1: Ch number needed, insert hook in 2nd ch from hook (see Photo E), yo, pull up lp, [insert hook in next ch, yo, pull up lp] across, leaving all lps on hook, do not turn.

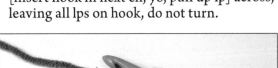

PHOTO E

To complete row 1, **work lps off hook** as follows: Yo, pull through 1 lp on hook (see *Photo F*), [yo, pull through 2 lps on hook] across (see *Photo G*), until 1 lp rem on hook.

PHOTO F

PHOTO G

Row 2: Sk first vertical bar, insert hook under next vertical bar (see *Photo H*), yo, pull up lp, [insert hook under next vertical bar, yo, pull up lp] across, do not turn.

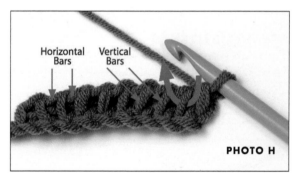

Horizontal Bars   Vertical Bars

PHOTO H

To complete row 2, **work lps off hook** as follows: Yo, pull through 1 lp on hook, [yo, pull through 2 lps on hook] across, until 1 lp rem on hook.

Pivotal: To make the Tunisian crochet wedge out slightly, work half of the row as normal, stop and work lps off hook. Work the next row as normal over the entire row. You can work a short row from either end.

Decrease (dec): Insert hook through 2 (or more) vertical bars **at the same time**, yo, pull up lp.

Increase (inc): Pull up lp in **horizontal bar** (see illustration) between vertical bars.

Horizontal Bar

Picot: Ch 3, sl st in top of tr just made.

Joining picot: Ch 1, drop lp from hook, insert hook through st on the piece that you want to join the flower to, pull dropped lp through the st on the piece, ch 1, sl st to top of tr just made.

To join a new section to a previously worked section along the end row sts: Take the hook out of last lp, insert into st at end of the row of the completed section that you want to join to, pick up the lp again and pull it through the picked-up st. Work the rest of the row in the normal way.

If the last row of Tunisian st looks too open, work sl st through each st: Hold yarn under your work, reach through with hook from front to back, pull up lp and pull through lp on hook.

Petal: (Sc, hdc, 2 dc, tr, **picot**—see *Special Stitches*, 2 dc, hdc, sc, sl st) in indicated st or sp.

Petal joining: (Sl st, sc, hdc, 2 dc, tr, **joining picot**—see *Special Stitches*, 2 dc, hdc, sc, sl st) in next ch sp as indicated.

SKIRT

Row 1: Make ch to fit first section (see *Photo B on page 118*), draw up lp in 2nd ch from hook and in each rem ch across, **work lps off hook** (see *Special Stitches*).

Row 2: Sk first vertical bar, keeping all lps on hook, work **TSS** (see *Special Stitches*) across, work lps off hook.

Next rows: Using Special Stitches and previous instructions, work rem rows and pieces as needed (see Photos I and J).

PHOTO I

PHOTO J

One section is made by beg at the widest point and working across to the narrow side. Sts are picked up along the wide edge, and the same section of the other side of the Skirt is worked. The narrow edges are held tog and ch-stitched closed. Because the WS is chosen for the finished side of the Skirt, the sections are flipped and then pinned to the template with the WS of these sections on the outside.

WAISTBAND

First the Waistband front is worked, and then the Waistband back is worked and the sides are joined as the back Waistband is worked.

The Waistband is folded over and stitched almost shut, and then the elastic is inserted.

The Waistband of the Skirt in the photo was rolled to the outside of the Skirt before stitching in place.

SMALL FLOWER

With size K hook, ch 3, **join** (see Pattern Note) in first ch to form ring, ch 5, *sl st in ring, ch 5, rep from * 4 times, join in first ch of beg ch-5. Fasten off.

Note: You may wish to make fewer than 5 petals if using the Small Flower to fill a sp between other motifs or sections. Also, you may choose to not connect all the petals to adjoining sections.

JOINING SMALL FLOWERS

With size K hook, ch 3, join in first ch to form ring, *ch 2, drop lp from hook, insert hook through a st on the piece that you want to join the Flower to, pull dropped lp, through the st on the piece, ch 2, sl st in ring, rep from * as many times as needed to join or [ch 5, sl st in ring] as many times as needed to complete Small Flower, join in first ch of beg ch-2. Fasten off.

LARGE FLOWER

Rnd 1: With size K hook, ch 5, join in first ch to form ring, ch 5 (counts as first hdc and ch-3), [hdc in ring, ch 3] 4 times, join in 2nd ch of beg ch-5.

Rnd 2: **Petal** (see Special Stitches) in first ch-3 sp and in each ch-3 sp around, join in beg sc. Fasten off.

JOINING LARGE FLOWERS

Rnd 1: With size K hook, ch 5, join in first ch to form ring, ch 5 (counts as first hdc and ch-3), [hdc in ring, ch 3] 4 times, join in 2nd ch of beg ch-5.

Rnd 2: Work **petal joining** (see Special Stitches) in as many ch sps needed to join petals, (see Photos K and L), (sc, hdc, 2 dc, tr, picot, 2 dc, hdc, sc, sl st) in each rem ch sp, join in beg sc. Fasten off.

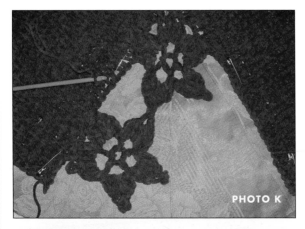

PHOTO K

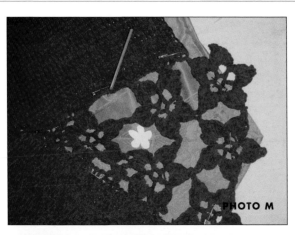

PHOTO M

PHOTO L

PHOTO N

JOINING LARGE FLOWER (OPTIONAL)

Sl st adjoining edges tog or sew a few sts from each petal to the Skirt.

FLOWER PLACEMENT

To establish where to place and join Flowers: Crochet 1 Large Flower and 1 Small Flower and trace around them on paper.

Cut them out and move around until you are happy with placement (*see Photos M and N*). The paper flowers will show you where the perfect connection points are for the crocheted flowers.

On the completed skirt (*see Photo O*), a Large Flower may be appliquéd to the front at the hip, if desired. ■

PHOTO O

Insider Shaping Secrets

Time and time again, many crocheters express a fear of tackling a garment that requires shaping for sleeves, necklines, armholes or other areas. It's really less complicated than you think. Proper shaping can produce results that are more flattering and comfortable.

Try thinking of each piece of a garment as a simple square or rectangle with stitches that are simply increased or decreased at the edges to create shaping. If you can work two stitches into one stitch, you already know how to increase, or add, stitches. And if you know how to combine stitches, you know how to decrease, or subtract, stitches.

SLEEVES

To shape a crocheted sleeve, you simply increase stitches at each edge, at regular intervals, to widen the shape from the wrist to the armhole. Then, you work even to desired length for a drop sleeve, or shape the cap per written instructions. If, at first, you have difficulty identifying the increases made at the ends of rows, place a stitch marker on each increase row, so you can quickly count your stitches and rows as you work.

ARMHOLES & NECKLINES

To shape curved armholes and necklines, center stitches are skipped to begin the opening, and then stitches are gradually decreased (by working stitches together) on either side of the initial opening to create a curve. You could slip stitch across those skipped stitches, and slip stitching on one side of a neckline or armhole may save a few seconds of time, but you will probably pay dearly in terms of comfort.

The amount of comfort is greater when a neckline is divided for a jacket or a placket opening than for a crewneck sweater when one side of the neck has skipped stitches and the other side of a jacket begins with slip stitches. To test this method, take a few minutes to make two small swatches.

SLIP-STITCH SWATCH

Row 1: Using hook and yarn of your choice, ch 22, dc in 4th ch from hook (*beg 3 sk chs count as first dc*) and in each ch across, turn. (*20 dc*)

Rows 2–4: Ch 3 (*counts as first dc*), dc in each dc across, turn.

Row 5: Sl st across each of first 5 dc for beg of neck shaping, sl st in next dc, ch 3, dc in each rem dc across, turn.

Row 6: Ch 3, dc in each dc across to last 2 dc, **dc dec** (*see Stitch Guide*) in last 2 dc, turn.

Row 7: Ch 2, dc in next dc (*counts as beg dc dec*), dc in each rem dc across. Fasten off.

SKIPPED-STITCHES SWATCH

Row 1: Using hook and yarn of your choice, ch 22, dc in 4th ch from hook (*beg 3 sk chs count as first dc*) and in each ch across, turn. (*20 dc*)

Rows 2–4: Ch 3 (*counts as first dc*), dc in each dc across, turn. At end of last row, fasten off.

Row 5: Sk first 5 dc, join in next dc, ch 3, dc in each rem st across, turn.

Row 6: Ch 3, dc in each st to last 2 dc, **dc dec** *(see Stitch Guide)* in last 2 sts, turn.

Row 7: Ch 2, dc in next dc *(counts as beg dc dec)*, dc in each dc across. Fasten off.

Note: Rows 6 and 7 of each swatch create the curve for the neckline or armhole opening. As you can see, not only do your swatches for the simulated neckline look different, they feel different. The first five stitches of the Slip-Stitch Swatch are firm and have little give, while the Skipped-Stitches Swatch has more elasticity, and, thus, is less restrictive and feels more comfortable on your body.

FLARES & RUFFLES

Our Ribbed Collar Cardigan *(photo on page 127)* features a flared peplum and collar which are shaped using a nontraditional method. Both of these flared pieces are worked from side to side with half of each row being worked in double crochet, while the other half of the same row is worked in half double crochet which creates a flare. This shaping method can be easily adapted to shape a skirt or other garments. Try working a jacket to the armhole using this method, and then work back and forth across the length of this piece and work even from the armhole up instead of side by side, and you'll create a flattering, sophisticated shape.

DECREASING BULK

Crochet garments always fit and feel best on the body when the bulk is decreased as you work the shaping or seaming. At ends of rows, you'll significantly decrease edge bulk when working in double or half double crochet as follows: Chain one *(does not count as a stitch)*, work the first stitch of the next row as a double or half double crochet.

The second advantage to this technique is that when garment pieces are assembled, the ends of the rows do not have a gap between the beginning chains and the next stitch and are much neater.

SEAMING TECHNIQUES

The seaming technique of choice for a garment also affects shape, drape and comfort. Invisible (woven) seams are less bulky than seams that are backstitched. Determine which seaming method best meets the needs of the yarn used and the design of the garment. For example, a child's jacket is likely to undergo more rough and tumble wear than the garment for an adult. For most children's garments, a backstitch seam may best fill your needs because this method is strong and durable. Backstitching creates a sturdy, firm seam that can take a lot of wear and tear.

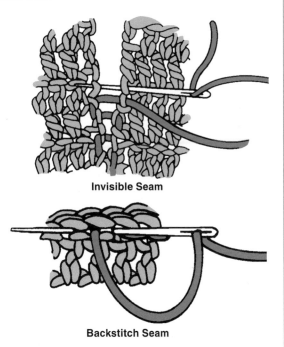

Invisible Seam

Backstitch Seam

On the other hand, a woman's jacket, vest or jacket is less likely to be submitted to the same abuse as a child's garment and may be finished with a woven seam which is less sturdy, but reduces the bulk and has more give than a backstitch seam. This method is a particularly good choice for lightweight yarns.

CROCHET SEAMS

Garment pieces can also be crocheted together using either slip stitch or single crochet. When the stitch of choice *(usually single crochet)* is worked with the wrong sides facing, the seam is raised and purposely becomes an exterior design element meant to enhance the overall appearance of a garment. When the seam is meant to be on the interior of a garment, the best choice would be a slip stitch rather than single crochet in order to reduce bulk. A crochet seam has some degree of elasticity and is a good choice for adult garments. The main drawback to using this technique is the risk of a chain becoming snagged and the whole seam unraveling before your eyes.

Using these simple insider shaping tips will help make your crocheted garments look better and feel more comfortable, and increase your overall satisfaction of the finished results.

RIBBED COLLAR CARDIGAN

SKILL LEVEL

INTERMEDIATE

FINISHED SIZES
Instructions given fit 30–32-inch bust *(small)*; changes for 34–36-inch bust *(medium)*, 38–40-inch bust *(large)*, 42–44-inch bust *(X-large)*, 46–48-inch bust *(2X-large)* and 50–52-inch bust *(3X-large)* are in [ ].

FINISHED GARMENT MEASUREMENT
Bust: 36 inches *(small)* [40 inches *(medium)*, 44 inches *(large)*, 48 inches *(X-large)*, 52 inches *(2X-large)*, 56 inches *(3X-large)*]

MATERIALS
- Cascade 220 Superwash medium (worsted) weight yarn (3½ oz/220 yds/100g per ball): 9 [9, 10, 10, 10, 11] balls #808 sunset orange
- Sizes H/8/5mm and I/9/5.5mm crochet hooks or size needed to obtain gauge
- Tapestry needle

GAUGE
Size I hook: 12 dc = 4 inches; 4 pattern rows = 2¾ inches

Take time to check gauge.

PATTERN NOTE
Chain-3 at beginning of row counts as first double crochet unless otherwise stated.

SPECIAL STITCHES
Cluster (cl): Holding back last lp of each st on hook, 2 dc in place indicated, yo, pull through all lps on hook.

Beginning decrease (beg dec): Ch 2 *(does not count as first dc)*, dc in next st.

CARDIGAN
BACK
Row 1 (RS): With size I hook, ch 55 [61, 67, 73, 79, 85], dc in 4th ch from hook *(beg 3 sk chs count as first dc)* and in each ch across, turn. *(53 [59, 65, 71, 77, 83] dc)*

Row 2: **Ch 3** *(see Pattern Note)*, dc in each st across, turn.

Row 3: Ch 3, [**dc dec** *(see Stitch Guide)* in next 3 sts, ch 3, **cl** *(see Special Stitches)* in 3rd ch from hook] across to last 4 sts, dc dec in next 3 sts, dc in last st, turn.

Row 4: Ch 3, 3 dc in each dc dec across, ending with dc in last st, turn.

Row 5: Ch 3, dc in each st across, turn.

Rows 6–13: [Rep rows 2–5 consecutively] twice. At end of last row, fasten off.

ARMHOLE SHAPING
Row 1 (WS): Sk first 4 [4, 7, 7, 10, 10] sts, join with sl st in next st, ch 3, dc in each st across leaving last 4 [4, 7, 7, 10, 10] sts unworked, turn. *(45 [51, 57, 63, 69, 75] dc)*

Row 2 (RS): **Beg dec** *(see Special Stitches)*, dc in next st, [dc dec in next 3 sts, ch 3, cl in 3rd ch from hook] across to last 6 sts, dc dec in next 3 sts, dc in next st, dc dec in last 2 sts, turn. *(13 [15, 15, 17, 17, 19] dc dec, 4 [4, 4, 4, 4, 4] dc)*

Row 3: Beg dec, 3 dc in each dc dec across, ending with dc dec in last 2 sts, turn. *(41 [47, 47, 53, 53, 59] dc)*

Rows 4 & 5: Ch 3, dc in each st across, turn.

Row 6: Ch 3, [dc dec in next 3 sts, ch 3, cl in 3rd ch from hook] across to last 4 sts, dc dec in next 3 sts, dc in last st, turn.

Row 7: Ch 3, 3 dc in each dc dec in each st across, dc in last st, turn.

Rows 8 & 9: Ch 3, dc in each st across, turn.

Row 10: Ch 3, [dc dec in next 3 sts, ch 3, cl in 3rd ch from hook] across to last 4 sts, dc dec in next 3 sts, dc in last st, turn.

Row 11: Ch 3, 3 dc in each dc dec across, ending with dc in last st, turn.

Row 12 [12–14, 12–14, 12–15, 12–16, 12–17]: Ch 3, dc in each st across, turn. At end of last row, fasten off.

RIGHT FRONT

Row 1 (RS): With size I hook, ch 28 [31, 34, 37, 40, 43], dc in 4th ch from hook *(beg 3 sk chs count as first dc)* and in each ch across, turn. *(26 [29, 32, 35, 38, 41] dc)*

Row 2: Ch 3, dc in each st across, ending with dc dec in last 2 sts, turn. *(25 [28, 31, 34, 37, 40 dc)*

Row 3: Beg dec, dc in next st, [dc dec in next 3 sts, ch 3, cl in 3rd ch from hook] across to last 4 sts, dc dec in next 3 sts, dc in last st, turn.

Row 4: Ch 3, 3 dc in each dc dec across, ending with dc in each of last 2 sts, turn. *(24 [27, 30, 33, 36, 39] dc)*

Row 5: Ch 3, dc in each st across, turn.

Row 6: Ch 3, dc in each st across, ending with dc dec in last 2 sts, turn. *(23 [26, 29, 32, 35, 38] dc)*

Row 7: Ch 3, [dc dec in next 3 sts, ch 3, cl in 3rd ch from hook] across to last 4 sts, dc dec in next 3 sts, dc in last st, turn.

Row 8: Ch 3, 3 dc in each dc dec across, ending with dc in each of last 2 sts, turn.

Row 9: Ch 3, dc in each st across, turn.

Row 10: Ch 3, dc in each st across, ending with dc dec in last 2 sts, turn. *(22 [25, 28, 31, 34, 37] dc)*

Row 11: Beg dec, dc in next st, [dc dec in next 3 sts, ch 3, cl in 3rd ch from hook] across to last 4 sts, dc dec in next 3 sts, dc in last st, turn.

Row 12: Ch 3, 3 dc in each dc dec across, ending with dc in each of in last 2 sts, turn.

Row 13: Ch 3, dc in each st across, turn. Fasten off.

ARMHOLE SHAPING

Row 1: Sk first 4 [4, 7, 7, 10, 10] sts, join with sl st in next st, ch 3, dc in each st across, turn. *(17 [20, 20, 23, 23, 26] dc)*

Row 2: Beg dec, [dc dec in next 3 sts, ch 3, cl in 3rd ch from hook] across to last 6 sts, dc dec in next 3 sts, dc in next st, dc dec in last 2 sts, turn. *(15 [18, 18, 21, 21, 24] dc)*

Row 3: Beg dec, 3 dc in each st across,

ending with dc in last st, turn. *(14 [17, 17, 20, 20, 23] dc)*

Row 4: Ch 3, dc in each st across, turn.

Row 5: Ch 3, dc in each st across, ending with dc dec in last 2 sts, turn. *(13 [16, 16, 19, 19, 22] dc)*

Row 6: Ch 3, dc in each of next 2 sts, [dc dec in next 3 sts, ch 3, cl in 3rd ch from hook] across to last 4 sts, dc dec in next 3 sts, dc in last st, turn.

Row 7: Ch 3, dc in each st across, turn.

Row 8: Beg dec, dc in each st across, turn. *(12 [15, 15, 18, 18, 21] dc)*

Row 9: Ch 3, dc in each st across, turn.

Row 10: Ch 3, dc in next st, [dc dec in next 3 sts, ch 3, cl in 3rd ch from hook] across to last 4 sts, dc dec in next 3 sts, dc in last st, turn.

Row 11: Ch 3, 3 dc in each st across, ending with dc dec in last 2 sts, turn. *(11 [14, 14, 17, 17, 20] dc)*

Row 12: Ch 3, dc in each st across, turn.

SMALL SIZE ONLY
Fasten off.

MEDIUM, LARGE, X-LARGE, 2X-LARGE & 3X-LARGE SIZES ONLY
Row [13, 13, 13, 13, 13]: Ch 3, dc in each st across, turn.

MEDIUM & LARGE SIZES ONLY
Row [14]: Ch 3, dc in each st across, turn. Fasten off.

X-LARGE, 2X-LARGE & 3X-LARGE SIZES ONLY
Row [14, 14, 14]: Beg dec, dc in each st across, turn. *([16, 16, 19] dc)*

Row [15, 15, 15]: Ch 3, dc in each st across, turn.

X-LARGE SIZE ONLY
Fasten off.

2X-LARGE & 3X-LARGE SIZES ONLY
Row [16, 16]: Ch 3, dc in each st across, turn.

2X-LARGE SIZE ONLY
Fasten off.

3X-LARGE SIZE ONLY
Row [17]: Beg dec, dc in each st across. Fasten off.

LEFT FRONT
Work same as Right Front, reversing shaping.

SLEEVE
MAKE 2.
Row 1: With size I hook, ch 28 [28, 34, 34, 34, 34], dc in 4th ch from hook *(beg 3 sk chs count as first dc)* and in each ch across, turn. *(26 [26, 32, 32, 32, 32] dc)*

Row 2: Ch 3, dc in each st across, turn.

Row 3: Ch 3, dc in same st, [dc dec in next 3 sts, ch 3, cl in 3rd ch from hook] across to last 4 sts, dc dec in next 3 sts, 2 dc in last st, turn.

Row 4: Ch 3, dc in next st, 3 dc in each dc dec across, ending with dc in each of last 2 sts, turn. *(28 [28, 34, 34, 34, 34] dc)*

Row 5: Ch 3, dc in same st, dc in each st across, ending with 2 dc in last st, turn. *(30 [30, 36, 36, 36, 36] dc)*

Rows 6–25 [6–25, 6–25, 6–26, 6–26, 6–26]: Continue in established pattern and **at the same time**, inc 1 st at each edge every other row 8 [8, 9, 9, 10, 10] times. At end of last row, fasten off. *(46 [46, 54, 54, 56, 56] dc at end of last row)*

SLEEVE CAP
Row 1: Sk first 4 [4, 7, 7, 10, 10] sts, join with sl st in next st, work in established pattern across leaving last 4 [4, 7, 7, 10, 10] sts unworked, turn.

Row 2: Work even in pattern across, turn.

Rows 3 & 4: Beg dec, work in pattern across, ending with dc dec in last 2 sts, turn.

Next rows: Work 3 [4, 5, 5, 6, 7] rows even in pattern.

UPPER CAP SHAPING
SMALL, MEDIUM, LARGE & X-LARGE SIZES ONLY
Rows 1–4: Ch 1, dc dec in first 3 sts, work in pattern across, ending with dc dec in last 3 sts, turn. At end of last row, fasten off. *(18 [18, 20, 20] sts at end of last row)*

2X-LARGE & 3X-LARGE SIZES ONLY
Rows [1–5]: Ch 2, dc dec in next 2 sts, work in pattern across, ending with dc dec in last 2 sts, turn. At end of last row, fasten off. *([22, 22] sts at end of last row)*

ASSEMBLY
Sew shoulder seams.

Fold 1 Sleeve in half lengthwise. Place fold at shoulder seam and sew into place.

Rep with rem Sleeve.

Sew side and Sleeve seams.

SLEEVE EDGING
Rnd 1: Working in starting ch on opposite side of row 1, with size I hook, join with sc at seam, sc in each ch around, join with sl st in beg sc.

Rnd 2: Ch 2, working from left to right, **reverse sc** *(see Stitch Guide)* in each st around, join in beg reverse sc. Fasten off.

OUTER EDGING
Working in ends of rows and in sts across back neck, with size H hook and RS facing, join with sc in end of first row at lower Front corner, sc in same row, evenly sp 51 [53, 55, 55, 57, 59] sc across to shoulder seam, evenly sp 19 [19, 19, 21, 23, 23] sts across back neck, evenly sp 52 [54, 56, 56, 58, 60] sc across to lower Front, 3 sc in corner, working in starting chs on opposite side of row 1 on Back and Fronts, sc in each ch across, sc in same st as beg sc, join with sl st in beg sc. Fasten off.

PEPLUM
Row 1: With WS facing and size H hook, join with **fpsc** *(see Stitch Guide)* around 2 sc at corner, fpsc around each st across bottom edge to next corner, ending with fpsc around 2 sts of next corner, leaving rem sts unworked, turn.

Row 2: Ch 14, dc in 4th ch from hook and in each of next 4 chs, hdc in each of next 6 chs, sl st in each of next 2 sts on row 1, turn.

Row 3: Sk last 2 sl sts, hdc in each of next 6 hdc, dc in each of next 6 sts, turn.

Row 4: Ch 3, dc in each of next 5 dc, hdc in each of next 6 hdc, sl st in each of next 2 sts on row 1, turn.

Next rows: Rep rows 3 and 4 alternately across, ending with row 3. At end of last row, fasten off.

COLLAR
Row 1: With WS facing and size H hook, join with sl st in first unworked st above row 1 of Peplum, ch 14, dc in 4th ch from hook and in each of next 4 chs, hdc in each of next 6 chs, sl st in each of next 2 sts on Outer Edging, turn.

Row 2: Sk last 2 sl sts, hdc in each of next 6 hdc, dc in each of next 6 sts, turn.

Row 3: Ch 3, dc in each of next 5 dc, hdc in each of next 6 hdc, sl st in each of next 2 sts on Outer Edging, turn.

Next rows: Rep rows 3 and 4 alternately across, ending with row 3. At end of last row, fasten off.

TIE
With size H hook, join with sl st at lower edge of Collar, make ch to measure 13 inches in length, sl st in 2nd ch from hook and in each ch across, sl st in beg sl st. Fasten off.

Rep on opposite side.

Tie in bow. ■

Crocheting Socks That Fit

It's a known fact that no two people have the same feet and that most people do not have feet that fit the "standard" sizes given in many sock patterns. For example, patterns for knit or crochet socks will often state general sizes, such as "fits woman's size medium." With a little guidance and the right information, it's easy to make comfortable socks that can be custom-fit to any foot.

GETTING THE RIGHT FIT

When making socks, do not use ony the length of the foot to determine the size you will make. A size 9 shoe doesn't necessarily mean you have a wide foot; you may have a narrow- or medium-width foot. The circumference of your foot and leg should determine the size of the sock you will make.

Using the foot illustration below as a guide, take the foot measurements of the sock recipient. For accuracy, if you are making socks for yourself, have a crochet or knit buddy take your measurements.

Measure the circumference of the foot at A, measuring the widest portion around the heel and arch. Your sock cuff must be able to stretch enough to fit around the foot, heel, arch and ankle.

While the person is standing, measure up from the floor at the heel to the height of the sock leg listed in the pattern (or to the height you want your sock). At this height, measure the circumference of the leg, using this measurement to determine the circumference of the sock leg.

Note: Do not use measurement B for kneesocks. This type of sock is measured differently and is normally shaped to fit the calf.

Measure around the ball of the foot at C to determine the circumference of the foot portion of the sock. This measurement should be about ½ inch narrower than the heel/arch measurement (A).

While the person is standing, measure the foot from the back of the heel to the longest

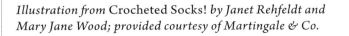

Illustration from Crocheted Socks! *by Janet Rehfeldt and Mary Jane Wood; provided courtesy of Martingale & Co.*

toe (D). This will give you an accurate foot length measurement. You will make your sock approximately ¾ to 1 inch shorter than the actual foot length measurement.

Note: If there is a finished sock length given in your pattern, it should be used as a guide or suggested finished length.

For toe-up socks, while the person is standing, measure the foot from the longest toe to just below and at the midpoint of the ankle (E) to determine when to begin the heel. For the best fit, toe-up socks should be tried on often while being crocheted to ensure a proper foot and heel fit.

CHOOSING YOUR SIZE

Final measurements in sock patterns are normally given for the foot circumference of the leg and foot with the narrowest size listed first, and each additional width from medium to the widest width in brackets. Once you have your measurements, pick the leg and foot circumference measurements given in the pattern that fit closest to your measurements. Follow the instructions for that size.

What if the sock recipient isn't present, or you want your socks to be a surprise? This is where the Pattern Sizing chart *(see next page)* comes in. If you do not have the sock recipient present, find out their shoe size, including width. Following the chart for the width size, use the appropriate circumference in the pattern to fit the person's shoe width. Then, use the chart based on standardized shoe sizing as a guide for the length of the sock.

Regardless of whether you use actual foot measurements or the chart, remember to take into account that socks stretch in both width and length. Your finished sock should be slightly narrower and shorter than your actual foot.

MAKING ADJUSTMENTS

You may find that your leg is narrower than your foot. Or you might have a wider leg with a narrower foot. To have your socks fit correctly, you would follow the numbers in the pattern that best fit your leg circumference, and then make adjustments to be able to follow the numbers in the pattern that best fit your foot circumference.

Example: Your leg is a medium but your foot measures to the narrow width. Work the leg of the sock to the medium-width numbers; then decrease the gusset down to the narrow size and use those numbers, not the medium-size numbers. If you are working a short-row heel, once the heel is complete, decrease stitches on the foot section to meet the narrow numbers of the pattern.

If the measurement at point A is more than 1 inch larger than the measurement at point B, you may have to use a wider size for the cuff portion, adding elastic thread to your cuff. When the cuff is completed, evenly space decreases around the base of the cuff until you have the number of stitches required for the leg pattern. After you've worked approximately half an inch into the leg, drop the elastic thread.

No matter what size you are making, if possible, try the sock on often to make sure of the fit. Ease or inch the sock up and over the foot. Do not yank or pull the sock on by the cuff. Each time you try the sock on, it will stretch the stitches and your gauge will change. Always squeeze the sock back down into shape and then continue crocheting.

GAUGE

Take time to make a gauge swatch, and do it in the round. The last thing you want is not to meet gauge. Adjust your hook size accordingly to obtain the gauge given in your pattern. If you're making a 7-inch circumference and your gauge is off, you may end up with socks that fit either a fashion doll or the Big Bird float in the Macy's Thanksgiving Day Parade®.

If you have too many stitches per inch, try a larger hook. If there are too few stitches per inch, try a smaller hook. Most sock patterns do not consider rounds per inch important unless there is a special patterning involved.

However, you may still need to adjust your gauge in this area. If your rounds are slightly short, try loosening up your tension; if you are slightly higher in rounds per inch, try tightening up your tension.

By determining the best size to comfortably fit your foot, and then matching gauge to achieve that size, your sock-making experience should be an enjoyable one with an outcome to your liking. ■

PATTERN SIZING

The measurements listed in the following charts are based on standardized measurements for men's and women's shoe widths and shoe sizes.

SHOE WIDTH

Approximate foot circumference at ball of foot (*C on diagram on page 131*)

Women				
Shoe Width	Narrow	Medium	Wide	Extra-Wide
Approx. Foot Circumference	6¾" to 7¼"	7½" to 8½"	9" to 9½"	9¾" to 11¼"
Men				
Shoe Width	Narrow	Medium	Wide	Extra-Wide
Approx. Foot Circumference	8½" to 8¾"	9" to 10"	10½" to 11"	12" to 13"

SHOE SIZE

Women's Shoe Size (Standard American)	Measurement of Actual Foot	Finished Length of Sock Foot
4 to 4½	8⅜"	7¾" to 8"
5 to 5½	8¾"	8¼" to 8½"
6 to 6½	9"	8½" to 8¾"
7 to 7½	9⅜"	9" to 9¼"
8 to 8½	9¾"	9¼" to 9½"
9 to 9½	10"	9½" to 9¾"
10 to 10½	10⅜"	10" to 10¼"
11 to 11½	10¾"	10¼" to 10½"
Men's Shoe Size (Standard American)	Measurement of Actual Foot	Finished Length of Sock Foot
8 to 9	10" to 10½"	9½" to 10"
10 to 11	10½" to 11"	10" to 10½"
12 to 13	11¼" to 11¾"	10½" to 11¼"
14	12"	11¼" to 11½"

Sizing chart from Crocheted Socks! *by Janet Rehfeldt and Mary Jane Wood; provided courtesy of Martingale & Co.*

Sock Hop

FAIR ISLE SOCKS

SKILL LEVEL
INTERMEDIATE

FINISHED SIZES
Instructions given fit woman's size small; changes for medium, large and X-large are in [ ].

FINISHED MEASUREMENTS
Foot circumference: 7¼ inches *(small)* [7¾ inches *(medium)*, 8½ inches *(large)*, 9¼ inches *(X-large)*]

Leg circumference: 7½ inches *(small)* [8 inches *(medium)*, 8¾ inches *(large)*, 9½ inches *(X-large)*]

MATERIALS
- Regia 4 Ply super fine (sock) weight yarn (1¾ oz/240 yds/50g per ball):
  - 2 [2, 2, 2] balls #1976 rose
  - 1 [1, 1, 1] ball #0600 white
- Sizes D/3/3.25mm and E/4/3.5mm crochet hooks or size needed to obtain gauge
- Tapestry needle
- Stitch markers

GAUGE
Size E hook: 24½ sts in foot pattern = 4 inches

Take time to check gauge.

PATTERN NOTES
Work in continuous rounds; do not turn or join unless otherwise stated.

Mark first stitch of each round.

Do not fasten off yarn at end of rounds; carry colors along the Leg.

When changing colors, always change colors in last stitch.

Join with slip stitch unless otherwise stated.

SPECIAL STITCH
Extended single crochet (ext sc): Insert hook in st, yo, pull lp through, yo, pull through 1 lp on hook, yo, pull through all lps on hook.

SOCK
MAKE 2.

CUFF
Row 1: Working from side to side, with size D hook and rose, ch 11, sl st in 2nd ch from hook and in each ch across, turn. *(10 sl sts)*

Row 2: Working in **back lps** *(see Stitch Guide)*, ch 1, sl st in each st across, turn.

Next rows: Rep row 2 until piece measures 7¼ [7¾, 8½, 9¼] inches from beg unstretched. **Do not fasten off.**

Sew row 1 and last row tog to form circle.

LEG

Rnd 1: Working in ends of rows, evenly sp 46 [50, 54, 58] sc across 1 edge of Cuff, **changing colors** (*see Stitch Guide and Pattern Notes*) to white, **join** (*see Pattern Notes*) in beg sc. (*46 [50, 54, 58] sc*)

Rnd 2: With size E hook, sc in first st, ch 1, sk next st, [sc in next st, ch 1, sk next st] around, **do not join** (*see Pattern Notes*).

Rnd 3: Insert hook in first st, yo with rose, pull lp through, complete sc, dc in next ch sp, [sc in next sc, dc in next ch sp] around. (*46 [50, 54, 58] sc*)

Rnd 4: Insert hook in next sc, yo with white, pull lp through, complete as sc, ch 1, sk next dc, [sc in next sc, ch 1, sk next dc] around.

Next rnds: Rep rnds 3 and 4 alternately until piece measures 7 inches from beg, including Cuff.

HEEL FLAP

Row 1: Carry unused color up along side of work, now working in rows, with white, sc in first st, sc in each of next 22 [22, 24, 26] sts, leaving rem sts unworked, turn. (*23 [23, 25, 27] sc*)

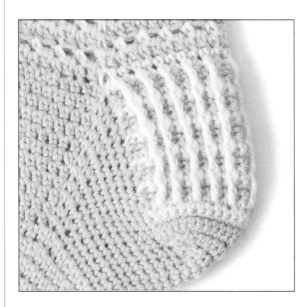

Row 2: With size D hook, ch 1, sc in first st and in each st across, changing to rose, turn.

Rows 3 & 4: Ch 1, sc in first st and in each st across, turn. Change to white in last st of last row.

Row 5: Ch 1, sc in first st, [**fptr** (*see Stitch Guide*) around next st on row 1, sk st behind fptr, sc in next st on this row] across, turn.

Row 6: Ch 1, sc in first st and in each st across, changing to rose, turn.

Rows 7 & 8: Ch 1, sc in first st and in each st across, turn. Change to white in last st of last row.

Row 9: Ch 1, sc in first st, [fptr around next fptr 3 rows below, sk st behind fptr, sc in next st on this row] across, turn.

Next rows: Rep rows 6–9 consecutively until Heel Flap measures 2¾ inches in length, ending with row 8 and rose. At end of last row, fasten off white.

HEEL TURN

Row 1 (RS): Ch 1, sc in first st, [**sc dec** (*see Stitch Guide*) in next 2 sts] twice, sc in each of next 5 [5, 6, 7] sts, sc dec in next 2 sts, sc in each of next 6 [6, 7, 8] sts, [sc dec in next 2 sts] twice, sc in last st, turn. (*18 [18, 20, 22] sc*)

Rows 2 & 3: Ch 1, sc in first st, [sc dec in next 2 sts] twice, sc in each st across to last 5 sts, [sc dec in next 2 sts] twice, sc in last st, turn. (*10 [10, 12, 14] sc*)

Row 4: Ch 1, sc in first st, [sc dec in next 2 sts] 1 [1, 2, 3] time(s), sc in each st across to last 3 [3, 5, 7] sts, [sc dec in next 2 sts] 1 [1, 2, 3] time(s), sc in last st, turn. (*8 [8, 8, 8] sc*)

Row 5: Ch 1, sc in each of first 3 sts, sc dec in next 2 sts, sc in each st across, **do not turn**. (*7 [7, 7, 7] sc*)

GUSSET

Rnd 1 (RS): Now working in rnds and in ends of rows, with size E hook, evenly sp 15 [15,

16, 17] sc along side edge of Heel Flap, place marker in last st, **ext sc** *(see Special Stitch)* in each of next 23 [27, 29, 31] sts across top of Foot, evenly sp 15 [15, 16, 17] sc on opposite side of Heel Flap, place marker in first st on this side of Gusset, sc in each of next 7 sts across Heel, place marker at beg of rnd, do not join. *(60 [64, 68, 72] sts)*

Rnd 2: Sc in each sc across to 3 sts before first marker, [sc dec in next 2 sts] twice, move marker, ext sc in each st across top of Foot, [sc dec in next 2 sts] twice, move marker, sc in each sc around to beg marker. *(56 [60, 64, 68] sts)*

Rnd 3: Sc in each sc around to top of Foot, ext sc in each st around Foot, sc in each sc around to beg marker.

Next rnds: Rep rnds 2 and 3 alternately until 44 [48, 52, 56] sts rem. Remove markers, leaving 1 marker to mark beg of rnds.

FOOT

Rnd 1: Ext sc in each st around.

Next rnds: Rep rnd 1 until piece measures 2 inches less than total length of Foot measured while standing.

TOE SHAPING

Note: *Place marker in sc at center bottom of Foot to mark beg of rnds, work in pattern to that marker. Fold Sock so that Heel is positioned correctly on Foot. Place marker at each side edge of Foot. While working Toe Shaping, move side markers as needed to keep them at side edges.*

Rnd 1: [Ext sc in each st around to 2 sts before marker at side edge, sc dec in next 2 sts, ext sc in marked st, sc dec in next 2 sts] around.

Next rnds: Rep rnd 1 until there are 20 sts rem, ending at side edge. At end of last rnd, leaving long end, fasten off.

Sew Toe end closed. ▪

SKILL LEVEL

EASY

FINISHED SIZES

Instructions given fit woman's size small; changes for medium, large and X-large are in [ ].

FINISHED MEASUREMENTS

Foot circumference: 7¼ inches *(small)* [8 inches *(medium)*, 8½ inches *(large)*, 9¼ inches *(X-large)*]

Leg circumference: 8¼ inches *(small)* [9 inches *(medium)*, 9¾ inches *(large)*, 10¼ inches *(X-large)*]

MATERIALS

- Fine (sport) weight yarn (3½ oz/414 yds/100g per ball): 414 [414, 828, 828] yds red/blue/green variegated
- Sizes D/3/3.25mm and E/4/3.5mm crochet hooks or sizes needed to obtain gauge
- Tapestry needle
- Stitch markers

GAUGE

Size D hook: 26 sts in pattern = 4 inches

Size E hook: 23 sts in pattern = 4 inches

Take time to check gauge.

PATTERN NOTES

Work in continuous rounds; do not turn or join unless otherwise stated.

Mark first stitch of each round.

Join with slip stitch unless otherwise stated.

SOCK
MAKE 2.

CUFF

Row 1: Working from side to side, with size D hook, ch 11, sl st in 2nd ch from hook and in each ch across, turn. *(10 sl sts)*

Row 2: Working in **back lps** *(see Stitch Guide)*, ch 1, sl st in each st across, turn.

Next rows: Rep row 2 until piece measures 8 [8¾, 9½, 10] inches from beg unstretched. **Do not fasten off.**

Sew row 1 and last row tog to form circle.

LEG

Rnd 1: Working in ends of rows around 1 edge of Cuff, evenly sp 48 [52, 56, 60] sc around, do not join *(see Pattern Notes)*. *(48 [52, 56, 60] sc)*

Rnd 2: With size E hook, sc in first st, hdc in next st, dc in next st, hdc in next st, [sc in next st, hdc in next st, dc in next st, hdc in next st] around. *(48 [52, 56, 60] sts)*

Rnd 3: [Sc in next st, hdc in next st, dc in next st, hdc in next st] around.

Next rnds: Rep rnd 3 until piece measures 3 inches from beg, including Cuff.

Next rnds: With size D hook, rep rnd 3 until piece measures 6 inches from beg, including Cuff.

HEEL FLAP

Row 1 (RS): Now working in rows, sc in each of next 24 [24, 26, 26] sts, leaving rem sts unworked, turn.

Row 2: Ch 1, sc in each st across, turn.

Next rows: Rep row 2 until Heel Flap measures 2¾ inches, ending with WS row.

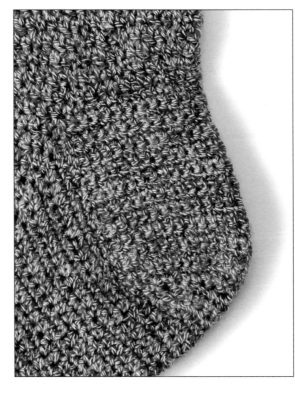

HEEL TURN

Row 1 (RS): Ch 1, sc in first st, [**sc dec** *(see Stitch Guide)* in next 2 sts] twice, *sc in each of next 5 [5, 6, 6] sts, [sc dec in next 2 sts] twice, rep from * once, sc in last st, turn. *(18 [18, 20, 20] sc)*

Row 2: Ch 1, sc in first st, [sc dec in next 2 sts] twice, *sc in each of next 2 [2, 3, 3] sts, [sc dec in next 2 sts] twice, rep from * once, sc in last st, turn. *(12 [12, 14, 14] sc)*

Rows 3 & 4: Ch 1, sc in first st, sc dec in next 2 sts, sc across to last 3 sts, sc dec in next 2 sts, sc in last st, turn. *(8 [8, 10, 10] sc at end of last row)*

GUSSET

Rnd 1 (RS): Now working in rnds, sc in each st across 8 [8, 10, 10] sts on Heel, place marker in first sc to mark beg of rnds, evenly sp 18 sc in ends of rows along edge of Heel Flap, place marker, work in same pattern as Leg across next 24 [28, 30, 34] sts on top of Foot, evenly sp 18 sc in ends of rows along edge of Heel Flap, place marker in first sc on Heel, **do not join**. *(68 [72, 76, 80] sc)*

Rnd 2: Sc around to 3 sts before first marker, [sc dec in next 2 sts] twice, move marker, work in pattern across 24 [28, 30, 34] sts on Top of Foot to next marker, [sc dec in next 2 sts] twice, move marker, sc in each sc around to beg marker. *(64 [68, 72, 76] sc)*

Rnd 3: Hdc in each sc along Heel and Gusset, work in pattern across next 24 [28, 30, 34] sts on Foot, hdc in each sc along Gusset to beg marker.

Next rnds: [Rep rnds 2 and 3 alternately] 4 [4, 4, 4] times. Remove markers. *(48 [52, 56, 60] sts at end of last rnd)*

FOOT

Rnd 1: Hdc in each sc around to top of Foot, work in pattern across next 24 [28, 30, 34] sts, place marker in first sc of top of Foot to mark beg of rnds, work in pattern around entire Heel top to top of Foot.

Rnd 2: Work in pattern around.

Next rnds: Rep rnd 2 until Foot measures 2 inches from longest toe.

TOE SHAPING

Note: Place marker in sc at center bottom of Foot to mark beg of rnds, work in pattern to that marker. Fold Sock so that Heel is positioned correctly on Foot. Place marker at each side edge of Foot. While working Toe Shaping, move side markers as needed to keep them at side edges.

Rnd 1: Sc around to 2 sts before next marker, sc dec in next 2 sts, sc in next st, sc dec in next 2 sts, sc in each st around before next marker, sc dec in next 2 sts, sc in next st, sc dec in next 2 sts, sc in each st around to beg marker. *(44 [48, 52, 56] sc)*

Next rnds: Rep rnd 1 until there are 16 [20, 20, 24] sts rem, ending at a side edge. Leaving long end, fasten off.

Sew end of Toe closed. ■

chapter nine
working with color

From learning how to select the right complementary colors for your projects to understanding the simple basics of color-change techniques, we've got some helpful tips to help you master the mysteries of working with color.

Using the Color Wheel

We all have our favorite colors and color combinations, but sometimes we just get stuck trying to decide which colors would go together well in our projects. Have you ever thought about using a color wheel to help you put together great color combos that can produce eye-catching results?

There are numerous styles of color wheels, as shown below and on the opposite page. The color wheel shown below is very basic and simple to use.

Locate the main color you'd like to use for your afghan. *Blending* colors can be chosen from the two wedges to the right or left, depending on the look you want to achieve. *Contrasting* colors are directly across from the main color.

Triad color schemes can be created by choosing the colors that create an equilateral triangle with your main color. On a 12-part color wheel, the lines of an equilateral triangle would select every fourth color. So, for example, if your main color is blue, the triad colors are yellow and red.

All colors on the color wheel are numbered according to value, so if you wish to create unusual color schemes, choose colors that are the same values. You can create an unlimited number of gorgeous color combinations using colors from any value group (all No. 3's, for example). For an exciting color scheme, choose black, gray, navy, brown or white, and accent with one or more vivid colors.

Let's say you are making an afghan as a gift. You might like to choose colors that reflect the personality of the recipient. Yellows are cheerful and bright. Reds are passionate and aggressive. Blues are calm and cool. Purples are regal and starlike. Oranges are warm and cozy. Greens, depending on whether they are more blue or more yellow, can be cool or vibrant.

If you are making an afghan or other decorative accessories for your own home, work up swatches in several possible color combinations. Look at them from a distance rather than close up, preferably in the location where you plan to use the pieces. You will get a more realistic view of how the color combination will look and which combinations you prefer.

Have fun experimenting with the color wheel and seeing what fabulous color combinations you can put together for your projects. The possibilities are virtually endless! ■

Color Magic Secrets

If there is anything in life that is truly magic, it's color! As everyday life seems to grow more fast-paced by the day, people often go about mundane daily duties while giving little thought to color. In spite of this seeming disinterest, responses to color are very real, can be scientifically measured and influence many day-to-day choices, often at times when color is the last thing on your mind.

COLOR PSYCHOLOGY

Manufacturers and merchants spend billions of dollars to capitalize on our responses to color because they know colors influence what we buy, how much we eat, as well how as how we are likely to feel and respond to their products in other ways. For example, red is often used in the decor of a fast-food restaurant because red stimulates and increases your appetite, so you'll spend more money on food when surrounded by red, and you'll be subconsciously dissuaded from lingering over the meal. Both red and yellow catch the eye and are used on food labels to stand out enticingly on store shelves, making them more visually appealing to the shopper.

When it comes to choosing colors for clothing and yarn, it's easy to become confused at the vast array of offerings in any store. Take the guesswork out of yarn choices with a small investment in a color wheel (see Fig. 1), a purchase that will almost guarantee you'll never make another color error again! Craft stores offer color wheels in sizes small and flat enough to slide into most handbags.

COLOR BASICS

Instructions included with the color wheel shown here are simple and easy to grasp. To begin, choose a color of yarn, such as red, and then match the shade and the color number on the color wheel as closely as possible. As you rotate the inner wheel, notice how the symmetrical spacing and cutout shapes automatically indicate harmonious combinations. For example, if the color value of your red is No. 4, the arrows on the inner wheel point to opposite and complementary shades to use with your red, all of which also have a value of No. 4.

Fig. 1

The more colors are combined with one another, the more sophisticated and fashion oriented they become. In addition, the value of a color is deepened when mixed with black and becomes lighter when mixed with white. The next step/nuance would be to add gray to create more hues.

COLOR PROPERTIES: VALUE & VISUAL WEIGHT

In looking at the color values shown in Fig. 2 on page 142, the primary colors of blue, yellow and red in Tier 1 cannot be mixed from other colors. The secondary colors in Tier 2 result from mixing two primary colors together: blue + red = purple; yellow + blue = green; red + yellow = orange. The tertiary colors in Tier 3 result from mixing one primary color with one adjacent secondary color: yellow/green, blue/green, blue/purple, red/purple, red/orange and yellow/orange.

When selecting yarn colors, two properties must be taken into consideration: the value of the colors and the visual weight. The lighter the color, the less it appears to weigh visually, while the darker the color, the heavier it seems. The most eye-catching color combinations are those that are the most opposite in value and weight, such as black and white, as well as other primary or strong colors combined with white. These opposites really stand out.

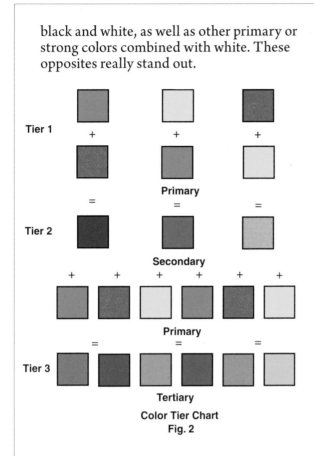

Tier 1 +
Primary
Tier 2 =
Secondary
Primary
Tier 3 =
Tertiary
Color Tier Chart
Fig. 2

Fig. 3

The most soothing combinations are monochromatics, but they can also be made to pop when one hue is very strong. For example, if you crochet a sweater in shades of tan, and then work the edging, collar or ribbing in a dark brown, the dark brown stands out and makes a strong, appealing statement. The goal is to achieve visual balance while using harmonious shades. Without a color wheel, this can be a daunting, risky task.

BEST COLORS TO WEAR

When it comes to colors, those we use in home decorating are not necessarily the most flattering when it comes to wearables. The colors a person wears should complement one's eyes, hair and skin coloring to be truly flattering. Colors fall into two basic groupings: warm and cool. Warm colors have golden undertones, while cool colors are based on blue. If your skin undertone is slightly blue (cool), then warm hues such as corals *(see Fig. 3)*, oranges and rusts probably

Fig. 4

shouldn't be in your personal color palette because they are visually discordant with your skin tone.

If your undertone is warmer, cool blues *(see Fig. 4)* and lavenders will tend to make you look wan and washed out.

Generally speaking, yellow is the single most

difficult color to wear. If yellow is a color you truly love, choosing the right shade will make all the difference. If your skin coloring is warm, select a banana shade that has a bit more red than lemon yellow, which is a slightly harsher yellow with green undertones. If your skin tone is cool, then opt for yellows with hints of greens or blues.

If you haven't yet discovered the secret of the two easiest-to-wear colors (*regardless of your own skin, hair and eye colors*), just give turquoise and coral a try! Before long, someone is sure to say, "Wow! That is *so* your color!" These clear colors have perfectly balanced values and are flattering for everyone. When you look at or wear either of these two colors, your psychological response is an automatic lifting of spirit—making you feel good while you're looking good.

For more information about the psychology of color, look up one of the many books available on the subject. The enlightening information found therein will take your ability to choose the right colors to an entirely new level.

Monochromatic color schemes always work when it comes to clothing or home decorating, as long as you begin with a basic color that flatters your own coloring. By varying the hues of the basic color, you add visual interest and impact. The more varied textures are introduced along with varied shades, the more sophisticated, interesting and pleasing you'll find your final outcome. For example, if you love green, try mixing and matching any shades from the lightest to darkest in varied amounts for the most impact, using one shade as an accent to optimize your end result.

The most sophisticated and difficult monochromatic color palette of all is undoubtedly that of neutrals: creams, grays and tans. Color wheels are unable to break down the intricate values of neutrals. It takes an expert eye and knowledge to maintain the shading and visual balance of these subtle color changes and hues.

If you truly love neutrals, go to your local home-improvement store and gather up paint chips to take home and study. Most paint manufacturers make it easy for you as they show color palettes in families with predetermined and matching values. For starters, look at the pale creams and you'll immediately notice distinct differences. Some chips have strong undertones of green or blue, while others are more yellow or orange; yet others have hints of brown or black. This is understandable because white is actually a combination of all colors, not an absence of color, and cream is just a subtle darkening of white.

COLOR TRENDS

When it comes to color, trends are not based on strong and growing demand for certain colors; rather, they are based on the findings from focused worldwide networks. Participants of these groups come from varied walks of life. Each member follows and studies such things as sports, politics, economics, music, arts, cuisine, leisure activities, decorating, fashion, the environment and cultural diversity, just to name a few. Each aspect of study provides useful information that allows the collective group to forecast colors with validity. When the core group comes to consensus, color chips are then developed and distributed to designers and manufacturers who further develop their own forecast for trends for yarn, fabric, paint, clothing, furniture and the like.

From season to season the hues of core colors change slightly to reflect worldwide changes as they occur within focus groups. Colors then become stronger, more muted or more convoluted to reflect global changes.

How drab the world would be without the magic of color. It is truly something to celebrate and enjoy! Thank goodness that the secrets of color can be revealed to enhance our daily lives with a simple, little color wheel. ■

Color Changes Made Easy

Color changes can add dimension and style to a variety of patterns, from afghans, rugs and pillows to purses, scarves and sweaters. Making color changes can sometimes seem daunting, but with a little practice and some helpful tips, it's an easy technique to accomplish.

SIMPLE & EASY

The simplest method of changing colors is to fasten off the first color and join the second color. This method works well when you have large areas worked in one color.

Another easy way to change from the working color to a new color is to work the last stitch to be done in the working color until two loops remain on the hook (*Photo A*), then draw the new color through the two loops on the hook (*Photo B*).

COLOR CHANGES & GRAPHS

When creating a piece that contains different colors, the objective is to make color changes that look smooth and consistent as though made with one continuous strand of yarn. There are a few simple tricks to help achieve this effect.

All your yarns should be the same weight to prevent puckering. To keep the elastic quality of crochet, be sure to maintain the proper tension when carrying yarn across the back. Strands that are too loose will snag and pull, creating unsightly holes and ragged edges where color changes occur. Strands pulled too tightly will result in puckered work and distorted stitches. For garments that need to stretch more than others, carry the unused color more loosely.

The following photos show a color-change sample that has been done correctly with proper tension maintained on the carried strand and a sample in which the yarn was carried too loosely, creating an unfinished look. The sample on the left shows color changing done smoothly and accurately. The sample on the right is too loose and holey with yarn colors bleeding into the other color sections

SECTIONS OF COLOR

Some patterns include sections that cover several stitches between color changes. One method of handling this type of color change is to work over the unused carried yarn with each stitch. This leaves no loose strands in the back, but will double the thickness of the item and the unused color may show through on the right side. To avoid extra thickness, you can work over the carried color every second or third stitch instead of every stitch.

To work over a carried strand of yarn, consider the strand a part of the stitch being worked into. Simply insert the hook in the stitch and underneath the strand of carried yarn, draw the working yarn through and complete the stitch as usual (*Photo C*).

PHOTO C

ONLY STITCHES APART

For color changes that are only a few stitches apart, use a ball of yarn or a bobbin wound with the new color for each color section. As you work, each new color is picked up from the nearest stitch of the same color on the row or round before to avoid leaving so many loose strands across the back. A technique called "twisting" (picking up the new color from under the first color) may be used. This twists the strands together to avoid forming a hole.

BOX IT UP

For multiple sections of colors, place the yarn balls or skeins on a tray or in a box in the order in which they will be used. As you complete the first row, turn your work as you normally would, bringing the box around to the front. Crochet the next row, turning the box to the back to coincide with turning the crocheted piece.

FOLLOWING COLOR CHARTS

Instructions for color-change designs are often published in chart form. Charts are easy to follow once you understand how to follow them.

Charts are drawn with the right side of the work facing you and are read from bottom to top. Each square represents one stitch. Odd-numbered rows on the chart are worked from right to left and even-numbered rows are worked from left to right. Thus, odd-numbered rows are worked on the right side

of the piece and even-numbered rows are worked on the wrong side. To help follow across the row, you might find it helpful to place a ruler or sheet of paper directly below the row being worked.

A chart that is not illustrated in full color for a pattern is usually accompanied by a color key that identifies the stitches and colors needed. A chart for a design that will be repeated in the work may show only one repeat of the design. The written instructions of the pattern usually give the first rows and stitches to position the design. From there, it will tell you to work according to the chart, giving any shaping or special instructions as needed.

BOTANICA PILLOWS

SKILL LEVEL

INTERMEDIATE

FINISHED SIZE

Approximately 14 x 14 inches

MATERIALS

- Red Heart Super Saver medium (worsted) weight yarn (7 oz/364 yds/198g per skein):
  2 skeins #385 royal (A)
  1 skein each #336 warm brown (B), #661 frosty green (C), #631 light sage (D) and #316 soft white (E)
- Size H/8/5mm crochet hook or size needed to obtain gauge
- Tapestry needle
- (2) 14 x 14-inch pillow forms

GAUGE

4 dc = 1 inch; 2 dc rows = 1 inch

PILLOW A
FRONT

Row 1 (RS): With A, ch 50, dc in 4th ch from hook (beg 3 sk chs count as a dc) and in each rem ch, turn. (48 dc)

Row 2: Ch 3 (*counts as dc on this and following rows*), dc in each rem dc and in 3rd ch of beg 3 sk chs, turn.

Row 3: Ch 3, dc in next 24 dc, changing to B in last dc, dc in next 2 dc, changing to A in last dc, dc in next 2 dc, changing to C in last dc, dc in next 8 dc, changing to A in last dc, dc in each rem dc and in 3rd ch of beg ch-3, turn.

Rows 4–28: Follow Chart A. At end of row 28, do not turn.

EDGING

Ch 1, 3 sc in first dc—*corner made*, sc in each dc to turning ch-3, 3 sc in 3rd ch of beg ch-3—*corner made*. Working across next side in ends of rows in sps formed by edge dc and turning chs, 2 sc in each row. Working across next side in unused lps of beg ch, 3 sc in first lp—*corner made*, sc in each lp to last lp, 3 sc in last lp—*corner made*. Working across next side in ends of rows in sps formed by edge dc and beg chs, 2 sc in each row, join with sl st in first sc.

Fasten off and weave in all ends.

BACK

Row 1 (RS): With A, ch 50, dc in 4th ch from hook (*beg 3 sk chs count as dc*) and in each rem ch, turn. (*48 dc*)

Row 2: Ch 3 (*counts as dc on this and following rows*), dc in each rem dc and in 3rd ch of beg 3 sk chs, turn.

Row 3: Ch 3, dc in each rem dc and in 3rd ch of beg ch-3, turn.

Rows 4–28: Rep row 3. At end of row 28, do not turn.

EDGING

Work same as Edging for Front.

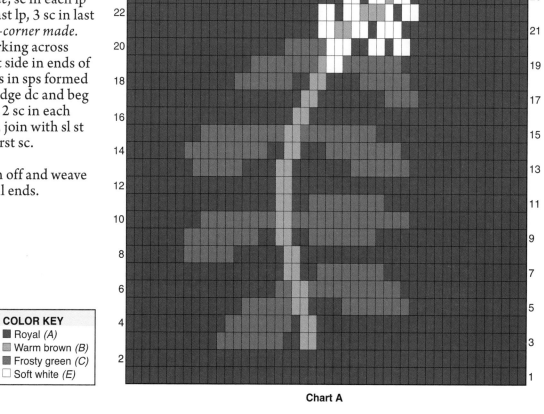

COLOR KEY
- ■ Royal (A)
- ■ Warm brown (B)
- ■ Frosty green (C)
- □ Soft white (E)

Chart A

ASSEMBLY

With A, sew Front and Back tog along 3 sides. Insert pillow form. Sew rem side.

PILLOW B
FRONT

Row 1 (RS): With A, ch 50, dc in 4th ch from hook *(beg 3 sk chs count as dc)* and in each rem ch, turn. *(48 dc)*

Row 2: Ch 3 *(counts as dc on this and following rows)*, dc in each rem dc and in 3rd ch of beg 3 sk chs, turn.

Row 3: Ch 3, dc in next 7 dc, changing to C in last dc, dc in next 7 dc, changing to A in last dc, dc in next 4 dc, changing to B in last dc, dc in next 2 dc, changing to A in last dc, dc in next 2 dc, changing

to D in last dc, dc in next 2 dc, changing to C in last dc, dc in next 3 dc, changing to A in last dc, dc in next 2 dc, changing to C in last dc, dc in next 4 dc, changing to A in last dc, dc in each rem dc and in 3rd ch of beg ch-3, turn.

Rows 4–28: Follow Chart B. At end of row 28, do not turn.

EDGING

Work same as Edging for Front of Pillow A.

BACK

Work same as Back for Pillow A.

ASSEMBLY

Follow Assembly instructions for Pillow A. ∎

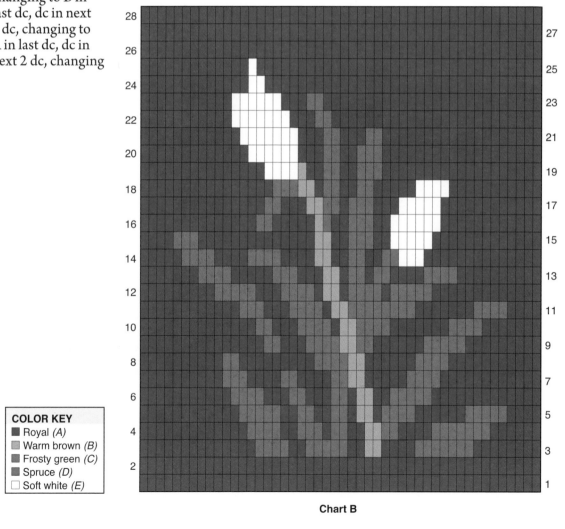

COLOR KEY
- ■ Royal *(A)*
- ■ Warm brown *(B)*
- ■ Frosty green *(C)*
- ■ Spruce *(D)*
- □ Soft white *(E)*

Chart B

chapter ten
professional touches

If you're sometimes stumped when it comes to finishing details like blocking, buttons and other closures, or decorative accents such as fringe, tassels and edgings, we'll show you how to give your crocheted projects a finished and polished look.

Blocking Basics

Blocking is an important step toward making your crocheted pieces look more professional. It's a way of "dressing" or finishing your projects using moisture and sometimes heat. Proper blocking of a crocheted garment or accessory can go a long way toward making it look and fit better, and it can help restore symmetrical balance to a misshapen afghan or rug. Blocking sets the stitches and can even enhance the drape of the fabric. Seaming and edging are easier on blocked pieces, and minor sizing adjustments may be made during the blocking process.

There are different methods for blocking crocheted pieces and knowing which one to use for a particular project can make all the difference in achieving a successful result. Choosing the correct blocking method depends on what the item is and what type of yarn or thread is used. Some items might not be suitable for blocking, such as 3-D pieces that are difficult to handle or very small items such as Christmas ornaments. Also, certain fibers might not be suitable for blocking.

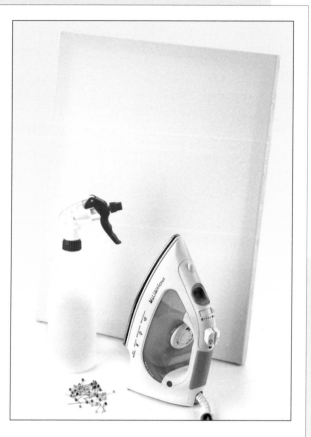

GETTING STARTED

You'll need a blocking board, rustproof pins, a steamer or steam iron, a spray bottle and your yarn or thread labels. A blocking "board" needs to be a flat surface that's large enough to hold the piece or pieces you want to block. Pieces should not hang over the edges of the blocking board.

If you don't have, or can't find, a commercially made blocking board, it's easy to create your own. Purchase a piece of plastic foam insulation board at your local home-improvement center or foam board from an office-supply store. In choosing the size, keep in mind that, while a larger board can block more pieces, it may be difficult to store. It might be better to purchase several smaller boards.

Cover the board with a thick towel and then with a clean cotton cloth, both of which have been washed so that they will not bleed onto your work. While solids usually work best, you can use a fabric with a large check print or stripes in order to have a blocking guide.

Your blocking board will need to be in a location where it can remain undisturbed until the blocking is finished, which can range from just a few minutes to more than a day, depending on the circumstances. The board needs to be able to handle pins, moisture and heat. To block large items such as afghans or shawls, for example, a guest-room bed or a large, well-padded table—even a sheet-covered carpeted floor—work great.

CHOOSE YOUR METHOD

Blocking methods may be described as wet, dry or cold. The actual method you choose will vary depending on yarn content, final use and your own preferences.

Consult the yarn label. If different fibers have been combined in the same item, the most delicate fiber takes precedence. Most natural fibers such as wool, cotton, linen and mohair may be either wet- or dry-blocked. Some synthetic fibers do not benefit from blocking and may, in fact, be ruined by careless blocking. Novelty and metallic fibers may need special care and may not be suitable for blocking.

While it's always advisable to make a test swatch for any pattern to check gauge, an added benefit to making a swatch is that you will also have a piece to practice blocking to make sure you are using the proper method. For example, did you know that too much heat can "kill" acrylic yarn, making it shiny and limp? It's better to wreck a swatch than a whole afghan.

Wet blocking is suitable only for those fibers which tolerate submersion. Wash the piece first, if desired, or thoroughly wet it and gently squeeze out excess water. Do not wring or twist! For two-diminsional pieces, lay the piece out flat, and gently pat and shape it into the desired finished measurements. Pin the piece securely in place using rustproof pins or blocking wires. For 3-D pieces, stuff the piece with rolled-up plastic grocery bags or other waterproof stuffing. For round pieces, blowing up a balloon to the desired size inside the item works well. Leave the piece undisturbed until it is completely dry. You can hasten the drying process by setting up a fan to blow over the area.

Dry blocking is suitable for fibers which can tolerate moisture and heat (steam). Pin the piece into the desired shape and size on the blocking board. Pins should be close together and evenly spaced so as not to distort the fabric. Blocking wires also work well.

Smooth all seams and areas that are puckered or rippled as much as possible with your fingers. Holding a steamer or steam iron an inch or more above the item, steam the fabric well. Move the iron slowly over the surface, never allowing it to touch the fabric; do not press. After steaming, leave the piece undisturbed until it is completely cool and dry.

Cold blocking can be used for fibers which can tolerate moisture but not heat. Pin the piece into shape on the blocking board as you did for dry blocking. Mist with a spray bottle

of clean water until the piece is completely wet. If stubborn areas resist lying flat, use additional pins as needed or press with your hand for a few seconds (*it's amazing how the gentle warmth from your skin can help!*). Leave the item undisturbed until it is completely dry. Again, a fan can help speed things up.

TIPS FOR BLOCKING AFGHANS & OTHER LARGE PIECES

Afghans and other large crochet pieces, such as tablecloths, bedspreads and shawls, can easily be blocked on a bed with a firm or extra-firm mattress, on a large, well-padded table or on a clean, carpeted floor.

Arrange the piece into a nice, even shape to the required or desired measurements, taking care not to over-stretch or distort the shape of the piece. Using rustproof pins, pin all edges down securely around the entire piece. If any stubborn areas don't want to lie down smoothly, adding a few extra pins in these spots usually does the trick.

If desired, the piece can be dry-blocked as previously instructed. But, for large pieces such as these, you can also achieve beautiful results by blocking without the use of steam.

Using a large spray bottle of chemical-free water, mist the piece thoroughly until it is lightly wet (semi-saturated). Use your hand to gently press each area as it is sprayed. It's amazing how just the heat from your skin acts like a low-heat iron of sorts on wet yarn or thread, but without the possible damage to yarn fibers an iron can cause.

After the piece is thoroughly wet down and "hand-pressed," have a fan blow on the project until it's completely dry. The results will be beautiful!

Now that you know the different ways to block your projects and which method works best for each, you'll feel more confident to take that extra step and give your projects a more finished look with the results you desire. But, don't forget to practice on a test swatch first! ▪

Right on the Button

The right button can make or break a sweater or jacket, but choosing the right one can sometimes be more difficult than you might think. Here are some hints for finding the perfect button that will enhance your garment rather than detract from it (or worse, cause an unexpected wardrobe malfunction), as well as some tips for applying them properly:

- Try to purchase your buttons before making the button bands. That way, you can pick the button without fear that the buttonhole will be too large or too small. Once the buttons are chosen, you can make the buttonhole to fit the button.

- Take along your gauge swatch when button shopping. If you have time, try stitching a small buttonhole band onto the swatch, using a couple of different-size buttonholes. At the store, you'll be able to try the buttons on your buttonholes to see how they look on your garment and which ones work best.

- Decide whether your garment needs buttons that stand out as part of the overall design, or whether they should be unobtrusive. You may want to match the yarn color, or you may find that a great-looking contrasting color gives the best appearance.

- Scale is important. Tiny buttons belong on garments made with fine yarns, and large buttons look better on garments made with heavy yarns.

- Shank buttons generally work better on thick fabrics—they are easier to apply and provide good stability.

- To sew on buttons, use sewing or embroidery thread in a matching color. A button can be stabilized to prevent wobbling, drooping or pulling through the crocheted fabric by adding a small "stay" button on the wrong side of the fabric. The designer button on the right side of the fabric and the stay button on the wrong side are sewn on at the same time in one operation. Choose a stay button that is flat and at least as large as the designer button. Use a button with two holes for a designer button with two holes or a shank. Use a four-hole stay button with a four-hole designer button.

- Mix button styles on one garment. You can create some fun, unique looks, and it's a great way to use some of those lovely one-of-a-kind buttons in your grandmother's button box!

- If you are using buttons that are non-washable or require special cleaning, fasten them onto the garment with button pins. These special safety pins have a curve to accommodate the button and allow easy removal of the button for cleaning.

- Make your own buttons. You can purchase a button-covering kit and cover them with matching fabric, or use Fimo® or Sculpey® modeling clay to make eye-catching, machine-washable buttons.

- You can also crochet simple buttons to complement your garment. If you decide to crochet your buttons, try one of the following.

CROCHETED RING BUTTON

FRONT   BACK

MATERIALS
- Yarn of choice
- Appropriate-size crochet hook and tapestry needle
- Purchased bone/plastic ring in desired size from craft store

SINGLE-ROUND OPTION
Rnd 1: Leaving 6-inch tail, **sc around ring** *(see illustration)* until completely covered. Leaving 8-inch tail, fasten off.

With tapestry needle, weave longer tail through every sc around and pull tight, bringing sts to inside of ring. If needed, work 1 or 2 sts across to tighten and secure the center. Using beg and ending tails, sew the button onto the garment.

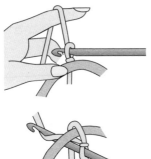

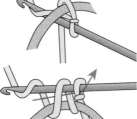

Single Crochet Around Ring

MULTIPLE-ROUND OPTION
Rnd 1: Leaving 6-inch tail, sc around ring until completely covered.

Rnds 2 & 3: Sc in each st around. At end of last rnd, leaving 8-inch tail, fasten off.

With tapestry needle, weave longer tail through every sc around and pull tight, bringing sts to inside of ring. If needed, work 1 or 2 sts across to tighten and secure the center. Using beg and ending tails, sew the button onto the garment.

CROCHETED STUFFED BUTTON

FRONT   **BACK**

MATERIALS
- Yarn of choice
- Appropriate-size crochet hook and tapestry needle

PATTERN NOTE
Join rounds with slip stitch unless otherwise stated.

BUTTON
Rnd 1: Leaving 8-inch tail, ch 2, 8 sc in 2nd ch from hook, **join** (*see Pattern Note*) in first sc. (*8 sc*)

Rnd 2: Ch 1, sc in same st, 2 sc in next st, [sc in next st, 2 sc in next st] 3 times, join in first sc. (*12 sc*)

Rnd 3: Sc in each sc around, join in first sc.

Rnd 4: Ch 1, [**sc dec** (*see Stitch Guide*) in next 2 sts] 6 times. Leaving 10-inch tail, fasten off.

Stuff small scraps of matching yarn into ball. With tapestry needle, weave 10-inch tail from last rnd through all sts on last rnd and pull tight. Thread the 8-inch tail down through center of button and use both ends to sew button to garment.

BUTTON PLACEMENT
It's easy to get even spacing for an odd number of buttonholes. Place pins at point where top and bottom holes will be. Fold piece in half so that pins are together. Place a third pin at center and unfold. Fold again so that center pin and top pin are together. Place a fourth pin at this fold, unfold. Fold again so that center pin and bottom pin are together. Place a fifth pin at this fold, unfold. If necessary, continue to split the difference between the pins until the desired number of holes is marked.

Here is a final tip: Sloppy, loose buttonholes look amateurish and don't stay closed very well. Remember that most yarns stretch slightly with use over time, so your new buttonholes should fit *snuggly* over your buttons.

Try applying these tips and techniques when using buttons on your garments to ensure successful results. Buttons really *can* make or break the finished look! ▪

Seeking Closure

From loops, cords and toggles to flowers, frogs and cables you can create a variety of eye-catching fasteners to give your crocheted garments dazzling detail. It all depends on the look you want, which type of fastener works best with your project and your choice of buttons, where applicable.

The Merriam-Webster dictionary defines "closure" as "an often comforting or satisfying sense of finality," and that definition perfectly describes what a crocheter feels when the last stitch of a "just-right" edging has been completed. As the piece is gently smoothed out for that final look, you feel good inside knowing the time spent executing every stitch has resulted in an edging that complements and enhances your crochet project. That final special touch makes all the difference between completing an ordinary and an extraordinary crochet project.

BASIC GUIDELINES FOR SELECTING AN EDGING

Whether your crochet project is a garment, an afghan or a table runner, the most complementary and compatible edgings should flatter the basic pattern stitch. For example, let's say the pieces of a jacket are worked in a shell pattern. Whether you want a tailored or romantic look, your choice of edgings could determine the final outcome and could make the difference between failure and success. To that end, a simple edging such as single crochet or reverse single crochet can provide a tailored look, while an edging worked in ruffles or another shell pattern can heighten the overall romantic look.

Avoid discordant combinations whenever possible. For example, if your pattern stitch is a basket weave or other geometric pattern with straight lines, then your edging should also include some straight lines. Should you choose to use a shell edging with soft, curved lines, instead of enhancing your basket-weave pattern stitch, the outcome would most likely be discordant and incompatible.

Choosing edgings can be likened to the art of interior decorating, where the rule of thumb is to replicate an architectural shape, such as an arched doorway, to create harmony and flow. A decorator who is working with any room is likely to include design details from that room such as a curved picture frame, carved elongated arches on table legs, curves in the pattern or edging of an area rug or curved shapes found in fabric used for pillows. The trick is not to overdo the shape, but to add a particular element more than once to enhance the overall appearance.

CONTRASTING-COLOR EDGINGS

When you edge a garment or afghan with a contrasting color (see Photo A) have you ever noticed how the side edges are never as crisp and even as the bottom and top edges? The uneven appearance is created by working over the ends of stitches and rows instead of working into the loops of the stitches at the top or the remaining loops of the beginning chains which will create a smooth line.

PHOTO A

Working a single row of single crochet into the loops of the stitches at the top or the remaining loops of the beginning chains and/or into the shaping eliminates that jagged transition and creates the desired smooth line. It is not necessary to work an extra row of single crochet at the top or bottom of the piece; simply work a row at each side for a more professional finish, as used in our jacket on the fronts and V-neck.

MOTIFS

Whether crocheted with yarn or thread, motifs can be used for surprising or dramatic closures. Try some of the following: squares, miniature doilies, triangles, leaves, flowers, animals, butterflies, ladybugs, bumblebees, tiny ice cream cones, teddy bears and the like. Instead of adding a button or bobble, you can sew on clear plastic snaps for closure, and then cover the snap location with a complementary motif.

BUTTON LOOPS

Here are four different ways to crochet button loops for garments.

Chained loop: Try this technique for decorative buttons as this simple look allows a fancy button to stand out *(see Photo B)*.

PHOTO B

Determine the number of chains needed to fit snugly around the button chosen for the garment, three chains for example. Place markers to indicate the button placement. Working in single crochet, at each marker, skip one less stitch *(two stitches using our example)* than number of chains required.

The instructions for our example would read as follows: *Ch 3, sk next 2 sts, sc in each st across to next marker, rep from * across.

Solid loop: This technique is best used for heavy and/or large buttons *(see Photo C)*.

PHOTO C

Determine the number of chains needed to fit snugly around the button chosen for the garment, five chains for example. Place markers to indicate the button placement. Working in single crochet, at each marker, work the same number of stitches as chains required *(five stitches using our example)*. Chain five, **turn**, working to the right, slip stitch in one less stitch than the number of chains required *(fourth stitch to the right in our example)*, **turn**. Work one to two more stitches than number of chains *(six or seven chains)* into chain space.

The instructions for our example would read as follows: *Sc in each st across to next marker, sc in each of next 5 sts, ch 5, **turn**, sl st in 4th st to right, **turn**, work 6 or 7 sc in ch-5 sp just made, rep from * across.

PHOTO D

PHOTO E

Picot loop: This technique is best used for plain buttons as the picots create the "wow" factor *(see Photo D)*.

Determine the number of chains needed to fit snugly around button, five chains for example. Place markers to indicate the button placement. Working in single crochet, at each marker, work the same of number of stitches as chains required *(five stitches using our example)*. Chain five, **turn**, working to the right, slip stitch in one less stitch than number of chains *(fourth stitch to the right in our example)*, **turn**. [(Single crochet, chain three, slip stitch in single crochet just made—*picot*) five times, slip stitch] in chain-5 space just made, slip stitch in next stitch on working row.

The instructions for our example would read as follows: *Sc in each st across to next marker, sc in each of next 5 sts, ch 5, **turn**, sl st in 4th st to right, **turn**, [(sc, ch 3, sl st in sc just made—*picot*) 5 times, sl st] in ch-5 sp just made, sl st in next st on working row.

Toggle: This technique is best used for jackets or at the neckline of a hoodie or slit-neck pullover. Toggles make a nice design element for pillows, hats, handbags, etc *(see Photo E)*.

To form a toggle, you will work as follows:

Row 1: Leaving 8-inch tail, form slip knot on hook, ch 2, sc in 2nd ch from hook, turn.

Row 2: Ch 1, 3 sc in sc, turn. *(3 sc)*

Row 3: Ch 1, 2 sc in first st, sc in next st, 2 sc in last st, turn. *(5 sc)*

Row 4: Ch 1, 2 sc in first st, sc in each of next 3 sts, 2 sc in last st, turn. *(7 sc)*

Work even across 7 sc for 3 or more rows to achieve look when piece is rolled up. Fasten off.

Roll piece with row 1 on top. Tack tog and sew bead to tip, if desired.

CROCHET I-CORD

Simple crochet I-cord works up quickly and can be used to create a variety of trims. Long lengths can be twisted or swirled into any kind of shape and simply sewn to a crochet project for a designer look. Try repetitions of loops, circles, or sew a cord to your crochet project just inside an edging to add another level to your finish work.

Crochet I-cord can be made in two ways.

BASIC CROCHET I-CORD

Chain desired length. Slip stitch in second chain from hook and in each remaining chain across (*see cord on left, Photo F*). Fasten off.

Corded closures: (top to bottom) figure eight, long double loop, spiral frog, and clover frog.

DOUBLE-EDGED CROCHET I-CORD

Chain desired length. Slip stitch in second chain from hook and in each remaining chain across. Turn and slip stitch in the remaining loop of each chain across (*see cord on right, Photo F*). Fasten off.

Depending upon the look you are seeking, the basic crochet I-cord tends to work best with heavier weight or textured yarns. For lighter weight yarns, double-edged crochet I-cord may best suit your needs.

CORDED CLOSURES

Corded crochet closures aren't just for garments—they can also be used in a variety of ways for decoration. Add one of the following shapes to the ends of a table runner along with tassels or add to the front of a purse or the flap of a pillow. These shapes make great embellishments for the brim of a hat, the front of a shawl, pockets, collars and hemlines. Run a series of the shapes from wrist to shoulder on a sleeve. Not just for adults, corded closures make terrific additions to items for babies and children too!

FIGURE EIGHT

(*Our example features double-edged crochet I-cord—see Photo G*)

Shape double-edged crochet I-cord into a figure eight and then sew ends tog. Wrap yarn around center several times and secure. Sew one loop and one button to right side. Sew one button to left side, leaving second loop free.

LONG DOUBLE LOOP

(*Our example features double-edged crochet I-cord—see Photo G*)

Shape double-edged crochet I-cord into a long loop and sew the ends tog. Wrap yarn around ends four to five times to form loops. Sew one loop and one button to right side. Sew one button to left side, leaving second loop free.

SPIRAL FROG

*(Our example features basic crochet I-cord—
see Photo G)*

Fold I-cord in half. Form each end into spiral.
Tie second length of cord into a knot for the
button and form remaining end into spirals
as with first half.

CLOVER FROG

*(Our example features basic crochet I-cord—
see Photo G)*

Fold I-cord in half with end of cord in center,
forming four equal loops. Tie another length
of I-cord in single knot for button and form
three equal loops.

POPCORN FLOWER

This pretty popcorn flower *(see Photo H)* adds
delightful dimension to a sweater that's
worked in basic stitches such as double
crochet, giving a "wow" look to an otherwise
plain design. Matching or contrasting
buttons *(these may either be purchased shank
buttons or round crocheted buttons)* sewn
to the sweater fasten through the center
openings of the flowers.

The flower pattern is worked as follows:

SPECIAL STITCH

Popcorn (pc): 5 dc in indicated st, drop lp
from hook, insert hook in top of first dc of
5-dc group, pull dropped loop through.

Rnd 1: With yarn of choice and appropriate
size hook, ch 5, sl st in first ch to form ring,
ch 1, 12 sc in ring, join with sl st in beg sc.
(12 sc)

Rnd 2: Ch 9, sl st in same st, *pc *(see Special
Stitch)* in next st**, (sl st, ch 9, sl st) in next st,
rep from * around, ending last rep at **, sl st
in same st as beg sl st. Fasten off.

Sew flowers to front sweater edge opposite
buttons.

CABLED BANDS

Whether you use cabled crochet bands to
edge Aran crochet work, or add it as a single
stand-out element to a garment with a plain
stitch *(see Photo I)*, these bands are sure to
add an elegant touch to any crochet project.

LEFT-SIDE BUTTON BAND

This option requires 8 stitches.

Rows 1 & 2: Work hdc or desired st or st pattern across, turn.

RIGHT-SIDE ROW

Note: Ch-2 will count as first hdc throughout rem pattern.

Row 3: Ch 2 *(see Note)*, work in established st or st pattern across to last 8 sts, **fpdc** *(see Stitch Guide)* around next st 2 rows below, hdc in each of next 5 sts on working row, fpdc around next st 2 rows below, hdc in last st, turn.

Row 4: Ch 2, hdc in each st across, turn.

Row 5: Ch 2, hdc in each st across to st above next fpdc, fpdc around next fpdc, hdc in each of next 5 sts, fpdc around next fpdc, hdc in last st, turn.

Row 6: Ch 2, hdc in each st across, turn.

Next rows: [Rep rows 5 and 6 alternately] until piece reaches desired length.

RIGHT-SIDE BUTTONHOLE BAND

This option requires 8 stitches.

Rows 1 & 2: Work hdc or desired st or st pattern across, turn.

RIGHT-SIDE ROW

Note: Ch-2 will count as first hdc throughout rem pattern.

Row 3: Ch 2 *(see Note)*, **fpdc** *(see Stitch Guide)* around next st 2 rows below, hdc in next st on working row, sk next 2 sts, fpdc around next st 2 rows below, fpdc around st 1 row below each sk st, hdc in next st on working row, fpdc around next st 2 rows below, work in established st or st pattern across, turn.

Row 4: Ch 2, hdc in each st across, turn.

Row 5: Ch 2, fpdc around next fpdc, hdc in next st on working row, fpdc around each of next 3 fpdc, hdc in next st on working row, fpdc around next fpdc, work in established st or pattern across, turn.

Row 6: Ch 2, hdc in each st across, turn.

Row 7: Ch 2, fpdc around next fpdc, sk next 2 fpdc, fpdc around next fpdc, fpdc around each fpdc just sk, hdc in next st on working row, fpdc in next st, work in established st or pattern across, turn.

Row 8: Ch 2, hdc in each st across, turn.

Row 9: Ch 2, fpdc around next fpdc, hdc in next st on working row, fpdc around next fpdc, ch 1 *(buttonhole)*, sk next fpdc, fpdc around next fpdc, hdc in next st on working row, fpdc around next fpdc, work in established st or pattern across, turn.

Row 10: Ch 2, hdc in each st and sp across, turn.

Next rows: [Rep rows 3–10 consecutively] until piece reaches desired length.

Sew buttons to button band opposite buttonholes.

No matter which style you choose, crochet closures are guaranteed to give you that feeling of comfort and satisfying sense of finality in your crocheted garments. ■

Pocket Panache

POCKET TYPES

Pockets can be a useful addition to any sweater. Not only are they practical, but they can also add a bit of detail to an otherwise plain sweater. The most common pocket types are patch, horizontal slit or vertical slit.

Patch pockets (*see Photo A*) are simple square or rectangular pieces which are stitched first, and then sewn onto the sweater fabric. While the patch pocket may be the easiest to execute, you must use extreme care when sewing the pocket onto the fabric. The seam should be nearly invisible, and the pocket must be placed exactly on the grain of the fabric.

Horizontal-slit or vertical-slit pockets, also known as horizontal-inset (*see Photo B*) or vertical-inset (*see Photo C*) pockets, have a single or double lining which is crocheted first, and then incorporated into the body of the sweater as it is worked. The double lining is generally used for finer-gauge fabrics and does not require that the inside of the pocket be sewn onto the sweater. The single lining is better suited for heavier yarns and must be sewn onto the wrong side of the sweater fabric. A pocket-opening border is usually added after the sweater is complete. This type of pocket has the advantage of being mostly hidden—the only part of the pocket that shows is the border. The crocheter who is uncomfortable with finishing work on the "public" side may be more satisfied with an inset pocket.

PATCH POCKET

1. Crochet a piece of fabric to desired size and shape. Use a simple square or rectangle, and experiment with unusual shapes or motifs, or try a 3-D piece.

2. Pin pocket onto right side of sweater. Take care to pin it straight both horizontally and vertically.

3. Working on right side, invisibly stitch pocket onto sweater. For a decorative look, try a whipstitch or a blanket stitch using a contrasting color.

PHOTO B

HORIZONTAL-INSET POCKET

1. Stitch the pocket lining. The lining may be worked in either the pattern stitch used in the sweater or in single crochet. The pocket lining should be unobtrusive yet functional, so stay away from any pattern stitch that will add excess weight or texture, or any that is too "holey" to be practical.

2. Stitch the sweater to desired length. The pocket should be positioned so that it is comfortable for the wearer's hand. Placement of special or decorative pockets, such as a watch pocket, may be somewhat different.

3. Referring to the sweater directions, work in pattern the required number of stitches to the pocket opening. Sometimes pockets are placed in the center of the piece, sometimes to one side. The instructions will state how many stitches to work.

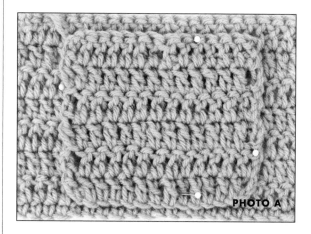

PHOTO A

4. Holding the pocket piece behind your work-in-progress, work stitches in pattern across the top of the pocket piece rather than into the main fabric. The number of stitches you work across the pocket and the number of stitches you skip on the main-fabric will probably be the same as the number you used in your pocket lining.

5. Continue working into remaining main-fabric stitches to end of row, keeping in established pattern. At this point, you have joined the pocket lining to the sweater fabric. There is a hole in the main fabric and the lining is loose against the back of the fabric.

6. Continue stitching sweater as directed. Fasten off.

7. When sweater is complete, work desired border (if any) along the top front pocket edge.

8. Sew side and bottom edges of pocket lining to back of fabric. If necessary, sew side edges of border to right side of fabric.

VERTICAL-INSET POCKET

POCKET OPENING

PHOTO C

1. Stitch the sweater to desired length between bottom of sweater and bottom of pocket, ending with a wrong-side row.

2. Referring to the sweater directions, work in pattern across the required number of stitches to make the pocket opening, leaving remaining stitches unworked. Vertical pockets are placed so that they lie toward the center of the garment. The sweater instructions will state how many stitches to work.

3. Turn work and continue in pattern on the stitches just worked until sweater reaches the desired height of the pocket opening, ending with a wrong-side row. Drop loop from hook. Do not fasten off. Place pin in stitch as holder.

4. With a new strand of yarn, chain the number required to match width and stitch pattern of pocket front, turn and work first row of the stitch pattern. Turn and place marker. You will end by working a right-side row. The stitch pattern used for the pocket lining should have the same row gauge as the main fabric.

5. With same yarn, working in stitch pattern, work in pocket lining stitches and in unworked stitches from sweater body, turn.

6. Work in stitch pattern across sweater body and pocket lining, turn. Continue working as stated until sweater body and pocket lining match height of pocket front, ending with a wrong-side row. Fasten off.

7. Put dropped loop back on hook. Leaving pocket lining stitches unworked, work in stitch pattern across pocket front stitches and across stitches on sweater body.

8. Continue working sweater as directed.

9. When sweater is complete, work desired border, if any, along the front pocket edge.

10. Sew side, top and bottom edges of pocket lining to back of fabric. If necessary, sew top and border edges of border to right side of fabric. ■

Fringe, Tassels & Edgings

Elegant fringe, luxurious tassels and decorative edgings are simple touches that can go a long way in enhancing the completed look of a crocheted project, especially items such as afghans, pillows, rugs, jackets, accessories and numerous other designs. Use these enhancements to add distinctive style to your projects, whether making them for yourself or to give as gifts.

SINGLE-KNOT FRINGE

Basic, single-knot fringe (see Photo A) is perhaps the most widely used type of fringe on crochet projects. It is easily created by cutting a specified number of strands of yarn the desired or specified length, folding them in half and securing them to the edge of the project, as shown in Figs. 1–4. When the single-knot fringe has been applied to the entire desired area, trim the ends even.

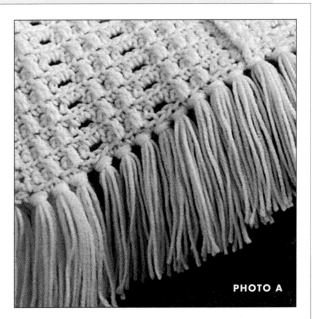

PHOTO A

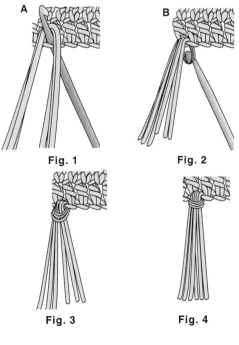

Fig. 1

Fig. 2

Fig. 3

Fig. 4

Single-Knot Fringe

Fringe adds an especially beautiful element to afghans. However, when deciding to fringe an afghan, it's helpful to consider whether the afghan will need to be laundered frequently or not. Over time, fringe often does not hold up well through extensive laundering.

DOUBLE-KNOT & TRIPLE-KNOT FRINGE

For a lacy, honeycomb-type edging that's very easy to make, try double-knot (see Photo B) or triple-knot fringe (see Photo C), which is sometimes referred to as macramé fringe. To make double-knot fringe, first work single-knot fringe completely across the indicated side. Keep in mind that since you will be adding more knots to make double-knot fringe, you'll want to cut the strands about twice as long as you want the finished fringe.

Then, with right side facing you and working from left to right, take half the strands from one single-knot fringe and half the strands from the next single-knot fringe and knot them together approximately 1½ inches lower than the single-knot fringe, as shown in Fig. 5. Continue across the edge, dividing each fringe and knotting it with the next.

Fig. 5
Double-Knot Fringe

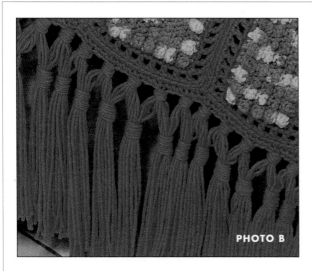

PHOTO B

CHAIN-LOOP FRINGE

Chain-loop fringe *(see Photo D)* is quite easy to work and creates an interesting, ruffled appearance. It is also a good choice for an afghan that will need to be cleaned regularly, as it will not fray or ravel when washed.

To make chain-loop fringe, as shown in the photo, join the desired color of yarn with a slip stitch at one corner of the afghan, *chain 30, slip stitch in next stitch on afghan, repeat from * across. Do this on both ends of the afghan, or all the way around. However, if you want to work chain loops across the ends of your rows, it's best to work a row of single crochet stitches first.

To make triple-knot fringe, first work single and double-knot fringe. Then, again working on right side from left to right, tie a third row of knots as shown in Fig. 6.

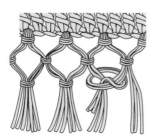

Fig. 6
Triple-Knot Fringe

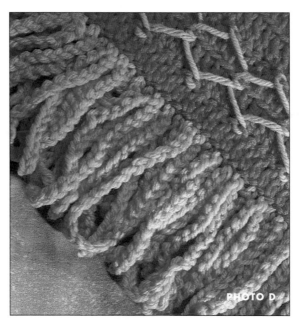

PHOTO D

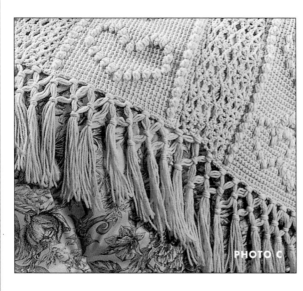

PHOTO C

TASSELS

Fringe is to an afghan what icing is to a cake, but tassels (see Photo E) lend a classic touch that adds richness to even a plain afghan. Practice making a few tassels to determine the best size for your project.

To create a basic tassel, cut a square of cardboard about two inches larger than your desired tassel length. Starting at one side, wrap the yarn around the cardboard at least five or six times. Take care not to pull the yarn tight or the strands will be too short when cut. After wrapping, tie a separate strand of yarn tightly around the loops at one edge of the cardboard and then cut the loops at the opposite edge. Now tie a second strand tightly around the loops about 1 inch from the first strand to form the "knot." Trim the ends even. Use the ends of the first strand to tie the tassel to your afghan.

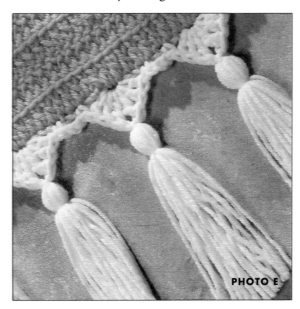

PHOTO E

THREE-TO-ONE RUFFLE

For real feminine appeal, add a lavish three-to-one ruffle (see Photo F). To add a ruffle like the one shown, work three double crochet stitches in each stitch across the afghan edge. Then, work two more rows, putting only one stitch in each stitch. Use treble crochet stitches if you want a wider ruffle.

PHOTO F

CROCHETED EDGINGS

Edgings and borders are an important part of many crocheted projects. They may be the main decorative element or just a finishing touch. They may conquer problems of curling or uneven edges. They may be worked directly onto the fabric or stitched separately and then sewn onto the fabric.

If working an edging directly onto a crocheted piece, always work the first row of an edging with the right side facing. To ensure a smooth, even edge, it's important to pick up stitches evenly when working the first, or "base," row of the edging.

Using a tape measure or ruler and your choice of stitch markers or pins, divide the side to be edged into evenly spaced intervals. Work the same number of stitches within each section, or if necessary, work one additional stitch

Lacy Fans

Violets

into every other section or two to maintain an even edge.

The number of stitches in each interval will depend on the gauge of the border stitches. A little experimentation will tell you how many stitches need to be worked to enable the edge to lie flat. If you start with too few stitches, the edge will be shortened. Too many stitches in the border will cause the edge to expand, creating a ruffled effect.

If you are working an edging in a contrasting color and are unhappy with the way the first row looks worked on the "unfinished" edges on your project, try working the base row of the edging in the same color as the project and then change to the contrasting color for the remaining rows.

Try experimenting with some of your favorite edging patterns to see what beautiful and unique looks you can create in your crochet projects. In the meantime, here are a few creative ideas to get you started.

LACY FANS
MULTIPLE OF 8 + 2.

Row 1 (RS): Ch 18, sc in **back bar** (see illustration) in 2nd ch from hook and in back bar of each rem ch across, turn.

Back Bar of Chain

Row 2: Ch 1, sc in first st, [ch 3, sk next 3 sts, sc in next st] across, turn.

Row 3: Ch 1, sc in first st, [ch 1, sk next ch sp, (dc, ch 1) 5 times in next st, sk next ch sp, sc in next st] across, turn.

Row 4: Ch 1, sc in first st, ch 3, sk next ch-1 sp, sc in next ch-1 sp, *[ch 3, sc in next ch-1 sp] 3 times**, ch 2, sk next 2 ch-1 sps, sc in next ch-1 sp, rep from * across, ending last rep at **, ch 3, sk next ch-1 sp, sc in last st. Fasten off.

VIOLETS
BACKGROUND
MULTIPLE NEEDED FOR 2 INCHES.

Row 1 (RS): With first color, ch 9, sc in **back bar** (see illustration above) of 2nd ch from hook, and in back bar of each ch across, turn.

Row 2: Ch 1, sc in each st across, turn.

Rows 3–5: Rep row 2. At end of last row, fasten off.

Double Cables

VIOLET
MAKE 1 FOR EVERY 2 INCHES ON BACKGROUND.
Ch 4, sl st in first ch to form ring, sl st in ring, [ch 3, dc in ring, ch 2, sl st in ring] 5 times. Fasten off.

With matching color, sew Violets to Background.

With yellow, embroider **French knot** (*see illustration*) in center of each Violet.

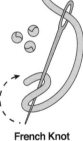

French Knot

DOUBLE CABLES

PATTERN NOTES
Leave stitches behind post stitches unworked.

Post stitches are worked around **post** (*see Stitch Guide*) of stitch 2 rows below throughout.

SPECIAL STITCH
Front post triple treble crochet (fptrtr): Yo 4 times, insert hook from front to back to front around indicated st, yo, draw lp through, (yo, draw through 2 lps on hook) 5 times.

BACKGROUND
MULTIPLE OF 6 + 2.
Row 1 (RS): Ch 14, sc in **back bar** (*see illustration on page 165*) of 2nd ch from hook and in back bar of each rem ch across, turn.

Row 2: Ch 1, sc in each st across, turn.

Row 3: Ch 1, sc in first st, *fptr (*see Stitch Guide*) around post of each of next 2 sts **2 rows below** (*see Pattern Notes*)**, sc in next st on working row, rep from * across, ending last rep at **, sc in last st on working row, turn.

Row 4: Rep row 2.

Row 5: Ch 1, sc in first st, *sk next 3 sts 2 rows below, **fptrtr** (*see Special Stitch*) around each of next 2 sts 2 rows below, sc in next st on working row, working in front of fptrtr just made, fptrtr around post of each of 2 sts just sk**, sc in next st on working row, rep from * across, ending last rep at **, sc in last st on working row, turn.

Next rows: [Rep rows 2–5 consecutively] until piece reaches desired length. At end of last row, fasten off.

Popped Popcorn

Picot Points

POPPED POPCORN

PATTERN NOTES
Leave stitches behind post stitches unworked.

Post stitches are worked around vertical **post** (*see Stitch Guide*) of indicated stitches 2 rows below throughout.

SPECIAL STITCH
Popcorn (pc): (Yo, insert hook in indicated st, yo, draw lp through, yo, draw through 2 lps on hook) 3 times, yo, pull through all lps on hook.

BACKGROUND
Row 1: Ch 14, sc in **back bar** (*see illustration on page 165*) of 2nd ch from hook and in back bar of each rem ch across, turn.

Row 2: Ch 1, sc in each of first 5 sts, **pc** (*see Special Stitch*) in next st, sc in each of next 5 sts, ch 1, sk next st, sc in last st, turn.

Row 3: Ch 1, sc in first st, sc in next ch-1 sp, sc in each of next 8 sts, **fptr** (*see Stitch Guide*) around post of each of next 2 sts **2 rows below** (*see Pattern Notes*), sc in last st, turn.

Row 4: Ch 1, sc in each of first 4 sts, ch 10, leaving rem sts unworked, turn.

Row 5: Sc in back bar of 2nd ch from hook and in back bar of each of next 8 chs, sc in next st, fptr around each of 2 sts, sc in last st, turn.

Next rows: [Rep rows 2–5 consecutively] until piece reaches desired length, ending last rep with row 3. Fasten off.

Push pc through each ch-1 sp on Background.

PICOT POINTS

BACKGROUND
MULTIPLE OF 2 + 3.
Row 1 (RS): Ch 5, sc in **back bar** (*see*

Knotted Loops

illustration on 165) of 2nd ch from hook, and in back bar of each ch across, turn.

Row 2: Ch 1, sc in each st across, turn.

Row 3: Ch 1, sc in first st, *ch 3, sl st in back bar of 3rd ch from hook**, sc in each of next 2 sts, rep from * across, ending last rep at **, sc in last st. Fasten off.

KNOTTED LOOPS

PATTERN NOTE
Using needle, thread 12 beads onto yarn for every multiple of 2 stitches on Background.

BACKGROUND
MULTIPLE OF 2 + 2.
Row 1: Ch 6, sc in **back bar** *(see illustration on page 165)* of 2nd ch from hook and in back bar of each rem ch across, turn.

Row 2: Ch 1, sc in first st, *pull 12 beads up to hook, leaving 2½-inch sp between 6th and 7th beads, hdc in next st, sc in next st, rep from * across. Fasten off.

KNOTS
With yarn in sp between 6th and 7th beads, tie knot at the bottom of each bead lp as shown in photo. ◾

chapter eleven
reinvent & recycle

If you're ready to throw away some of your damaged or worn-out clothing, or perhaps you'd simply like to change the look, you can easily reinvent and recycle these garments into chic new wardrobe pieces with a little creative crochet.

Makeover Magic

If you're tempted to throw out that snagged, stained or just plain tired piece of clothing, don't be so hasty! With a little bit of creative crochet added for pizzazz, you can give a fun, new look and longer life to your garments.

There are all sorts of reasons why crocheters need creative ideas to make over sweaters, jackets or other crochet wearables. Perhaps you've grown bored with a plain pullover, or a mustard blotch lingers after repeated efforts at stain removal, or worse yet, an ink mark now mars a fashion favorite. Who hasn't snagged a beloved sweater on an earring, ring or bracelet when dressing in a hurry. Life is full of unexpected spills that, at first, seemingly ruin a treasured garment. Before you toss it out, however, consider some ways to salvage your disaster and possibly create a new and better look than the original. Where there is a will, there usually is a way to use the art of crochet to make it work.

The goal when performing makeover magic is to create a finished look that is intentional rather than homemade, add-on or last-minute. Need ideas? Visit any website that sells designer clothing (Nordstrom, Neiman Marcus, Bloomingdale's, or Saks Fifth Avenue, etc.), and you'll find ideas galore lurking only a few clicks away. When leafing through your favorite magazines or catalogs, clip out ideas that appeal to you and save them in a file folder. A simple, yet appealing clipping I saved shows a simple shell worn by Jessica Simpson. Her white scoop-neck top features flutter sleeves of lacy crochet, which can be easily duplicated by folding two doilies in half (use one for each sleeve) and sewing one to each armhole in order to measure approximately one third of the distance between the shoulder and underarm seams. Make your own motif or use one you've saved from your grandma's collection.

Choose any weight and type of yarn that suits the garment in your closet that is begging for a makeover. A chenille or suede type of yarn can be used for a rustic, country look, while a yarn with metallic threads can turn a plain-Jane sweater into an evening delight. Check out your stash. Those tiny bits of leftover novelty-fur yarn or a variegated yarn might be just the ticket. Feel free to adapt a pattern stitch by working more or fewer rows or rounds. Add a picot edging for a girly look.

Experiment with different yarns and different hook sizes to get the look that is most complementary to your garment.

QUICK & EASY CROCHET I-CORD
The simplest and most adaptable solution is a basic crochet I-cord (see Photo A and instructions on page 157). The ways it can be used to hide flaws while adding design elements are limited only by your imagination.

It's so easy to make in any size thread or weight of yarn using any size of hook, that yards and yards can be made quickly.

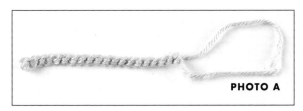

PHOTO A

CROCHET I-CORD
Make a chain (ch) to desired length. Slip stitch (sl st) in 2nd chain from hook and in each chain across. Fasten off.

PHOTO B

LOOPED I-CORD
Form I-cord into a series of loops (see Photo B). Use around outer edges, sleeve edges, hems or as all-over patterns. To add more visual appeal, sew a bead, a tiny button or a sequin to the center of every or every other loop. Embroider French knots (see illustration on page 166) in loop centers using yarn of a different color.

PHOTO C

Crochet I-cord can be used to create names of people, places, sports teams, pets, monograms, designs, etc. Easily molded, a few twists and turns of I-cord can create a stylized Christmas tree, a crochet frog closure, a series of spirals, flowers, hearts and other shapes. Add crocheted flowers, bows or decorative pompoms to I-cord (see Photo C) for added pizzazz, or braid three different-color lengths of I-cord together to create striking edgings and shapes.

For ideas, turn to the crochet stitch dictionaries on your bookshelves or other patterns to make flowers, leaves or other shapes.

MOTIFS

Eye-catching crochet motifs and edgings can add delightful trim elements to any garment.

DOILY & LACY MOTIFS

As mentioned before, any lacy, round motif can be folded in half to create flutter sleeves. A single motif can also be sewn to the front of a pullover. For a completed look, add crochet edging to the neckline and bottom edge of the top. Sew a motif to

the center back of a jacket or cardigan to make a statement (see Photo D). Smaller motifs can be sewn around the bottom of any sweater. Add a few around the lower sleeves or scatter a few along a sleeve. Add tiny pearls or other beads for a dressy look.

PHOTO D

TRIANGLE, FLAT FLOWER, DOUBLE-PETAL FLOWER, LEAF & STAR MOTIFS

Motifs of any size or shape can be used in dozens of different ways to breathe new life into an old or damaged wearable. Here are a few ideas for starters.

Sew crochet flowers around the hemline and lower sleeves, or around the outer edge of a jacket, to turn an everyday garment into something spectacular. Sew crochet leaves around the bottom of a garment to create an edgy, high-fashion look. Individual leaves in the same or varied sizes can cover up a multitude of sins or just add eye candy.

Use crochet I-cord to make the stem of a flower, add a crochet flower at the top, and a few crochet leaves and voilà!—a blah sweater or jacket is suddenly transformed into a work of art. Marching across the shoulder line of a striped garment, or down one side, crochet stars are sure to lift your spirits. Use a single star as a sleeve elbow patch for more impact and a cohesive look, or as a cute cover-up on a snagged pocket *(see Photo E)*.

PHOTO E

EDGINGS

Whether whimsical, delicate or bold, edgings sewn to a hemline or lower sleeve *(see Photo F)* are quick to crochet and sure to please. Seek out the edging you like best amongst your crochet books.

PHOTO F

Any of the ideas provided can be used as makeover magic for store-bought clothing made of woven fabric as well. Transform a pair of slacks into more fashionable capri pants by cutting off the worn and tattered hem. Turn up a ½-inch and use iron-on fusible webbing to hold it in place; then add trims or edgings for an entirely new look. Popular candidates for personalized fashion statements include jean jackets as they can be embellished any way you like. If you're unable to resist, feel free to transform hats, handbags and other items as well. I'm sure you'll find that makeover magic is fun, easy and empowering. Enjoy!

TRIM INSTRUCTIONS

PATTERN NOTES

Join rounds with a slip stitch unless otherwise stated.

Chain-3 at beginning of round counts as first double crochet unless otherwise stated.

SPECIAL STITCHES

Chain-3 picot (ch-3 picot): Ch 3, sl st in top of last st made.

Chain-5 picot (ch-5 picot): Ch 5, sl st in indicated place.

Cluster (cl): Keeping last lp of each st on hook, 3 dc in indicated place, yo, draw through all lps on hook.

Shell: 7 dc in indicated place.

MOTIFS
LITTLE FLOWER
USES 2 COLORS: A & B

Rnd 1: Using A, ch 2, 7 sc in 2nd ch from hook, **join** (see Pattern Notes) in first sc. Fasten off.

Rnd 2: Join B with sc in any sc, ch 1, sc in same sc as beg ch-1, *(sc, ch 1, sc) in next sc, rep from * around, join in first sc. Fasten off.

LACE MOTIF
(SEE PHOTO D ON PAGE 171)

Rnd 1: Ch 6, **join** (see Pattern Notes) in 6th ch from hook, ch 8, sl st in 5th ch from hook (counts as dc and 1 picot), *4 dc in ring, **ch-5 picot** (see Special Stitches), rep from * 7 times, 3 dc in ring, join in 3rd ch of beg ch-8.

Rnd 2: Sl st in next dc and in next picot, **ch 3** (see Pattern Notes), (dc, ch 2, 2 dc) in same picot, *ch 3, (2 dc, ch 2, 2 dc) in next picot, rep from * 7 times, ch 3, join in beg ch-3.

Rnd 3: Sl st in next dc and next ch sp, ch 3, (dc, ch 2, 2 dc) in same ch sp, *ch 6, (2 dc, ch 2, 2 dc) in next ch sp, rep from * 7 times, ch 6, join in beg ch-3.

Rnd 4: Sl st in next dc and next ch sp, ch 3, (dc, ch 2, 2 dc) in same ch sp as beg ch-3, *ch 8, sk next ch sp, (2 dc, ch 2, 2 dc) in next ch sp, rep from * 7 times, ch 8, sk last ch sp, join in beg ch-3.

Rnd 5: Ch 1, sc in first st, sc in next dc, *(2 dc, **ch-3 picot**—see Special Stitches, 2 dc) in next ch sp, sc in each of next 2 dc, 9 dc in ch-8 sp**, sc in each of next 2 dc, rep from * around, ending last rep at **, join in first sc. Fasten off.

TRIANGLE
USES 3 COLORS: A, B & C

Rnd 1: Using A, ch 4, **join** (see Pattern Notes) in 4th ch from hook to form ring, **ch 3** (see Pattern Notes), 11 dc in ring, join in top of beg ch-3.

Rnd 2: Ch 5, sk next 3 dc, sl st in next dc, [ch 5, sk next 3 dc, sl st in next dc] twice, join in 3rd ch of beg ch-5. Fasten off.

Rnd 3: Join B in any ch-5 sp, ch 3, 6 dc in same sp as beg ch-3, [ch 3, 7 dc in next ch-5 sp] twice, ch 3, join in 3rd ch of beg ch-5. Fasten off.

Rnd 4: Join C in any ch-3 sp, ch 3, 8 dc in same sp as beg ch-3, sc in each of next 7 sts, [ch 3, 9 dc in next ch-3 sp, sc in each of next 7 dc] twice, join in top of beg ch-3. Fasten off.

FLAT FLOWER

Ch 5, **join** (see Pattern Notes) in 5th ch from hook to form ring, *ch 10, sc in ring, rep from * 12 times, join in first sc. Fasten off. Sew bead to center of flower.

DOUBLE PETAL FLOWER
USES 2 COLORS: A & B (VARIEGATED)

Rnd 1: Using A, ch 2, 9 sc in 2nd ch from hook, **join** (see Pattern Notes) in first sc. Fasten off.

Rnd 2: Join B in **front lp** (see Stitch Guide) of any sc, ch 5, sl st in same lp, working in front lps only, (sl st, ch 5, sl st) in each st around. **Do not join.**

Rnd 3: Working in rem lps of rnd 1, sl st in first lp, ch 9, sl st in same lp as beg ch-9, (sl st, ch 9, sl st) in each lp around. Fasten off.

LEAF

Row 1: Ch 17, sc in 3rd ch from hook, sc in each ch across to last ch, 3 sc in last ch, working in opposite side of beg ch, sc in each ch to last 3 chs. Leaving rem chs unworked, turn.

Row 2: Ch 1, sk first sc, sc in each sc to center sc, 3 sc in center sc, sc in each sc across to last 3 sc, sk last 3 sc, turn.

Rows 3–5: Rep row 2.

Row 6: Ch 1, sk first sc, sc in each sc to center sc, sc in center sc, ch 9 for stem, sl st in 2nd ch from hook and each rem ch, continuing around Leaf, sc in each sc to with last 2 sts. Leaving rem sts unworked, fasten off.

STAR

Rnd 1: Ch 5, **join** (see Pattern Notes) in 5th ch from hook to form ring, ch 1, 15 sc in ring, join in first sc.

Rnd 2: *Ch 9, sc in 4th ch from hook, hdc in each of next 2 chs, dc in each of next 3 chs, sk next 2 sc**, sl st in next sc, rep from * around, ending last rep at **, join in joining st of rnd 1. Fasten off.

EDGINGS

CURLICUES & ROUNDS

Row 1: Ch 13 or a multiple of 6 + 7, sc in 2nd ch from hook and each rem ch across, turn.

Row 2: Ch 1, sc in each of first 3 sc, *ch 16, 3 sc in 2nd ch from hook and each rem ch across,

join (see Pattern Notes) in same sc as ch-16, sc in each of next 3 sc**, ch 3, 10 sc in 2nd ch from hook, join to first sc, sl st in same sc as ch-3 on row 1, sc in each of next 3 sc, rep from *, ending last rep at **. Fasten off.

CHAINLESS EDGING

Row 1: *Ch 5, sl st in 5th ch from hook, **picot** (see Special Stitches) twice in same ch as first sl st, ch 4, **cl** (see Special Stitches) in same ch as ch-4, rep from * to desired length. Fasten off.

OVERLAPPING SHELLS

Row 1: Ch a multiple of 8 + 12, sc in 5th ch from hook (beg 4 sk chs count as first sc and ch-3), *ch 3, sk next ch, sc in next sc, rep from * to last ch, ch 1, hdc in last ch, turn.

Row 2: Ch 1, sc in first ch sp, ch 3, sc in next ch-3 sp, *shell (see Special Stitches) in next ch-3 sp, sc in next ch-3 sp**, [ch 3, sc in next ch-3 sp] twice, rep from *, ending last rep at **, ch 3, sc in last ch sp, turn.

Row 3: Ch 4 (counts as dc and ch-1), sc in next ch-3 sp, *2 dc in each of next 7 dc, sc in next ch-3 sp**, ch 3, sc in next ch-3 sp, rep from *, ending last rep at **, ch 1, dc in last st, turn.

Row 4: Ch 1, sc in first ch-1 sp, *[2 dc in next dc of shell 2 rows below, dc in next dc] 3 times, 2 dc in each of next 3 dc, [dc in next dc, 2 dc in next dc] twice, dc in next dc**, sc in next ch-3 sp, rep from *, ending last rep at **, sc in last ch-1 sp. Fasten off. ■

Changing the Look

Have you ever wanted to modify the depth of a V-neck or the length of the sleeves on some of your favorite crochet sweater and top patterns, but didn't know how? It's easy once you understand the mathematical basics involved. You'll need just a few tools to work out your own modifications: pencil, eraser, graph or science paper, handheld calculator, knitting gauge measure and scratch paper.

The three-quarter-sleeve Ruffled V-Neck Pullover (shown on page 179) serves as the example for this article. It was purposely designed to be worked in plain half double crochet. After you understand the basic principles of adapting both necklines and sleeves, you can then try working a different sweater using your own design elements such as stripes, different stitch patterns, or working other types of edgings as desired. When shaping both V-necks and sleeves, you must create an angle whether working increases (for sleeves) or decreases (for V-neck).

HOW TO BEGIN V-NECK SHAPING

The starting point requires the following: gauge, total number of body stitches, number of stitches required for neck opening, length and the number of rows required from the armhole to the shoulder, along with the number of stitches needed for each shoulder.

Gauge is the single most important element that determines the final fit and measurements of any garment and **must** be accurate. While you need to make a sample swatch to determine gauge, you'll find that gauge is often given (as in our pullover) as follows:

GAUGE
Size H hook: 14 half double crochet (hdc) = 4 inches; 11 rows = 4 inches

GAUGE TIP
While the number of stitches per inch tends to remain constant as you crochet, the number of rows per inch tends to change so slightly, it is almost impossible to measure perfectly until you have crocheted at least 12 or more inches in length. You'll find it helps to always work both the front and back before penciling in numbers for sleeves. Using a tape measure, count the number of rows over at least 12 inches and make adjustments to your row gauge, if necessary.

To modify a V-neck or sleeves, you need precise information. To do that you need to break down the stitch and row counts to equal 1 inch. Using your calculator, divide 14 half double crochet by 4 inches and the result is 3½ half double crochet to equal 1 inch. To determine the number of rows per inch, divide 10 rows by 4 inches for a result of 2¾ rows per inch. These numbers are vital when it comes to adapting a pattern to fit your personal needs and measurements.

As a rule, the shaping for a V-neck starts on the same row as the armhole shaping. However, in the future, you might want to crochet a pullover with a deeper V-neck to be worn over a tank top, turtleneck or other top. Or you might want a higher neckline with only a 4-inch drop (the measurement from shoulder line to bottom of neckline). Once you understand the basics, you can modify the depth of the neckline to fit your wants and needs.

Note that the chart shows the left side of the garment as worn on the body. Therefore, the numbers shown represent only half of the upper body.

HOW TO READ THE CHART
Using the chart for size medium (see Fig. 1 on next page), the beginning row indicates how many stitches (five) are to be skipped for the armhole opening, and indicates that 28 half double crochet are required for the left front. You end with 17 half double crochet remaining for the shoulder, as noted. A total of 23 rows is required to achieve the desired armhole depth of 8½ inches. You need to decrease 11 stitches, or one-half of 22 (the total number of stitches required for the neck opening over 23 rows). As noted on the chart, the 11 stitches must be decreased as evenly as possible over 23 rows to achieve the straightest line or angle.

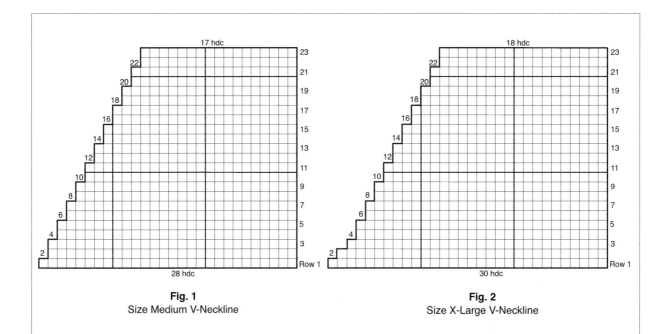

Fig. 1
Size Medium V-Neckline

Fig. 2
Size X-Large V-Neckline

This means you will decrease **one stitch** (by working two stitches together at the neckline edge only) every **two rows 11 times.** Deciding how and when to decrease is easy to calculate for this particular size. When you divide the total number of rows (23) by the number of stitches to be decreased (11), it's easy to see that two times 11 equals 22 rows, plus one extra row, but the decreases cannot always be worked out so simply.

Using size X-large as the next example (*see Fig. 2*), you'll see that you need to decrease 12 stitches over 23 rows for the neck opening, and that does not work out as easily or evenly as for size medium, although you might think so at first. Begin by drawing your own chart outline on graph paper, and then draw a line from the beginning of the neck opening to the shoulder. Then draw in your decreases, row by row as evenly as possible, following the line as closely as the stitches and rows allow.

RULES OF THUMB

When creating an angle, and the number of rows cannot be divided equally by the number of stitches to be decreased, it's best to work the first decreases closely (every row or every other row) for a few rows, and then decrease the number of rows in between

decreases evenly to create the straightest line, as shown in the chart for size X-large. Conversely, if you work all the decreases too quickly and then work many rows evenly, the neckline becomes distorted. The same rules apply for shaping sleeves; however, instead of decreasing, stitches must be increased.

While you may be perfectly satisfied with a neckline shape as in Fig. 3, remember it is not a true V-neck.

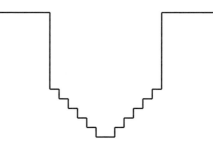

Fig. 3
Stitches decreased too quickly

HOW TO BEGIN SLEEVE SHAPING

When a sleeve is a set-in, like in our accompanying sweater, or a drop sleeve, the upper width of the sleeve must be the same as the measurement around the entire armhole opening, meaning both front and back body pieces, in order for the pieces to fit together.

The starting point for sleeve shaping requires the following: the gauge, the total number of stitches required for the upper sleeve, the number of stitches for the wrist, as well as the number of rows required from the wrist to the armhole. A drop sleeve ends when you reach the desired length to the underarm; however, a set-in sleeve continues evenly from that point until the length from the underarm to the top equals the number of stitches skipped for the armhole opening.

Our pattern gives you the instructions for making three sleeve lengths: short, three-quarter and full length, based on the Craft Yarn Council of America's sizing standards. To determine sleeve length and the subsequent number of rows to achieve the desired length, you must apply the gauge. For example, a full-length sleeve for size medium is 17½ inches in total length. You must know the total number of rows required to achieve the finished length if you are to know how many increases are required to gradually widen the sleeve as you work.

If you wish to have a 2-inch rib at the bottom of your sleeve, then those 2 inches must be deducted from the total number of rows worked for the body of the sleeve: 17½ inches less 2 inches = 15½ inches. Using the gauge of 2¾ rows per inch times 15½ inches, you would need 42 rows. However, be sure to double-check your gauge as you work because it can easily differ slightly as you work, as mentioned earlier.

In this case, if worked to 42 rows, instead of measuring 15½ inches, the length is actually 16 inches or ½ inch too long; therefore, the pattern has you working 40 rows for the true measurement.

Knowing the number of rows required for a full-length sleeve means you can easily calculate the number of rows needed for a three-quarter length sleeve. Simply multiply 40 rows by 75 percent (.75), and you'll see

30 rows are needed. Remember to then deduct the number of rows and/or the number of inches needed for the ribbing or other edging.

To determine the length of a standard short sleeve, simply multiply the number of rows required for a full-length sleeve (40 rows) by 25 percent. If your arms are longer or shorter, simply adjust the number of rows and inches to meet your needs.

Should you be interested in making other modifications to printed crochet patterns, and you have Internet access, the Craft Yarn Council of America has free downloadable Standards & Guidelines available at www.yarnstandards.com.

Developed by leading yarn companies, fiber producers, needle and hook manufacturers, and publishers, the Standards & Guidelines include measuring, fit and sizing information for babies, children, women and men, as well as other essential information about yarn categories, gauge ranges, yarn label information and more. Be sure to visit www.yarnstandards.com and download this valuable information.

RUFFLED V-NECK PULLOVER

SKILL LEVEL

◼◼◼▢
INTERMEDIATE

FINISHED SIZES
Instructions given fit size small; changes for medium, large, X-large, 2X-large, 3X-large, 4X-large and 5X-large are in [ ].

FINISHED GARMENT MEASUREMENT
Bust: 34 inches (*small*) [38 inches (*medium*), 42 inches (*large*), 46 inches (*X-large*), 50 inches (*2X-large*), 54 inches (*3X-large*), 58 inches (*4X-large*), 62 inches (*5X-large*)]

MATERIALS

- Red Heart Designer Sport acrylic light (light worsted) weight yarn (3 oz/279 yds/85g per ball): 6 [6, 7, 7, 8, 9, 10, 11] balls #3730 blush rose
- Sizes G/6/4mm and H/8/5mm crochet hooks or size needed to obtain gauge
- Tapestry needle

3 LIGHT

GAUGE

Size H hook: 14 hdc = 4 inches; 11 hdc rows = 4 inches

Take time to check gauge.

PATTERN NOTES

Chain-1 at beginning of row **does not count** as first half double crochet unless otherwise stated.

Join with slip stitch as indicated unless otherwise stated.

Chain-3 at beginning of row counts as first double crochet unless otherwise stated.

PULLOVER
BACK
RIBBING

Row 1 (RS): With size G hook, ch 9, sc in 2nd ch from hook and in each of last 7 chs, turn. *(8 sc)*

Rows 2–61 [2–67, 2–75, 2–81, 2–89, 2–95, 2–103, 2–109] (WS): Working in **back lps** *(see Stitch Guide)*, ch 1, sc in each st across, turn. At end of last row, **do not turn**.

BODY

Row 1 (RS): Working in ends of rows, with size H hook, **ch 1** *(see Pattern Notes)*, **hdc dec** *(see Stitch Guide)* in first 2 rows, hdc in end of each row across, turn. *(60 [66, 74, 80, 88, 94, 102, 108) hdc)*

Rows 2–32: Ch 1, hdc in each st across, turn. At end of last row, fasten off. Piece should measure 13½ inches from beg.

ARMHOLE SHAPING

Row 1: With RS facing, sk first 4 [5, 8, 10, 13, 16, 19, 22] sts, **join** *(see Pattern Notes)* in next st, ch 1, hdc in same st and in each st across leaving last 4 [5, 8, 10, 13, 16, 19, 22] sts unworked, turn. *(52 [56, 58, 60, 62, 62, 64, 64] hdc)*

Rows 2–21 [2–23, 2–23, 2–23, 2–24, 2–25, 2–26, 2–28]: Ch 1, hdc in first st and in each st across, turn. At end of last row, fasten off.

FRONT

Work same as Back to Armhole Shaping.

LEFT ARMHOLE & NECK SHAPING

Row 1: With RS facing, sk first 4 [5, 8, 10, 13, 16, 19, 22] sts, join in next st, ch 1, hdc in same st and in each of next 25 [27, 28, 29, 30, 30, 31, 31] sts, leaving rem sts unworked, turn. *(26 [28, 29, 30, 31, 31, 32, 32] hdc)*

Row 2: Ch 1, hdc dec in first 2 sts, hdc in each st across, turn. *(25 [27, 28, 29, 30, 30, 31, 31] hdc)*

SMALL SIZE ONLY

Row 3: Ch 1, hdc in first st and in each st across with hdc dec in last 2 sts, turn. *(24 hdc)*

Row 4: Ch 1, hdc dec in first 2 sts, hdc in each st across, turn. *(23 hdc)*

Row 5: Ch 1, hdc in first st and in each st across, turn.

Rows 6–21: [Rep rows 4 and 5 alternately] 8 times. At end of last row, fasten off. *(15 hdc at end of last row)*

MEDIUM SIZE ONLY

Row [3]: Ch 1, hdc in first st and in each st across, turn.

Rows [4–23]: [Rep rows 2 and 3 alternately] [10] times. At end of last row, fasten off. *([17] hdc at end of last row)*

LARGE SIZE ONLY

Row [3]: Ch 1, hdc in first st and in each st across, turn.

Rows [4–23]: [Rep rows 2 and 3 alternately] [10] times. At end of last row, fasten off. (*[18] hdc at end of last row*)

X-LARGE SIZE ONLY
Row [3]: Ch 1, hdc in first st and in each st across with hdc dec in last 2 sts, turn. (*[28] hdc*)

Row [4]: Ch 1, hdc dec in first 2 sts, hdc in each st across, turn. (*[27] hdc*)

Row [5]: Ch 1, hdc in first st and in each st across, turn.

Rows [6–23]: [Rep rows 4 and 5 alternately] [9] times. At end of last row, fasten off. (*[18] hdc at end of last row*)

2X-LARGE SIZE ONLY
Row [3]: Ch 1, hdc in first st and in each st across with hdc dec in last 2 sts, turn. (*[29] hdc*)

Row [4]: Ch 1, hdc dec in first 2 sts, hdc in each st across, turn. (*[28] hdc*)

Rows [5 & 6]: Rep rows [3 and 4]. (*[26] hdc at end of last row*)

Row [7]: Ch 1, hdc in first st and in each st across, turn.

Rows [8–24]: [Rep rows 4 and 7 alternately] [8] times, ending last rep at row [4]. At end of last row, fasten off. (*[18]hdc at end of last row*)

3X-LARGE SIZE ONLY
Row [3]: Ch 1, hdc in first st and in each st across with hdc dec in last 2 sts, turn. (*[29] hdc*)

Row [4]: Ch 1, hdc dec in first 2 sts, hdc in each st across, turn. (*[28] hdc*)

Row [5]: Ch 1, hdc in first st and in each st across, turn.

Rows [6–25]: [Rep rows 4 and 5 alternately] [10] times. At end of last row, fasten off. (*[18] hdc at end of last row*)

4X-LARGE SIZE ONLY
Row [3]: Ch 1, hdc in first st and in each st across with hdc dec in last 2 sts, turn. (*[30] hdc*)

Row [4]: Ch 1, hdc dec in first 2 sts, hdc in each st across, turn. (*[29] hdc*)

Row [5]: Ch 1, hdc in first st and in each st across with hdc dec in last 2 sts, turn. (*[28] hdc*)

Row [6]: Ch 1, hdc in first st and in each st across, turn.

Rows [7–26]: [Rep rows 5 and 6 alternately] [10] times. At end of last row, fasten off. (*[18] hdc at end of last row*)

5X-LARGE SIZE ONLY
Row [3]: Ch 1, hdc in first st and in each st across with hdc dec in last 2 sts, turn. (*[30] hdc*)

Row [4]: Ch 1, hdc dec in first 2 sts, hdc in each st across, turn. (*[29] hdc*)

Row [5]: Ch 1, hdc in first st and in each st across with hdc dec in last 2 sts, turn. (*[28] hdc*)

Row [6]: Ch 1, hdc in first st and in each st across, turn.

Rows [7–26]: [Rep rows 5 and 6 alternately] [10] times. (*[18] hdc at end of last row*)

Rows [27 & 28]: Ch 1, hdc in first st and in each st across, turn. At end of last row, fasten off.

RIGHT ARMHOLE & NECK SHAPING SMALL SIZE ONLY
Row 1: With RS facing, join in next-to-last hdc of first row of Left Armhole and Neck Shaping, ch 1, hdc in same st and in each of next 25 sts, leaving rem sts unworked, turn. (*26 hdc*)

Row 2: Ch 1, hdc in first st and in each st across with hdc dec in last 2 sts, turn. (*25 hdc*)

Row 3: Ch 1, hdc dec in first 2 sts, hdc in each of last 23 sts, turn. *(24 hdc)*

Row 4: Ch 1, hdc in first st and in each st across with hdc dec in last 2 sts, turn. *(23 hdc)*

Row 5: Ch 1, hdc in first st and in each st across, turn.

Rows 6–21: [Rep rows 4 and 5 alternately] 8 times. At end of last row, fasten off. *(15 hdc at end of last row)*

MEDIUM SIZE ONLY
Row [1]: With RS facing, join in next-to-last hdc of first row of Left Armhole and Neck Shaping, ch 1, hdc in same st and in each of next [27] sts, leaving rem sts unworked, turn. *([28] hdc)*

Row [2]: Ch 1, hdc in first st and in each st across with hdc dec in last 2 sts, turn. *([27] hdc)*

Row [3]: Ch 1, hdc in first st and in each st across, turn.

Row [4]: Ch 1, hdc in first st and in each st across with hdc dec in last 2 sts, turn. *([26] hdc)*

Rows [5–23]: [Rep rows 3 and 4 alternately] [10] times, ending last rep with row [3]. At end of last row, fasten off. *([17] hdc at end of last row)*

LARGE SIZE ONLY
Row [1]: With RS facing, join in next-to-last hdc of first row of Left Armhole and Neck Shaping, ch 1, hdc in same st and in each of next [28] sts, leaving rem sts unworked, turn. *([29] hdc)*

Row [2]: Ch 1, hdc in each st across with hdc dec in last 2 sts, turn. *([28] hdc)*

Row [3]: Ch 1, hdc in first st and in each st across, turn.

Rows [4–23]: [Rep rows 2 and 3 alternately] [10] times. At end of last row, fasten off. *([18] hdc at end of last row)*

X-LARGE SIZE ONLY
Row [1]: With RS facing, join in next-to-last hdc of first row of Left Armhole and Neck Shaping, ch 1, hdc in same st and in each of next [29] sts, leaving rem sts unworked, turn. *([30] hdc)*

Row [2]: Ch 1, hdc in first st and in each st across with hdc dec in last 2 sts, turn. *([29] hdc)*

Row [3]: Ch 1, hdc dec in first 2 sts, hdc in each st across, turn. *([28] hdc)*

Row [4]: Ch 1, hdc in first st and in each st across with hdc dec in last 2 sts, turn. *([27] hdc)*

Row [5]: Ch 1, hdc in first st and in each st across, turn.

Rows [6–23]: [Rep rows 4 and 5 alternately] [9] times. At end of last row, fasten off. *([18] hdc at end of last row)*

2X-LARGE SIZE ONLY
Row [1]: With RS facing, join in next-to-last hdc of first row of Left Armhole and Neck Shaping, ch 1, hdc in same st and in each of next [30] sts, leaving rem sts unworked, turn. *([31] hdc)*

Row [2]: Ch 1, hdc in first st and in each st across with hdc dec in last 2 sts, turn. *([30] hdc)*

Row [3]: Ch 1, hdc dec in first 2 sts, hdc in each of st across, turn. *([29] hdc)*

Rows [4 & 5]: Rep rows [2 and 3]. *([27] hdc at end of last row)*

Row [6]: Rep row 2. *([26] hdc)*

Row [7]: Ch 1, hdc in first st and in each st across, turn.

Rows [8–24]: [Rep rows 3 and 7 alternately]

[8] times, ending last rep with row 3. At end of last row, fasten off. *([18] hdc at end of last row)*

3X-LARGE SIZE ONLY

Row [1]: With RS facing, join in last st of first row after Armhole and Neck Shaping, ch 1, hdc in same st and in each of next [30] sts, leaving rem sts unworked, turn. *([31] hdc)*

Row [2]: Ch 1, hdc in first st and in each st across with hdc dec in last 2 sts, turn. *([30] hdc)*

Row [3]: Ch 1, hdc dec in first 2 sts, hdc in each st across, turn. *([29] hdc)*

Row [4]: Ch 1, hdc in each st across with hdc dec in last 2 sts, turn. *([28] hdc)*

Row [5]: Ch 1, hdc in first st and in each st across, turn.

Rows [6–25]: [Rep rows 4 and 5 alternately] [10] times. At end of last row, fasten off. *([18] hdc at end of last row)*

4X-LARGE SIZE ONLY

Row [1]: With RS facing, join in last st of first row of Left Armhole and Neck Shaping, ch 1, hdc in same st and in each of next 31 sts, leaving rem sts unworked, turn. *([32] hdc)*

Row [2]: Ch 1, hdc in first st and in each st across with hdc dec in last 2 sts, turn. *([31] hdc)*

Row [3]: Ch 1, hdc dec in first 2 sts, hdc in each st across, turn. *([30] hdc)*

Row [4]: Ch 1, hdc in first st and in each st across with hdc dec in last 2 sts, turn. *([29] hdc)*

Row [5]: Ch 1, hdc dec in first 2 sts, hdc in each st across, turn. *([28] hdc)*

Row [6]: Ch 1, hdc in first st and in each st across, turn.

Rows [7–26]: [Rep rows 5 and 6 alternately] [10] times. At end of last row, fasten off. *([18] hdc at end of last row)*

5X-LARGE SIZE ONLY

Row [1]: With RS facing, join in next-to-last hdc of first row of Left Armhole and Neck Shaping, ch 1, hdc in same st and in each of next [31] sts, leaving rem sts unworked, turn. *([32] hdc)*

Row [2]: Ch 1, hdc in first st and in each st across with hdc dec in last 2 sts, turn. *([31] hdc)*

Row [3]: Ch 1, hdc dec in first 2 sts, hdc in each st across, turn. *([30] hdc)*

Row [4]: Ch 1, hdc in first st and in each st across with hdc dec in last 2 sts, turn. *([29] hdc)*

Row [5]: Ch 1, hdc dec in first 2 sts, hdc in each st across, turn. *([28] hdc)*

Row [6]: Ch 1, hdc in first st and in each st across, turn.

Rows [7–26]: [Rep rows 5 and 6 alternately] [10] times. At end of last row, fasten off. *([18] hdc at end of last row)*

THREE-QUARTER–LENGTH SLEEVE
MAKE 2.
RIBBING

Row 1 (RS): With size G hook, ch 9, sc in 2nd ch from hook and in each ch across, turn.

Row 2 (WS): Working in back lps, ch 1, sc in each st across, turn.

Rows 3–37 [3–41, 3–41, 3–41, 3–45, 3–45, 3–47, 3–47]: Rep row 2. At end of last row, do not turn.

BODY
SMALL, MEDIUM, LARGE & X-LARGE SIZES ONLY

Row 1: With size H hook, working in ends of rows, ch 1, 2 hdc in end of first row, hdc in each of last 36 [40, 40, 40] rows, turn. *(38 [42, 42, 42] hdc)*

Row 2: Ch 1, 2 hdc in first st, hdc in each st across with 2 hdc in last st, turn. *(40 [44, 44, 44] hdc)*

Rows 3 & 4: Ch 1, hdc in first st and in each st across, turn.

Rows 5–26: [Rep rows 2–4 consecutively] 8 times, ending last rep with row 2. (*56 [60, 60, 60] hdc at end of last row*)

Rows 27 & 28 [27–30, 27–32, 27–34]: Ch 1, hdc in each st across. At end of last row, fasten off.

2X-LARGE & 3X-LARGE SIZES ONLY

Row [1]: With size H hook, working in ends of rows, ch 1, 2 hdc in end of first row, hdc in each of last [44, 44] rows, turn. (*[46, 46] hdc*)

Rows [2 & 3]: Ch 1, hdc in first st and in each st across, turn.

Row [4]: Ch 1, 2 hdc in first st, hdc in each st across with 2 hdc in last st, turn. (*[48, 48] hdc*)

Rows [5–28]: [Rep rows 2–4 consecutively] 8 times. (*[64, 64] hdc at end of last row*)

Rows [29–38, 29–39]: Ch 1, hdc in each st across. At end of last row, fasten off.

4X-LARGE SIZE ONLY

Row [1]: With size H hook, working in ends of rows, ch 1, 2 hdc in end of first row, hdc in each of last [46] rows, turn. (*[48] hdc*)

Row [2]: Ch 1, hdc in first st and in each st across, turn.

Row [3]: Ch 1, 2 hdc in first st, hdc in each st across with 2 hdc in last st, turn. (*[50] hdc*)

Rows [4–11]: [Rep rows 2 and 3 alternately] [4] times. (*[58] hdc at end of last row*)

Rows [12 & 13]: Ch 1, 2 hdc in first st, hdc in each st across with 2 hdc in last st, turn. (*[62] hdc*)

Row [14]: Ch 1, hdc in first st and in each st across, turn.

Rows [15–20]: [Rep rows 12–14 consecutively] [twice]. (*[70] hdc at end of last row*)

Rows [21–39]: Ch 1, hdc in each st across. At end of last row, fasten off.

5X-LARGE SIZE ONLY

Row [1]: With size H hook, working in ends of rows, ch 1, 2 hdc in end of first row, hdc in each of last [46] rows, turn. (*[48] hdc*)

Row [2]: Ch 1, 2 hdc in first st, hdc in each st across with 2 hdc in last st, turn. (*[50] hdc*)

Row [3]: Ch 1, hdc in first st and in each st across, turn.

Row [4]: Ch 1, 2 hdc in first st, hdc in each st across with 2 hdc in last st, turn. (*[52] hdc*)

Rows [5–11]: [Rep rows 3 and 4 alternately] [4] times, ending last rep with row [3]. (*[58] hdc at end of last row*)

Rows [12 & 13]: Ch 1, hdc in first st and in each st across, turn.

Row [14]: Ch 1, 2 hdc in first st, hdc in each st across with 2 hdc in last st, turn. (*[60] hdc*)

Rows [15 & 16]: Ch 1, hdc in first st and in each st across, turn.

Rows [17–34]: [Rep rows 14–16 consecutively] [6] times. (*[74] hdc at end of last row*)

Rows [35–47]: Ch 1, hdc in each st across. At end of last row, fasten off.

SHORT SLEEVE
MAKE 2.
RIBBING

Row 1 (RS): With size G hook, ch 9, sc in 2nd ch from hook and in each ch across, turn.

Row 2 (WS): Working in back lps, ch 1, sc in each st across, turn.

Rows 3–52 [3–54, 3–54, 3–54, 3–58, 3–58, 3–64, 3–68]: Rep row 2. At end of last row, **do not turn.**

BODY
SMALL SIZE ONLY
Row 1 (RS): With size H hook, working in ends of rows, ch 1, hdc in end of each row across, turn. *(52 hdc)*

Row 2: Ch 1, hdc in first st and in each st across, turn.

Row 3: Ch 1, 2 hdc in first st, hdc in each st across with 2 hdc in last st, turn. *(54 hdc)*

Rows 4 & 5: Ch 1, hdc in each st across, turn.

Row 6: Rep row 3. *(56 hdc)*

Rows 7–9: Ch 1, hdc in first st and in each st across, turn. At end of last row, fasten off.

MEDIUM, LARGE, X-LARGE, 2X-LARGE & 3X-LARGE SIZES ONLY
Row [1] (RS): With size H hook, working in ends of rows, ch 1, hdc in end of each row across, turn. *([54, 54, 54, 58, 58] hdc)*

Row [2]: Ch 1, 2 hdc in first st, hdc in each st across with 2 hdc in last st, turn. *([56, 56, 56, 60, 60] hdc)*

Rows [3 & 4]: Ch 1, hdc in each st across, turn.

Row [5]: Rep row [2]. *([58, 58, 58, 62, 62] hdc)*

Rows [6 & 7]: Rep rows [3 and 4].

Row [8]: Rep row [2]. *([60, 60, 60, 64, 64] hdc)*

Rows [9–12, 9–14, 9–16, 9–17, 9–18]: Ch 1, hdc in each st across, turn. At end of last row, fasten off.

4X-LARGE SIZE ONLY
Row [1] (RS): With size H hook, working in ends of rows, ch 1, hdc in end of each row across, turn. *([64] hdc)*

Rows [2 & 3]: Ch 1, hdc in first st and in each st across, turn.

Row [4]: Ch 1, 2 hdc in first st, hdc in each st across with 2 hdc in last st, turn. *([66] hdc)*

Rows [5 & 6]: Rep rows [2 and 3].

Row [7]: Rep row [4]. *([68] hdc)*

Rows [8 & 9]: Rep rows [2 and 3].

Row [10]: Rep row [4]. *([70] hdc)*

Rows [11–23]: Ch 1, hdc in first st and in each st across, turn. At end of last row, fasten off.

5X-LARGE SIZE ONLY
Row [1] (RS): With size H hook, working in ends of rows, ch 1, hdc in end of each row across, turn. *([68] hdc)*

Rows [2 & 3]: Ch 1, hdc in first st and in each st across, turn.

Row [4]: Ch 1, 2 hdc in first st, hdc in each st across with 2 hdc in last st, turn. *([70] hdc)*

Rows [5–10]: [Rep rows 2–4 consecutively] [twice]. *([74] hdc)*

Rows [11–26]: Ch 1, hdc in first st and in each st across, turn. At end of last row, fasten off.

LONG SLEEVE
MAKE 2.
RIBBING
Row 1 (RS): With size G hook, ch 9, sc in 2nd ch from hook and in each ch across, turn.

Row 2 (WS): Working in back lps, ch 1, sc in each st across, turn.

Rows 3–28 [3–30, 3–30, 3–30, 3–30, 3–30, 3–32, 3–34]: Rep row 2. At end of last row, do not turn.

BODY
Row 1 (RS): With size H hook, working in ends of rows, ch 1, hdc in end of each row across, turn. *(28 [30, 30, 30, 30, 30, 32, 34] hdc)*

Row 2: Ch 1, hdc in first st and in each st across, turn.

Row 3: Ch 1, 2 hdc in first st, hdc in each st

across with 2 hdc in last st, turn. *(30 [32, 32, 32, 32, 32, 34, 36] hdc)*

Rows 4 & 5: Rep row 2.

Rows 6–43 [6–46, 6–46, 6–46, 6–52, 6–52, 6–58, 6–60]: [Rep rows 3–5 consecutively] 13 [14, 14, 14, 16, 16, 18, 19] times, ending last rep with row 4 [4, 4, 4, 4, 4, 3, 3]. At end of last row, fasten off. *(56 [60, 60, 60, 64, 64, 70, 74] hdc at end of last row)*

Last rows: [Rep row 2] 4 [5, 5, 6, 7, 8, 10, 14, 17] times. At end of last row, fasten off.

ASSEMBLY
Sew shoulder seams.

Fold 1 Sleeve in half lengthwise. Place fold at shoulder seam, sew in place.

Rep with rem Sleeve.

Sew side and Sleeve seams.

NECK EDGING

Rnd 1: With RS facing and size G hook, join with sc in first st of Back neck, sc in each of next 21 [21, 21, 23, 25, 25, 27, 27] sts, working in ends of rows, evenly sp 25 [27, 27, 27, 28, 28, 30, 31] sc to bottom of V, sc in sp between 2 center hdc at bottom of V, working in ends of rows, evenly sp 25 [27, 27, 27, 28, 28, 30, 31] sc across, join in beg sc. Fasten off.

Row 2: Now working in rows, with RS facing and size H hook, working in back lps, join with sc in first sc of lower right at V, sc in each st around, leaving center sc at lower left front unworked, turn.

Rows 3 & 4: Working in both lps, **ch 3** *(see Pattern Notes)*, [2 dc in next st, dc in next st] across, turn.

Row 4: Ch 6, sl st in 3rd ch from hook, [dc in next st, ch 3, sl st in top of last st] across to last st, dc in last st. Fasten off. ■

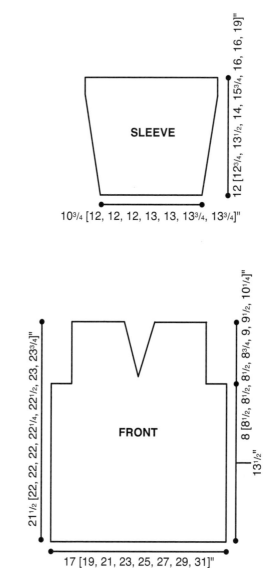

SLEEVE

12 [12¾, 13½, 14, 15¾, 16, 16, 19]"

10¾ [12, 12, 12, 13, 13, 13¾, 13¾]"

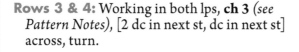

BACK

21½ [22, 22, 22, 22¼, 22½, 23, 23¾]"

8 [8½, 8½, 8½, 8¾, 9, 9½, 10¼]"

13½"

17 [19, 21, 23, 25, 27, 29, 31]"

FRONT

21½ [22, 22, 22, 22¼, 22½, 23, 23¾]"

8 [8½, 8½, 8½, 8¾, 9, 9½, 10¼]"

13½"

17 [19, 21, 23, 25, 27, 29, 31]"

Note: Measurements include Ribbing.

chapter twelve
not your ordinary crochet

Crochet is so much more than just making basic stitches. Creative techniques from felting, filet, Fair Isle and crocheting on fabric to mosaic patterns, beadwork, Swedish embroidery and cross-stitch on crochet, can take your projects from simple to spectacular.

Fabulous Felted Crochet

If you've never discovered the fun of felting your favorite crochet projects, these easy, step-by-step instructions will show you how. Included are instructions for two colorful, eye-catching purses to stitch and felt using either 100 percent wool or wool-blend yarn.

What is felting? Felting is a process by which wool fibers are tightened into a dense, strong material that is incredibly tough and long-wearing. Several ancient cultures used felted wool to make their shelters during their travels. Felting is also what happens when a favorite wool sweater gets turned into something resembling a pot holder. Unplanned and uncontrolled, felting is a bad thing. However, with planning, control and a great choice of colors, felting is a fabulous way to make useful, fun objects and terrific gifts.

The most important part of felting is the choice of yarn. Felting only works with animal hair fibers that have not been chemically treated to be washable. The best fiber is wool. A wool/mohair blend also works very well, with slightly different results.

Blends that contain acrylic or any other fibers generally will not work. Any yarn that says "superwash" on the label will never felt. Both Brown Sheep and Cascade produce excellent feltable yarns that come in a large assortment of colors.

Brown Sheep's Lamb's Pride yarns are an 85 percent wool/15 percent mohair blend. These yarns felt with a nice dense texture that tends to be thicker and fuzzier because of the mohair in the blend. Some of the heathered colors will be especially fuzzy and are a great choice for furry projects like slippers or stuffed toys.

Cascade's 220 Wool is 100 percent wool. It felts to a smoother surface that is great for things with a more tailored look, like nice square corners on a tote bag. 220 Wool also comes in heathers (220 Wool Heathers) and in a series of marled or two-color plied yarns (220 Wool Quatro) that give a tweedy look when felted.

The second most important part of making your felted project is the way you stitch it. Because crochet already tends to be dense in structure, it needs to be opened up more for proper felting.

If a medium (worsted) weight yarn, normally used with a size G or H hook, is felted, the resulting texture will bear a strong resemblance to plywood. If the same yarn is crocheted with a size J hook, it will look too loose and have gaps showing between the stitches before felting, but will felt to a closed up, dense fabric with a nice hand. Stitch choice also affects the result.

Single crochet will tend to be stiffer and double crochet might still have a few gaps. Half double crochet is the proverbial "just right" stitch for most projects, having a nice hand and flexibility, but no gaps.

In theory, almost any small-project pattern can be turned into a feltable pattern if the hook size is changed and a good felting yarn is used. If you choose to convert a pattern, plan to make a test piece before committing a lot of time and yarn as the other variables in the felting process can also affect results.

Once a piece is completed, it's time to go to the washer. Using a washing machine is the easiest way to felt unless the sample is very small. Placing the project into a zippered pillow cover prevents any fibers from getting into the washer and also protects things like purse straps from getting caught and stretched. Add a few towels for help in agitation and load balance. Use half the soap needed for a normal load. A gentle soap is best, but used in smaller quantities, regular laundry soap will also work. Set the load for the hottest water available for the wash cycle and a cold rinse. Turn it on and let it go.

One of the creative parts of felting is that the process can be stopped anytime. A lightly felted or "fulled" fabric with fully visible stitches is achieved after a short cycle in the wash. A fully felted fabric will have no visible stitches at all and can take as may as five washer cycles depending on the washer. Most projects are felted to someplace in the middle, as desired. Check the piece after the first load. Does it have a long way to go, or is it almost where it should be? If it has a long way to go, put it back in the washer and let it go though as many cycles as needed.

If it's nearly there, put it back in, but stay close and open the washer every few minutes to check the progress. With things like hats, try the damp piece on to see if it fits. If it's still too large, keep going, when it fits, stop.

When the required level of felting is reached, take the project out of the pillow cover and arrange it as needed to dry. Do NOT put it in the dryer, or that fabulous hat for your mother will fit her cat instead! Arrange the items on a dry towel, out of direct sunlight. If it's something flat like mittens, simply lay them out. For dimensional projects like hats, purses or tote bags, put something inside them that will help hold the desired shape—a bowl under a hat, a plastic-wrapped box of soda cans in a big tote, etc.—a couple of plastic grocery bags work especially well to shape slippers.

This next step is hard ... walk away from the project. Let it dry completely—without touching it. On a large project, this can take several days. In a desperate pinch for time, a hair dryer on a low heat setting can be used.

Gauge is normally important, and would normally be discussed much earlier in the project. In felting, gauge is not nearly as important because the piece is purposefully being crocheted in an open, loose manner and then is felted down to the desired size.

Gauge has very little effect on fit when a hat that looks like a huge ugly sack 36 inches around is made and then felted down to be an adorable, turned-brim, dressy, winter hat that fits a 22½-inch head.

A fun thing to try is to include a synthetic, non-felting yarn, such as a novelty or eyelash yarn as a carry along with the wool. When the wool felts, the synthetic yarn stands up or pops for a great trim. Try it for a furry edge on a hat, stripes on a purse or cuffs on mittens.

Felting can be used for any size project. In general, the larger the amount of yarn, the harder it is to control the process. For example, it is much more difficult to be sure of even results in a large project, like a coat, than it is to be sure of the results in smaller objects like purses, hats or slippers. A whole group of smaller pieces can be felted in one load as long as colors are separated into different pillow covers. It is very satisfying to see several purses or a whole row of pairs of slippers done at one time, lined up drying for family gifts. Have a great time playing with great yarns!

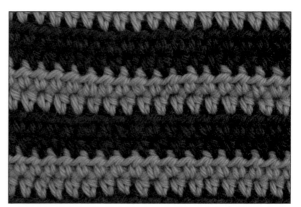

4. Unfelted "before" half double crochet swatch.

1. Diamonds swatch: Notice the puckering between the diamonds at the bottom; this sample did not have the thread carries snipped as called for in pattern.

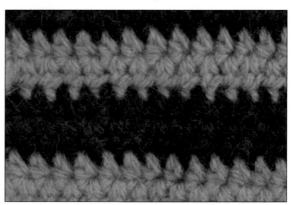

2. Unfelted "before" half double crochet swatch.

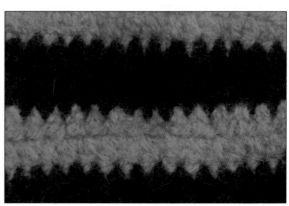

5. Lightly felted or "fulled": one wash cycle.

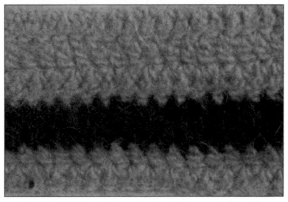

3. Plain, half double crochet rows: two wash cycles.

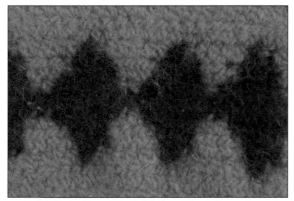

6. Plain, half double crochet rows: two wash cycles.

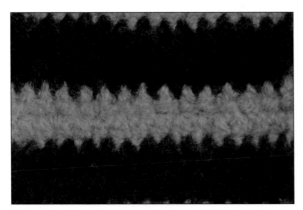

7. *Still further: three wash cycles, notice it's getting hard to count the stitches.*

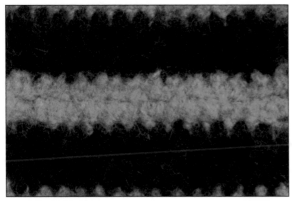

8. *Fully felted: four wash cycles, cannot count the green stitches accurately.*

DIAMOND BAG

SKILL LEVEL

INTERMEDIATE

FINISHED SIZE
Before felting: 12½ x 16 x 39 inches, including straps

After felting: 10½ x 12¾ x 26 inches, including straps

MATERIALS

- Brown Sheep Co. Lamb's Pride wool/mohair blend medium (worsted) weight yarn (3¾ oz/190 yds/106g per skein):
    1 skein each #M78 Aztec turquoise (*A*) and #M89 roasted coffee (*B*)
- Size J/10/6mm crochet hook
- Tapestry needle
- Stitch markers

GAUGE

Because this piece will be felted, gauge is not critical. There should be sp showing between sts when bag is held up to the light.

PATTERN NOTES

When **changing colors** (*see Stitch Guide*) always change in the last stitch made. Carry yarn loosely across back of work, a finger should easily fit in the carried loop.

The carried yarn will be trimmed later.

The Bag shown was washed through 2 normal-length, hot-water/cold-rinse washer loads for this degree of felting.

It is critical that after the first cycle, the thread carries on the inside of the diamond pattern are snipped in the center. These carries will felt faster than the rest of the Bag and will distort the pattern unless snipped. One washer cycle completes enough felting so that no stitches will come apart. After the Bag is dry, trim any remaining bits of the thread carries.

Join with slip stitch as indicated unless otherwise stated.

BAG

Rnd 1: With A, loosely ch 28, working in **back lps** (*see Stitch Guide*), hdc in 3rd ch from hook (*first 2 sk chs count as first hdc—place marker*), hdc in each rem ch across to last ch, 5 hdc in last ch (*place marker in first and 5th st*), working on opposite side and in rem lps of beg ch, hdc in each ch across with 4 hdc in last ch, (*place marker at beg of last 4 sts, you should have 5 hdc between first and last markers around end*), **join** (*see Pattern Notes*) in 2nd ch of beg ch-2. (*60 hdc*)

Rnd 2: Sl st in next st, ch 2, [hdc in each st across to first marker, 2 hdc in each of next 5 sts (*move markers on each rnd as you work*)] around, join in 2nd ch of beg ch-2. (*70 hdc*)

Rnd 3: Ch 2, hdc in each st across to first marker, [2 hdc in next st, hdc in next st] 5 times, hdc in each st across to marker, [2 hdc in next st, hdc in next st] 5 times, join in 2nd ch of beg ch-2. (*80 hdc*)

Rnd 4: Ch 2, *hdc in each st across to marker, [2 hdc in next st, hdc in each of next 2 sts] twice, 2 hdc in next st, hdc in next st, 2 hdc in next st, [hdc in each of next 2 sts, 2 hdc in next st] twice, rep from *, join in 2nd ch of beg ch-2. (*92 hdc*)

Rnd 5: Ch 2, *hdc in each st across to marker, 2 hdc in next st, [hdc in each of next 3 sts, 2 hdc in next st] 5 times, rep from *, join in 2nd ch of beg ch-2. Remove markers. (*104 hdc*)

Rnds 6–9: Ch 2, hdc in each st around, join in 2nd ch of beg ch-2.

Rnd 10: Ch 2, hdc in same st, hdc in each st around, join in 2nd ch of beg ch-2. (*105 hdc*)

Rnd 11: Ch 2, hdc in each of next 5 sts, **changing colors** (*see Pattern Notes*) to B in last st made, [hdc in next st, changing to A, hdc in each of next 6 sts, changing to B] around to last st, hdc in last st, changing to A, join in 2nd ch of beg ch-2.

Rnd 12: Ch 2, hdc in each of next 4 sts, changing to B, hdc in each of next 2 sts, changing to A, *hdc in each of next 5 sts, changing to B, hdc in each of next 2 sts, changing to A, rep from * around, join in 2nd ch of beg ch-2.

Rnd 13: Ch 2, hdc in each of next 3 sts, *changing to B, hdc in each of next 3 sts, changing to A**, hdc in each of next 4 sts, rep from * around, ending last rep at **, join in 2nd ch of beg ch-2.

Rnd 14: Ch 2, hdc in each of next 2 sts *changing to B, hdc in each of next 4 sts, changing to A**, hdc in each of next 3 sts, rep from * around, ending last rep at **, join in 2nd ch of beg ch-2.

Rnd 15: Ch 2, hdc in next st, *changing to B, hdc in each of 5 sts, changing to A**, hdc in each of next 2 sts, rep from * around, ending last rep at **, join in 2nd ch of beg ch-2.

Rnd 16: Ch 2, *changing to B, hdc in each of 6 sts** changing to A, hdc in next st, rep from * around, ending last rep at **, join in 2nd ch of beg ch-2.

Rnd 17: Ch 2, hdc in each st around, join with sl st in 2nd ch of beg ch-2.

Rnd 18: Ch 2, hdc in each of next 5 sts, *changing to A in last st made, hdc in next st, changing to B**, hdc in each of next 6 sts, rep from * around, ending last rep at **, join in 2nd ch of beg ch-2.

Rnd 19: Ch 2, hdc in each of next 4 sts, *changing to A, hdc in each of next 2 sts, changing to B**, hdc in each of next 5 sts, rep from * around, ending last rep at **, join in 2nd ch of beg ch-2.

Rnd 20: Ch 2, hdc in each of next 3 sts, *changing to A, hdc in each of next 3 sts, changing to B**, hdc in each of next 4 sts, rep from * around, ending last rep at **, join in 2nd ch of beg ch-2.

Rnd 21: Ch 2, hdc in each of next 2 sts, *changing to A, hdc in each of next 4 sts, changing to B**, hdc in each of next 3 sts, rep from * around, ending last rep at **, join in 2nd ch of beg ch-2.

Rnd 22: Ch 2, hdc in next st *changing to A, hdc in each of next 5 sts, changing to B**, hdc in each of next 2 sts, rep from * around, ending last rep at **, join in 2nd ch of beg ch-2.

Rnd 23: Ch 2, *changing to A, hdc in each of next 6 sts**, changing to B, hdc in next st, rep from * around, ending last rep at **, join in 2nd ch of beg ch-2. Fasten off B.

Rnds 24–28: Ch 2, hdc in each st around, join 2nd ch of beg ch-2. At end of last rnd, fasten off.

Rnd 29: Join B in first st, ch 2, hdc in each st around, join in 2nd ch of beg ch-2.

Rnds 30 & 31: Ch 2, hdc in each st around, join in 2nd ch of beg ch-2. At end of last rnd, fasten off.

Do not work in yarn ends, they can be clipped off after felting.

STRAP
MAKE 2.
Row 1: With B, loosely ch 110, hdc in 3rd ch from hook and in each rem ch across, turn.

Rows 2 & 3: Ch 2, hdc in each st across, turn. At end of last row, fasten off.

Sew long edges tog forming a tube.

Loosely sew the ends of Strap to desired position inside of Bag, keeping the Strap lined up the full width of the top strip. Loose stitching is needed because these sts will felt a little faster than the rest of the bag and could distort if they get too tight.

STRIPED BAG

SKILL LEVEL
◼◼◼▢
INTERMEDIATE

FINISHED SIZE
Before felting: 12½ x 16 inches

After felting: 9½ x 12 inches

MATERIALS

- Cascade 220 Wool medium (worsted) weight wool yarn (3½ oz/220 yds/100g per hank): 1 hank each #8555 black and #7814 chartreuse
- Size J/10/6mm crochet hook
- Tapestry needle
- Purse handles
- Stitch marker

GAUGE
Because this piece will be felted, gauge is not critical. There should be sp showing between sts when bag is held up to the light.

PATTERN NOTES

The Bag shown was washed through 4 normal-length, hot-water/cold-rinse washer loads for this degree of felting.

Join with slip stitch as indicated unless otherwise stated.

BAG

Rnd 1: With chartreuse, rep rnds 1–9 of Diamond Bag. Remove markers. *(104 hdc)*

Rnd 10: Ch 2, hdc in each st around, join in 2nd ch of beg ch-2. At end of last rnd, fasten off.

Rnd 11: Join black in first st, ch 2, hdc in each st around, join in 2nd ch of beg ch-2.

Rnd 12: Ch 2, hdc in each st around, join in 2nd ch of beg ch-2. Fasten off.

Rnd 13: Join chartreuse with sl st in first st, ch 2, hdc in each st around, join in 2nd ch of beg ch-2.

Rnd 14: Ch 2, hdc in each st around, join in 2nd ch of beg ch-2. Fasten off.

Rnds 15–32: [Rep rnds 11–14 consecutively] 5 times, ending last rep with rnd 12. At end of last rnd, fasten off.

Felt to desired degree. When drying, put several round cans, such as soup or vegetable cans, in bottom to help maintain flat bottom with rounded ends shape. This purse is more fully felted than the Diamonds Bag. After drying, clip any ends, add the handles.

Attach handles according to manufacturer's instructions. ▪

Fair Isle Crochet

The rugged Shetland Islands lie off the west coast of Scotland. The islands are known for their Shetland sheepdogs, which look like a very small collie, and their Shetland ponies, again a reduced version of a pony.

One of the most famous of the Shetlands is Fair Isle, which is the most remote, occupied island in Britain. Here the weather is harsh, and for hundreds of years the islanders have tended their sheep, spun and dyed their wool, and created a distinctive style of knitting garments that is known all over the world as Fair Isle.

From such a bleak environment it is surprising to see the bright and colorful garments with their typical rows of geometric designs. Although many colors are used in the knitwear, only two colors are used in any one row. The knitters alternate the colors, carrying the color not in use loosely across the wrong side, a technique called "stranding."

This stranding technique can also be used to create crocheted garments in the Fair Isle style, like the sweater design featured here. Be sure to carry the unused color loosely, so that the work will not draw in and pucker. If the stranding is too loose, it may catch and pull as the garment is worn.

FAIR ISLE SWEATER

SKILL LEVEL

EXPERIENCED

FINISHED SIZES

Instructions given fit 30–32-inch bust (small); changes for 34–36-inch (medium), 38–40-inch (large) and 42–44-inch (X-large) bust are in [ ].

FINISHED GARMENT MEASUREMENT

Bust: 38 inches (small) [42 inches (medium), 46½ inches (large), 49½ inches (X-large)]

Here is what the crocheted Fair Isle looks like on the front of the garment (see Photo A) and what the stranding looks like on the wrong side (see Photo B).

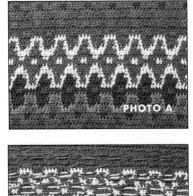

PHOTO A

PHOTO B

MATERIALS

- Lion Brand Wool-Ease medium (worsted) weight yarn (3 oz/197 yds/85g per ball):
    4 [4, 5, 6] balls #099 fisherman (A)
    2 [2, 3, 3] balls each #139 dark rose heather (B), #403 mushroom (C), #115 blue mist (D), #180 forest green heather (E) and #152 Oxford gray (F)
- Size E/4/3.5mm and F/5/3.75mm crochet hooks or size needed to obtain gauge
- Tapestry needle
- Blue sewing thread
- Sewing needle

GAUGE

Size F hook: 5 hdc = 1 inch; 7 hdc rows = 2 inches

PATTERN NOTES

Join with slip stitch as indicated unless otherwise stated.

Each square on chart equals 1 half double crochet stitch.

BODY
BACK

Notes: When working chart rows, work from outer edge to center, then reverse and work remainder of row from center to outer edge. Work between colored lines indicated for size.

Row 1: With F hook and F, ch 91 [101, 111, 119], sc in 2nd ch from hook and in each rem ch across, turn. *(90 [100, 110, 118] sc)*

Rows 2–24: Ch 2, hdc in each st across, **changing colors** *(see Stitch Guide)* according to chart, turn.

Rows 25–59 [25–61, 25–63, 25–63]: Ch 2, hdc in each st across, turn.

LEFT SHOULDER

Row 60 [62, 64, 64]: Ch 2, hdc in each of next 26 [29, 33, 36] sts leaving rem sts unworked, turn. *(27 [30, 34, 37] hdc)*

Row 61 [63, 65, 65]: Ch 2, hdc in each st across, **do not turn**. Fasten off.

RIGHT SHOULDER

Row 60 [62, 64, 64]: Sk next 36 [40, 42, 44] sts on row 59 [61, 63, 63] of Back, **join** *(see Pattern Notes)* A in next st, ch 2, hdc in each st across, turn. *(27 [30, 34, 37])*

Row 61 [63, 65, 65]: Ch 2, hdc in each st across. Fasten off.

FRONT

Notes: When working chart rows, work from outer edge to center, then reverse and work remainder of row from center to outer edge. Work between colored lines indicated for size.

Row 1: Rep row 1 of Back.

Rows 2–55 [2–57, 2–59, 2–59]: Ch 2, hdc in each st across, changing colors according to Front chart *(page 199)*, turn.

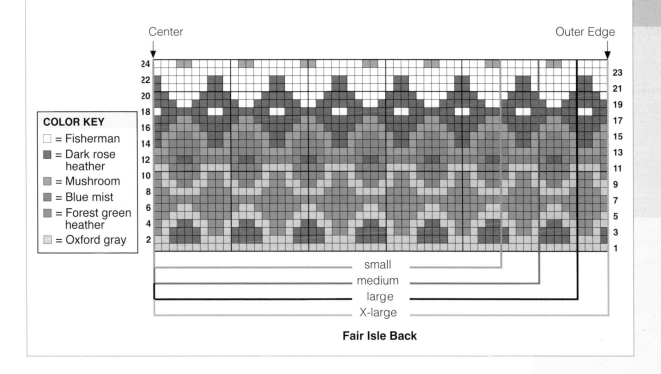

COLOR KEY
- ☐ = Fisherman
- ■ = Dark rose heather
- ■ = Mushroom
- ■ = Blue mist
- ■ = Forest green heather
- ☐ = Oxford gray

small
medium
large
X-large

Fair Isle Back

LEFT SHOULDER

Rows 56 [58, 60, 60]: Ch 2, changing colors according to chart, hdc in each of next 29 [32, 36, 39] sts, leaving rem sts unworked, turn. *(30 [33, 37, 40] sts)*

Note: For rem rows of Left Shoulder, work even-numbered rows on chart from right to left and odd-numbered rows on chart from left to right.

Row 57 [59, 61, 61]: Ch 2, sk next st, changing colors according to chart, hdc in each st across, turn. *(29 [32, 36, 39] hdc)*

Row 58 [60, 62, 62]: Ch 2, changing colors according to chart, hdc in each st across to last st, leaving last st unworked, turn. *(28 [31, 35, 38] hdc)*

Row 59 [61, 63, 63]: Rep row 57 [59, 61, 61]. *(27 [30, 34, 37] hdc)*

Rows 60 & 61 [62 & 63, 64 & 65, 64 & 65]: Ch 2, changing colors according to chart, hdc in each st across. At end of last row, fasten off.

RIGHT SHOULDER

Note: For rows of right shoulder, work even-numbered rows on chart from left to right and odd-numbered rows on chart from right to left.

Row 56 [58, 60, 60]: Sk next 30 [34, 36, 38] sts on row 55 [57, 59, 59] of Front, join color indicated on chart in next st, ch 2, changing colors according to chart, hdc in each of next 29 [32, 36, 39] sts, turn. *(30 [33, 37, 40] hdc)*

Row 57 [59, 61, 61]: Ch 2, changing colors according to chart, hdc in each st across to last st, leaving last st unworked, turn. *(29 [32, 36, 39] hdc)*

Row 58 [60, 62, 62]: Ch 2, sk next st, changing colors according to chart, hdc in each st across, turn. *(28 [31, 35, 38] hdc)*

Row 59 [61, 63, 63]: Rep row 57 [59, 61, 61]. *(27 [30, 34, 37] hdc)*

Rows 60 & 61 [62 & 63, 64 & 65, 64 & 65]: Ch 2, changing colors according to chart, hdc in each st across. At end of last row, fasten off.

Sew shoulder seams.

SLEEVE
MAKE 2.
RIBBING

Row 1: With F hook and F, ch 14, sc in 2nd ch from hook and in each rem ch across, turn. *(13 sc)*

Rows 2–40 [2–42, 2–42, 2–44]: Working in **back lps** *(see Stitch Guide)* only, ch 1, sc in each st across, turn. At end of last row, **do not fasten off**.

ARM

Row 1: With F hook and F, ch 1, working in ends of rows, sc in end of each row across, turn. *(40 [42, 42, 44] sc)*

Note: When working Sleeve chart, work between lines indicated for size.

Row 2: Ch 2, changing colors according to Sleeve chart *(page 199)*, hdc in each st across, turn.

Row 3: Ch 2, changing colors according to chart, hdc in same st as beg ch-2, hdc in each st across to last st, 2 hdc in last st, turn. *(42 [44, 44, 46] hdc)*

Rows 4 & 5: Ch 2, changing colors according to chart, hdc in each st across, turn.

Rows 6–8: Rep rows 3–5. *(44 [46, 46, 48] hdc)*

Rows 9 & 10: Rep row 3. *(48 [50, 50, 52] sts at end of last row)*

Rows 11 & 12: Rep row 4.

Rows 13 & 14: Rep row 3. *(52 [54, 54, 56] sts at end of last row)*

Rows 15 & 16: Rep row 4.

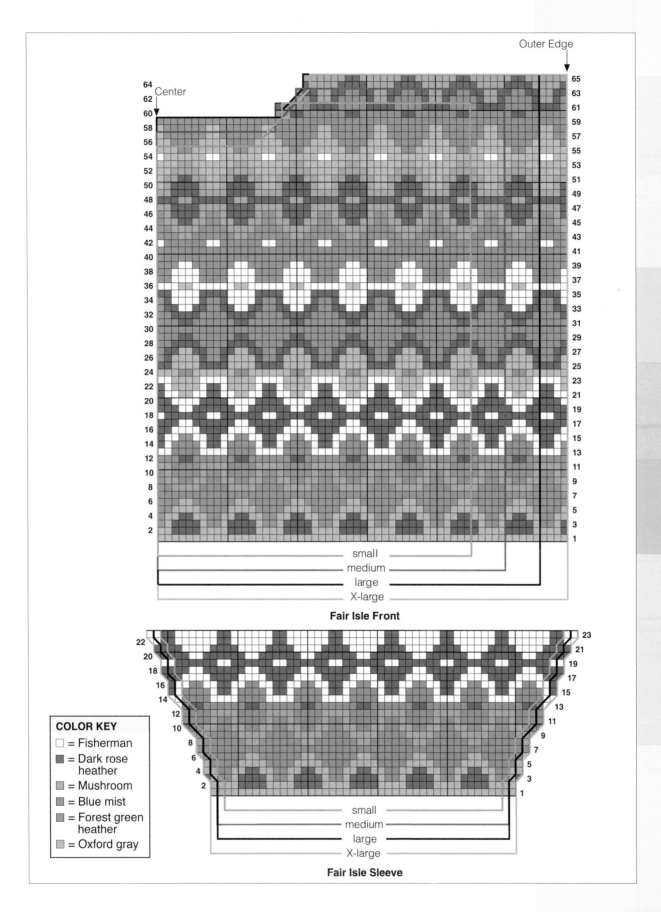

Fair Isle Front

Fair Isle Sleeve

COLOR KEY

- ☐ = Fisherman
- ■ = Dark rose heather
- ■ = Mushroom
- ■ = Blue mist
- ■ = Forest green heather
- ■ = Oxford gray

Rows 17–20: [Rep rows 3–5 consecutively] twice, ending last rep with row 3. *(56 [58, 58, 60] sts at end of last row)*

Row 21: Rep row 4.

Rows 22 & 23: Rep rows 3 and 4. *(58 [60, 60, 62] sts at end of last row)*

Row 24: With A, ch 2, hdc in each st across, turn.

Row 25: Ch 2, hdc in same st, hdc in each st across to last st, 2 hdc in last st, turn. *(60 [62, 62, 64] hdc)*

Rows 26 & 27: Ch 2, hdc in each st across, turn.

Row 28: Rep row 25. *(62 [64, 64, 66] sts)*

Row 29: Ch 2, hdc in each st across, turn.

Row 30: Ch 2, hdc in same st, hdc in each st across to last st, 2 hdc in last st, turn. *(64 [66, 66, 68] hdc)*

Rows 31–54 [31–54, 31–56, 31–56]: [Rep rows 29 and 30 alternately] 12 [12, 13, 13] times. *(88 [90, 92, 94] sts at end of last row)*

Rows 55–66 [55–68, 57–70, 57–70]: Ch 2, hdc in each st across, turn. At end of last row, fasten off.

ASSEMBLY
Matching center of last row on Sleeve to shoulder seam, sew Sleeve to Front and Back.

Sew Sleeve and side seams.

NECK RIBBING
Rnd 1: Working around neck opening, with E hook and D, join with sc in either shoulder seam, sc in end of each row and in each st and seam around, ending with an even number of sts, join in first sc.

Row 2: Working in rows, ch 5, sc in 2nd ch from hook, sc in each ch across, sl st in each of first 2 sts on rnd 1, turn. *(4 sc made)*

Row 3: Working the following rows in back lps only, ch 1, sk sl sts, sc in each st across, turn.

Row 4: Ch 1, sc in each st across, sl st in each of next 2 sts on rnd 1, turn.

Next rows: [Rep rows 3 and 4 alternately], ending with row 3. At end of last row, fasten off, leaving 6-inch end for sewing.

Sew row 2 and last row tog through back lps.

WAIST RIBBING
Row 1: With F hook and F, ch 14, sc in 2nd ch from hook, sc in each ch across, turn. *(13 sc)*

Next rows: Working in back lps only, ch 1, sc in each st across, turn, until piece measures 35 [39, 43, 47] inches. At end of last row, fasten off, leaving 6-inch end.

Sew first and last rows tog through back lps. Easing to fit, sew Waist Ribbing to bottom of Front and Back. ▪

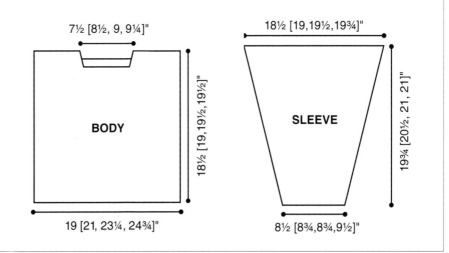

BODY

7½ [8½, 9, 9¼]"

18½ [19,19½,19½]"

19 [21, 23¼, 24¾]"

SLEEVE

18½ [19,19½,19¾]"

19¾ [20½, 21, 21]"

8½ [8¾,8¾,9½]"

Experimenting With Mosaic Crochet

With its colorful bits of glass, tile, ceramic or stone set closely together to form one larger pattern, mosaic design is something like fitting many little puzzle pieces together to make a beautiful picture. In this same technique, we can create lovely mosaic patterns in crochet using different colors of thread or yarn for our "puzzle" pieces.

Although this type of crochet work likely predates 1923, J. & P. Coats Book No. 16, *Centerpieces and Edgings* by Anne Orr and published in that year, claims, "We also introduce Mosaic Crochet, a new method of producing color effects in this work; and while this crochet permits the use of all sorts of beautiful colors, it is simply done and very rapidly gains wonderful effects, as most of it is arranged for coarse sizes of crochet cotton."

If you're artistically inclined, you can draw your own design on graph paper, but basically, any motif that has been charted out for filet crochet can be worked in mosaic crochet, as per the aforementioned book's further admonition, "Note the illustrations on pages 12, 13 and 15, which are shown in color and yet worked in filet stitchery. The actual pieces are made in filet crochet and are very beautiful in this method, but the color plates are added to help the worker visualize how they would appear if made by the Mosaic Crochet method."

On a chart for filet crochet, some of the squares represent spaces (generally the background) and some of the squares represent blocks (the "picture"). For mosaic crochet, all the squares on the chart represent blocks, the background being worked in the main color and the picture worked in blocks of contrasting colors.

The statement in *Centerpieces and Edgings* that mosaic crochet "permits the use of beautiful colors" and "gains wonderful effects" probably stops short of the claim that "it is simply done" and "very rapidly" gains those wonderful effects; and likely there is an advantage to using the finer cotton threads as opposed to the coarse cotton threads.

Depending upon how many colors are used in one row, following the color changes and carrying the thread not in use across the back of the work requires some manual dexterity and does tend to slow down one's progress. As for using the more coarse threads, the more detail you want in your design, the more blocks you need, and the more blocks you need the larger your finished piece becomes. In order for your finished piece not to be of epic proportions, it's often necessary to use the finer threads.

There are several ways to handle the thread not in use. You can use a separate bobbin or small ball of thread for every area of a different color and not carry the color not in use at all. While the number of bobbins attached may become quite cumbersome on rows requiring many colors, this method will eliminate any unnecessary bulk and unsightly, telltale traces of the thread not in use.

Or you can carry the thread not in use across the back of the work, either working over it with the thread in use on every stitch, or on every fifth or sixth stitch, for example.

Each method has its advantages and disadvantages. If you work over the thread on every stitch, you can sometimes see traces of the color not in use on the right side of the work if there is a bold contrast between the color of the working thread and the thread not in use. It also makes for a stiffer, heavier piece, but for something like a pot holder, a hot pad or rug, this is not necessarily a disadvantage. It also eliminates any long, unsightly strands across the back of the work.

Working over the thread not in use only every fifth or sixth stitch will produce "floaters" across the back of the work, but it assures that the color not in use will not be seen on the right side and that the issue of extra bulk from working over every stitch will be avoided.

The following Mosaic Rose Doily is worked over on every fifth or sixth stitch to eliminate any possible unwanted color show-through.

In spite of any awkwardness you may feel at first, you're sure to be pleased with the results of the doily.

MOSAIC ROSE DOILY

SKILL LEVEL
INTERMEDIATE

FINISHED SIZE
10 x 15 inches

MATERIALS
- Size 20 crochet cotton:
  415 yds each white, dark rose, medium pink, light pink, light green and dark green

- Size 10/1.15mm steel crochet hook or size needed to obtain gauge

GAUGE
12 tr = 1 inch

PATTERN NOTES
Chain-4 counts as first treble crochet unless otherwise stated.

For small areas worked in 1 color, carry color not in use across wrong side of work, working over it with color in use every 5th or 6th stitch.

For large areas worked in 1 color, do not carry color not in use across back of work. Use bobbins or wind small balls of thread for each large area worked in same color.

Always change color in last stitch worked.

Each square on chart stands for 1 block. When working from chart, read all odd-numbered rows from right to left and all even-numbered rows from left to right.

Join with slip stitch as indicated unless otherwise stated.

SPECIAL STITCHES
Foundation treble crochet (foundation tr):
Yo twice, insert hook in indicated st, yo, pull up lp, yo, pull through 1 lp on hook *(base)*, [yo, pull through 2 lps on hook] 3 times.

Block: Tr in each of next 3 sts.

Beginning block (beg block): Ch 4 *(see Pattern Notes)*, tr in each of next 3 sts.

Beginning block increase (beg block inc): Ch 6 for first block, ch 3 more for each additional block to be inc, tr in 5th ch from hook and in each rem ch across.

End block increase (end block inc): Foundation tr in same st as last tr worked, [foundation tr in base of last foundation tr worked] twice for first block, [foundation tr in base of last foundation tr worked] 3 times for each additional block to be inc.

Beginning block decrease (beg block dec): Sl st in each of first 3 sts for each block to be dec, sl st in next st, ch 4 for first tr.

End block decrease (end block dec): Leave 3 sts unworked for each block to be dec.

Shell: (3 tr, ch 2, 3 tr) in indicated sp.

Beginning shell (beg shell): (Ch 4, 2 tr, ch 2, 3 tr) in indicated st.

Cluster (cl): Holding back last lp of each st on hook, 3 tr in indicated ch sp, yo, pull through all 4 lps on hook.

Beginning cluster (beg cl): Ch 3, holding back last lp of each st on hook, 2 tr in indicated ch sp, yo, pull through all 3 lps on hook.

DOILY

Row 1 (RS): With white, ch 43, tr in 5th ch from hook (*first 4 chs count as first tr*) and in each ch across, turn. (*40 tr*)

Row 2: Ch 12, tr in 5th ch from hook, tr in each ch across (*3 beg blocks inc*), tr in each st across, **foundation tr** (*see Special Stitches*) in same st as last tr worked, [foundation tr in base of last foundation tr worked] twice (*first block inc*), [foundation tr in base of last foundation tr worked] 6 times (*2 additional blocks inc*), turn. (*58 tr, 19 blocks*)

Rows 3–5: Using Special Stitches as needed, work from chart, **changing colors** (*see Pattern Notes and Stitch Guide*) and inc blocks at beg and end of rows as indicated.

Row 6: Beg block with A, 27 more blocks with white, changing to dark green in last tr of 27th block, block twice with dark green, changing to light green in last tr of 2nd block, block with light green, changing to dark green in last tr of block, block twice with dark green, changing to white in last tr of 2nd block, block 6 times with white, turn. (*39 blocks*)

Rows 7–32: Continue to work from chart, inc and dec blocks at beg and end of rows and

changing colors as indicated. At end of row 32, turn. **Do not fasten off.** (*40 tr at end of row 32*)

BORDER

Rnd 1 (RS): Work as follows:

A. *Ch 7, sk next 3 sts, sl st in next st, [ch 7, sk next 4 sts, sl st in next st] 7 times, [ch 7, sk next 3 unworked sts on next row, sl st in next st, ch 7, sk next 4 sts, sl st in next st] twice;

B. ch 7, sk next 3 unworked sts on next row, sl st in next st, [ch 7, sk next 3 sts, sl st in next st] twice, [ch 7, sk next 3 unworked sts on next row, sl st in next st, ch 7, sk next 4 sts, sl st in next st, ch 7, sl st in end of next row] twice, [ch 7, sl st in end of next row] twice;

C. ch 7, sk next row, sl st in end of next row, ch 7, sl st in end of next row, [ch 7, sk next row, sl st in end of next row] 3 times, [ch 7, sl st in end of next row] twice, ch 7, sk next row, sl st in end of next row, [ch 7, sl st in end of next row] twice;

D. ch 7, sl st in top of end of next row, ch 7, sk next 4 sts, sl st in next st, ch 7, sl st in end of next row, ch 7, sl st in top of end of next row, ch 7, sk next 4 sts, sl st in next st, ch 7, sl st in top of end of next row, [ch 7, sk next 3 sts, sl st in next st] twice, ch 7, sl st in top of end of next row**;

E. [ch 7, sk next 4 sts, sl st in next st, ch 7, sl st in top of end of next row] twice, rep from * around, ending last rep at **;

F. ch 7, sk next 4 sts, sl st in next st, ch 7, sl st in top of end of next row, ch 7, sk next 4 sts, sl st in next st, ch 3, tr in top of first st of next row to form last ch-7 sp. (*92 ch-7 sps*)

Rnd 2: [Ch 7, sl st in next ch sp] 10 times, *ch 7, (sl st, ch 7) twice in next ch sp, sl st in next ch sp, [ch 7, sl st in next ch sp] 31 times, ch 7, (sl st, ch 7) twice in next ch sp, sl st in next ch sp*, [ch 7, sl st in next ch sp] 11 times, rep between *, ch 2, dtr in sl st at base of beg ch-7 to form last ch-7 sp. (*96 ch-7 sps*)

Rnd 3: Beg shell (*see Special Stitches*) in sp just formed, *ch 5, sk next ch sp, 7 tr in center ch of next ch sp, ch 5, sk next ch sp**, **shell** (*see Special Stitches*) in next ch sp, rep from * around, ending last rep at **, **join** (*see Pattern Notes*) in 4th ch of beg ch-4.

Rnd 4: Beg cl (*see Special Stitches*), *ch 3, **cl** (*see Special Stitches*), ch 4, sl st in next ch sp, ch 4, tr in each of next 7 tr, ch 4, sl st in next

ch sp, ch 4**, cl, rep from * around, ending last rep at **, join in top of beg cl.

Rnd 5: Sl st in next ch sp, beg cl in same ch sp, *ch 6, **tr dec** (*see Stitch Guide*) in next 2 ch sps, ch 6, tr dec in next 7 tr, ch 6, tr dec in next 2 ch sps, ch 6**, cl in next sp, rep from * around, ending last rep at **, join in top of beg cl. Fasten off. ■

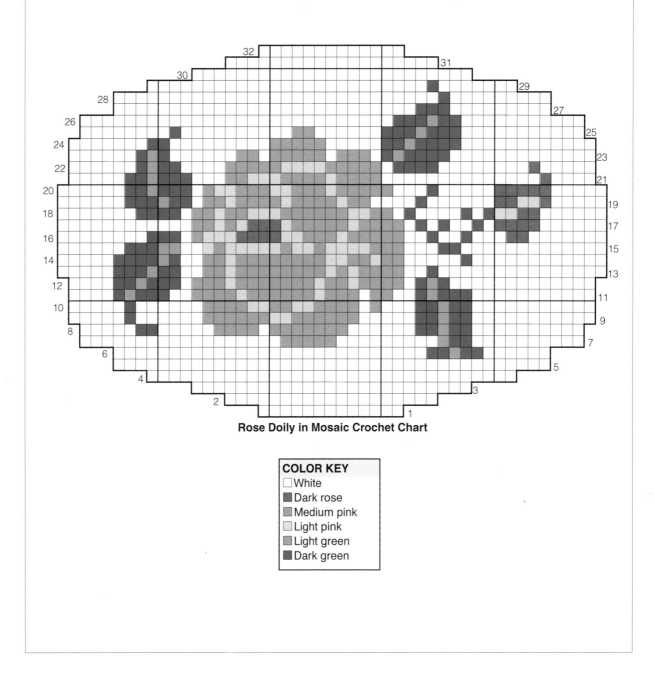

Rose Doily in Mosaic Crochet Chart

COLOR KEY
☐ White
■ Dark rose
■ Medium pink
□ Light pink
■ Light green
■ Dark green

A Tutorial in Filet Crochet

Isn't it remarkable that just two basic stitches can create beautiful pieces of lacy crochet work? If you've never tried filet crochet, here is an easy guide and simple project to get you started!

Filet crochet is an openwork technique that was very popular in the mid 1800s. "Queen Victoria, in an act of royal generosity, accepted gifts of Irish crocheted lace for her gowns. Special crochet thread was produced by enterprising textile manufacturers and during this peak in crochet's popularity, filet crochet was the favorite."[1] "Filet" is the French word meaning "net." Filet crochet consists of open meshes and solid blocks, which, when worked together, give the work a lacy quality. Although it may look intricate and complicated, it is one of the easier crochet techniques. It is so easy, in fact, that crocheters can create their own designs with graphs.

Using only two simple stitches, the chain and double crochet, this technique readily lends itself to using those stitches and chains to create pictures, such as animals, religious symbols, flowers or monograms. Some have described it, saying it is almost "like drawing with thread. Like a pencil drawing, it uses light and shadow to create an image where there was none before."[1] "Filet charms the artist in the crocheter, as well as acting as a challenge to one's skill resulting in a real crochet masterpiece to treasure."[4]

For best results, filet crochet is done with fine cotton threads, and those threads, traditionally, are either white or ecru in color. Ranging from size 3 to size 100, the finest available, threads require steel crochet hooks to create the series of open spaces and solid blocks in combinations to create pictorial designs. Like any kind of crochet, the thread must fit the hook: The larger the design or picture, the finer the thread must be. Probably the most sought after pattern is that of "The Last Supper" charted for filet crochet. This pattern is available online at: www.lacis.com; just type "Last Supper" in the search box.

"Like most 'facts' about [filet] crochet, there are many theories as to why it is mostly done in the color white. The most popular is that white has a religious significance because of its association with holiness and purity. Since nuns first taught it, this seems a logical theory. Other reasons for the use of white can also be put forth. Cotton is naturally white, and dyeing is expensive. Also, since many of the articles made of filet crochet are used as home decorations, and since white blends with all colors, the choice of white is a natural."[1]

Designs charted on graph paper are provided for the crocheter to follow. The design chart will usually include a note directing one to follow the chart from right to left for the right side and from left to right for the wrong side. "Since filet squares all blend into each other, the last stitch of one square is the first stitch of the next. Therefore, an isolated square may consist of four stitches (two sides to the square and two stitches in the center), but on a chart, each square requires only three stitches because it will share its last stitch as the first stitch of the next square."[1] While following the chart, it is best to mark off each row with a pencil as it is completed or use a magnetic board to keep track of progress.

To form a space, work two chains and skip over two stitches of the previous row. An open square or mesh on the chart or graph indicates a space. Filling the space with two double crochet stitches creates a solid block in the designs. On the chart, a solid square or "X" indicates a block.

It is thought that filet crochet must have two double crochets in each block and two chains in each space. However, some sources suggest that a space can consist of only one chain and a block of only one double crochet. "If you desire a fuller, heavier texture to your work, the double mesh crochet stitch should be used instead of the regular double crochet. This stitch gives more definition to the design. It is worked in a slightly different manner than the regular double crochet stitch.

If included in a pattern, this slightly irregular double crochet would be stated as follows: Yo hook, insert hook in next ch, pull thread through (*3 lps on hook*), yo hook and pull thread through only 1 ch, yo hook and pull thread through 3 rem lps on hook."[2]

"Once finished, the crochet work may require an outside edge to give it body and to prevent it from stretching. Slip stitch or single crochet will suffice, but there are also many elegant edgings to choose from. Blocking is necessary to acquire the proper size, to make the piece lay flat, and to give it a neat, pressed appearance."[2] Blocking can easily be accomplished by using steel pins to pin the piece evenly all around the sides and then covering it with a damp cloth for at least 24 hours or until the cloth is dry.

CREATING YOUR OWN DESIGN CHART

Start by charting your desired design on graph paper with a pencil. "To begin the piece, count the meshes in the first row of the pattern; make three times as many chain stitches as there are meshes and add 1 more chain, then chain 5 more to make the turning. Now work a double crochet in the 9th chain from the hook. This forms the first open mesh. Chain 2, skip 2 stitches on the foundation chain and work a double crochet into the next chain. Repeat this across the foundation chain. Always work in the 2 strands at the top of the stitches to make the work firm. The meshes should be square. If their width exceeds their height, either the chain stitches or the tops of the double crochets are too loose. If the first mesh of your first row is a solid block, work 2 double crochets in place of the 2 chain stitches."[3]

References:

[1] Rankin, Chris. *The Filet Crochet Book.* Sterling Publishing Co. Inc., 1990.

[2] Svinicki, Eunice and Thompson, Karla. *Old-Fashioned Crochet.* Van Nostrand Reinhold Co., 1981.

[3] Kirchmaier, Hugo. *The New Filet Crochet Book: Number 2.* House of White Birches, 1978.

[4] Blakley Kinsler, Gwen. "Filet Crochet" *Old-Time Crochet.* Spring 1999, page 12.

[5] Harding, Deborah. "Look What You Can Make from a Simple Ball of String" *Family Circle.* March 1976, page 92.

FLORAL FILET SACHET

SKILL LEVEL

■ ■ ■ ▢
INTERMEDIATE

FINISHED SIZE
3¾ x 4½ inches

MATERIALS
- DMC Cebelia size 30 crochet cotton (567 yds per ball):
  1 ball blanc
- Size 12/1.00mm steel crochet hook or size needed to obtain gauge
- Fabric scrap for Insert
- Polyester fiberfill
- Sewing needle
- Sewing thread
- Concentrated scented oil of choice

GAUGE
12 dc = 1 inch; 6 dc rows = 1 inch

PATTERN NOTE
Join with slip stitch as indicated unless otherwise stated.

SPECIAL STITCHES
Block: Dc in each of next 3 sts or 2 dc in next ch sp, dc in next st.

Mesh: Ch 2, sk next ch sp, dc in next st, or ch 2, sk next 2 sts, dc in next st.

Beginning mesh (beg mesh): Ch 5, sk next 2 dc or next ch sp, dc in next st.

SACHET
FRONT
Row 1: Ch 44, dc in 8th ch from hook (*first 8 chs count as sk 2 chs, dc and ch-2*), [ch 2, sk next 2 chs, dc in next ch] across, turn.

Row 2: Beg mesh (*see Special Stitches*), **mesh** (*see Special Stitches*) 7 times, **block** (*see Special Stitches*) twice, mesh 3 times, turn.

Rows 3–19: Using Special Stitches as needed, work according to Chart across each row, turn. At end of last row, **do not turn or fasten off**.

Rnd 20: Working around outer edge in sts and in ends of rows, ch 1, 3 sc in end of each of first 19 rows, working in starting ch on opposite side of row 1, 3 sc in each ch sp across with 3 sc in last ch, 3 sc in end of each row across, 3 sc in each ch sp across, **join** (*see Pattern Note*) in beg sc. Fasten off. (*192 sc*)

EDGING
Rnd 1: Working in **front lps** (*see Stitch Guide*), join with sc in center corner st at any corner, [ch 5, sk next 3 sts, sc in next st] around, ending with ch 2, sk last 3 sts, join with dc in beg sc forming last ch sp. (*48 ch sps*)

Rnd 2: Ch 5, (dc, ch 5, sc in 4th ch from hook, {ch 2, dc} twice) in same ch sp as beg ch-5, sk next ch sp, [(dc, ch 2, dc, ch 5, sc in 4th ch from hook, {ch 2, dc} twice) in next ch sp, sk next ch sp] around, join in 3rd ch of beg ch-5. Fasten off.

BACK
Row 1: Ch 44, dc in 8th ch from hook, [ch 2, sk next 2 chs, dc in next ch] across, turn.

Rows 2–19: Beg mesh, mesh across, turn.

Rnd 20: Rep rnd 20 of Front.

INSERT
Using Back as pattern, fold fabric, place Back on fold, allowing ¼-inch seam, cut fabric ¼ inch larger around edges.

Sew RS tog across 2 edges, turn RS out and stuff with fiberfill. Scent fiberfill with oil as desired. Sew end closed.

FINISHING
Holding Front and Back WS tog, working through both thicknesses and in **back lps** (*see Stitch Guide*), join in any st, sl st in each st around, inserting Insert before closing, join in beg sl st. Fasten off. ■

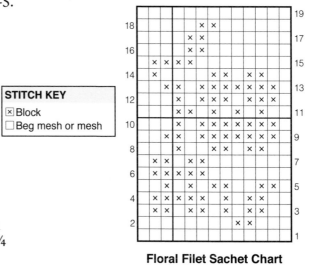

STITCH KEY
⊠ Block
☐ Beg mesh or mesh

Floral Filet Sachet Chart

Flatwork Bead Crochet

Bead crochet has evolved over many years and flatwork bead crochet is one of the most exciting and challenging techniques in beadwork. Bead crochet is for those who like technically precise crochet—and endless possibilities! If you have never worked with beads, use size 6 beads and fingering-weight yarn until you get the feel of it. Like any type of crochet, with a little practice you will begin to enjoy a beautifully relaxing rhythm with your bead crochet.

The Hope of Spring Brooch featured with this article is a great project for exploring the technique of flatwork bead crochet. Also included below are photos of some more challenging projects that will hopefully inspire you to experiment with flatwork bead crochet.

TIPS & TRICKS

As for any type of crochet, beads, thread, bead needle and hook need to be compatible.

Size 10 thread and big-eye or twisted-wire needles are compatible with size 11, 10 or 8 beads.

Nymo and Conso threads work well, but the colors are limited.

Use thread that matches the lightest bead in the design. Thread can influence the color of beads in some cases.

Threads can be matched to the various colors of beads. Flatwork bead crochet is worked in the jacquard method of carrying colors along the work and changing thread colors as bead colors are changed. This is a more advanced method and requires patience.

Beads are loaded onto thread in the reverse order in which they are used, i.e., the first bead on is the last bead used.

When loading beads according to a chart, load a series of beads, double-check chart count, and THEN move them past the needle. Frequent count checks save time later.

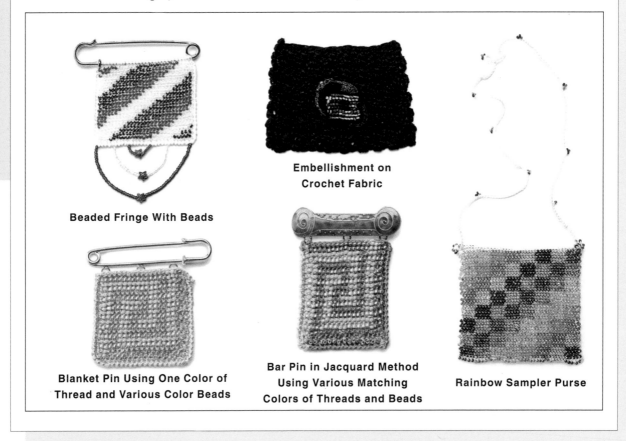

Beaded Fringe With Beads

Embellishment on Crochet Fabric

Blanket Pin Using One Color of Thread and Various Color Beads

Bar Pin in Jacquard Method Using Various Matching Colors of Threads and Beads

Rainbow Sampler Purse

CROCHETING THE PROJECT

You may crochet the first row of bead crochet with a smaller size hook than the rest of the rows because the first row tends to be looser. The stitches used for the first row, and others, will, most likely, be listed as follows:

Front bead single crochet (front bead sc): Insert hook from back to front in indicated st, pull bead down to hook, yo, draw lp through st, yo, draw through 2 lps on hook. Front bead sc sts fall to the front of the work and lay horizontally on the row.

Back bead single crochet (back bead sc): Insert hook from front to back in indicated ch or st, yo, draw lp through, pull bead close to hook, yo, pull through both lps on hook.

Start crochet in upper right corner of chart with the last bead that was loaded. This first row is the top of the finished piece even though it appears to be the bottom row of the work in progress.

Work the stitches tightly, pushing each bead snug to the last one worked and tightening the stitch.

Look at the front of your work every row or two to be sure the design is progressing according to the chart.

The last stitch of each row is often tight and difficult to see; be sure not to skip it.

If you find an extra bead on the thread, move it 4 inches from project and 4 inches from the strung beads. Crush it with needle-nose pliers. If thread gets cut by your pliers, rejoin.

If you are missing a bead, cut the thread and add the bead; rejoin and continue.

Block finished flatwork when finished by pinning it on an ironing board in at least four corners and covering it with a damp cloth for 24 hours.

Create your own design on graph paper. When charting your own design, place colors as you want to see them in the finished piece. Start loading beads in the lower right corner, load beads on the next row from the left side of the chart, alternate the direction of stringing with each row.

Block finished flatwork when finished by pinning work on an ironing board and pinning the four corners in a bit of a diagonal stretch. Pin along all four sides, as well. Cover with a damp cloth and let it dry for 24 hours.

OTHER BEAD-CROCHET STITCHES

Bead double crochet (bead dc): Probably best worked with beads falling to back of work. Yo, insert hook in indicated st, yo, pull up lp, pull up bead, yo, pull thread through first 2 lps, yo, pull up 2nd bead, yo, finish dc.

Bead half double crochet (bead hdc): Yo, insert hook in st, yo, pull up lp, pull up 2 beads, yo, pull thread through all 3 lps on hook.

Bead popcorn (bead pc): Also best worked with beads falling on back of work. Work 5 bead dc in indicated st, remove hook from 5th bead dc, insert hook in top of first bead dc and in 5th bead dc, yo, pull sts tog, ch 1 to lock.

USES

There are many uses for flatwork bead crochet. Only your imagination can limit you. You can derive inspiration from some of the decorative bar pins and chart a simple design that complements the bar pin and use matching beads. Inexpensive blanket pins can be used in place of bar pins. A charted design can become the focal point for a purse, a headband or an ornament. A friend's initial can be charted to create a personalized gift or coin purse.

FINISHING TECHNIQUES

Use reverse single crochet with or without beads to give a finished look to any flatwork bead crochet.

Bead fringe may be added to flatwork bead crochet to give a finished look or to complement the design.

HOPE OF SPRING BROOCH

SKILL LEVEL

■■□□
EASY

FINISHED SIZE

2 inches square, excluding pin back and Fringe

MATERIALS

- Size 4 very fine metallic thread:
  22 yds silver
- Size 6/1.80mm steel crochet hook or size
  needed to obtain gauge
- Large-eye beading needle
- Size 8 seed beads:
  1 oz each lime, purple and teal
- 5-ring ½ x 1½-inch bar pin
- Straight pins

GAUGE

11 sc = 1 inch; 11 sc rows = 1 inch

PATTERN NOTES

Every bead single crochet row is a right-side row, because with this method, beads fall on the front of each row.

Work bead single crochet stitch tightly.

Thread beads onto thread in color order, starting at lower right corner of Chart.

Start crochet in lower right corner of Chart. The last bead loaded will be the first bead used.

Count stitches after working each row to maintain accurate count.

Front bead single crochets fall to front of work and lay horizontally on row.

Back bead single crochets fall to back of work and lay vertically on row.

Join rounds with slip stitch as indicated unless otherwise stated.

SPECIAL STITCHES

Front bead single crochet (front bead sc): Insert hook from back to front in indicated st, pull bead down to hook, yo, draw lp through st, yo, draw through 2 lps on hook. Front bead sc sts fall to the front of the work and lay horizontally on the row.

Back bead single crochet (back bead sc): Insert hook from front to back in indicated ch or st, yo, draw lp through, pull bead close to hook, yo, pull through both lps on hook.

BROOCH
BODY

Row 1: With WS of bar pin facing, join with sc in first bar-pin ring, 2 sc in same ring, ch 3,

2 sc in next ring, ch 3, 3 sc in next ring, [ch 3, 2 sc in ring] twice, turn. (12 sc, 4 ch sps)

Row 2: Ch 1, sc in each of first 2 sts, 3 sc in next ch sp, sc in each of next 2 sts, 3 sc in next ch sp, sc in each of next 3 sts, 3 sc in next ch sp, sc in each of next 2 sts, 2 sc in next ch sp, sc in each of last 3 sts, turn. (23 sc)

Row 3: Ch 1, sc in each st across, turn.

Row 4 (RS): Ch 1, sc in each of first 6 sts, **back bead sc** (see Special Stitches) in each of next 4 sts, sc in each of next 3 sts, back bead sc in each of next 4 sts, sc in each of last 6 sts, turn.

Rows 5–24: Continue working according to Chart, working back bead sc and **front bead sc** (see Special Stitches) as indicated. At end of last row, fasten off.

EDGING
Rnd 1: With RS facing, join with sc in upper left corner, work sc evenly sp in ends of rows and sts around with 3 sc in each corner, **join** (see Pattern Notes) in beg sc.

Rnd 2: Working from left to right, **reverse sc** (see Stitch Guide) in each st around, join in beg reverse sc. Fasten off.

Block with damp cloth, if necessary.

FRINGE
Mark bottom of piece with 7 evenly sp pins in order to place Fringe evenly sp along edge.

Attach thread to lower right-hand corner of back of Brooch. String 9 beads, alternating purple and teal. Moving over slightly, secure thread. Move over again with needle to next pin, string 11 beads, alternating purple and teal, rep process stringing 13 beads alternately. String 15 beads in lime and secure.

Rep for other side of Brooch, stringing 13, 11 and 9 beads alternately with purple and teal. Fasten off. ▪

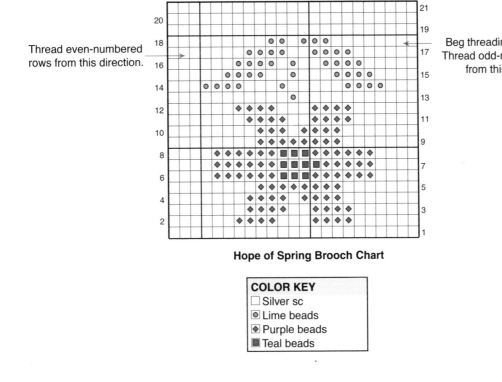

Hope of Spring Brooch Chart

Thread even-numbered rows from this direction.

Beg threading beads here. Thread odd-numbered rows from this direction.

COLOR KEY
☐ Silver sc
◉ Lime beads
◆ Purple beads
▪ Teal beads

Tambour Crochet

Tambour crochet is a type of Asian embroidery that is closely related to crochet and considered to have most directly influenced the development and spread of crochet lace patterns. Heralded in the mid-1700s as "the new Chinese needlework," tambour's origins have been traced to China, Turkey, Persia, India and North Africa.

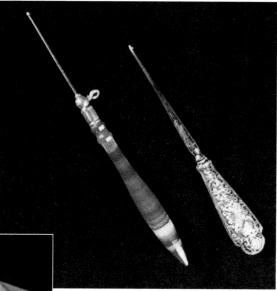

The tambour hook and crochet hook are almost identical in design.

It was first introduced to Europe through Saxony and Switzerland. There, it was worked only on white muslin and cambric with white thread and used to embellish dresses, curtains, caps, borders and a variety of other white trimmings. However, the original Asian tambour work was much more colorful.

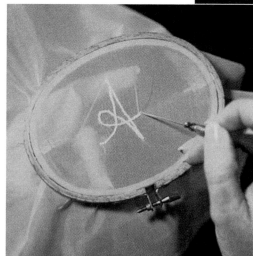

Tambour is worked on fabric stretched over a hoop.

The European peasants that took up the new technique did such excellent work with their newly found skill that their work was not only eagerly bought on the continent but also shipped back to the East, from whence it originated.

Tambour embroidery is worked with a hook almost identical to a crochet hook except that it generally has a sharper point at the tip for piercing the fabric upon which it is worked. The desired design is first sketched on a background material, and the fabric is then stretched on a tambour frame ("tambour" is the French word for "drum"). The thread is held underneath the fabric; the hook is inserted down into the fabric, and a loop of the thread is drawn through to the right side of the fabric.

The hook is then inserted a little farther along the fabric, the thread from underneath is drawn through the fabric and through the loop on the hook. The work progresses in this manner until the desired design has been completed. It is thought that at

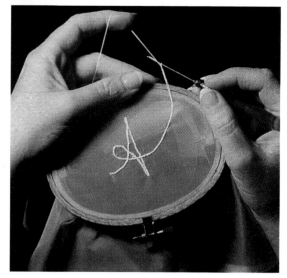

It is thought the tambour technique led to crochet when stitchers just kept tambouring off the edge of the hoop, creating "stitches in the air."

some point in time, probably the end of the 18th century, the fabric was eliminated and the stitch was worked on its own, developing into what the French called "crochet in the air." In fact, it is thought that the tambour technique led to crochet when stitchers just kept tambouring off the edge of the hoop, creating "stitches in the air."

In the late 1920s, McCall's introduced at least one transfer pattern for a technique they described as "crocheted chain embroidery for table linen." The advertising stated, "The crocheted chain-stitch used for this table set is something new, though suggested by the old tambour work of our great-grandmothers. It is most interesting to do and quicker with the crochet hook than with an embroidery needle." Their pattern called for size 5 pearl, or perle, cotton and a size 7 or 8 steel crochet hook.

You can use tambour crochet (or "surface chain") to decorate almost anything you can embroider, from clothing to a variety of home accessories. If you've never tried this technique, the beautiful Tambour-Work Doily included here might inspire you to give it a try.

TRY THE TAMBOUR TECHNIQUE IN A PRETTY PANSY-ADORNED DOILY

The delicate butterfly taking center stage in this lovely pansy doily calls for two strands of embroidery floss and a size 10 steel crochet hook, but you'll want to adjust the weight of the thread and the size of the hook to be appropriate for the fabric on which you will working when you create your own tambour-work projects.

Try to keep your stitches small and uniform in size. Our pattern uses an iron-on transfer for the butterfly design, but if you're artistically inclined, you might want to try drawing your own designs on fabric. Our instructions also call for a purchased hem-stitched linen circle, but you can easily create your own following the tips in our article Crocheting on Fabric on page 220.

TAMBOUR-WORK DOILY

SKILL LEVEL

■■■□
INTERMEDIATE

FINISHED SIZE
13½ inches in diameter

MATERIALS
- Size 10 crochet cotton:
  300 yds each shaded yellows (C) and shaded purples (D)
  225 yds white (A)
  150 yds green (B)
- 6-strand embroidery floss:
  1 skein each purple, lilac, gold, aqua and black
- Sizes 7/1.65mm and 10/1.15mm steel crochet hooks or size needed to obtain gauge
- Hemstitched 9¼-inch-radius linen circle
- Embroidery needle
- Butterfly iron-on transfer
- Embroidery hoop
- Dressmaker's carbon and ballpoint pen or pencil (optional)

GAUGE
With larger hook: Pansy = 2 inches from tip of first lower petal to tip of 3rd lower petal

Take time to check gauge.

PATTERN NOTE
Join with slip stitch as indicated unless otherwise stated.

SPECIAL STITCHES
Surface chain (surface ch): With crochet hook, make a slip knot at end of 2-strand length of embroidery floss. Drop lp with slip knot from hook. Holding slip knot on WS of work, insert hook from RS to WS at point where embroidery will beg, place dropped lp on hook, draw through to RS of work. *Insert hook from RS to WS at next point on work, draw up a lp with embroidery floss from WS to RS of work and through lp on hook, rep from * as necessary along outline, ending with drawing up entire length of

floss to RS of work and through lp on hook, holding hook at WS of work, insert hook from WS of work to RS at end of last ch made, draw entire length of floss through to WS, tie securely.

Dropped loop join (dropped lp join): Drop lp from hook, insert hook from RS to WS in indicated st or sp, pick up dropped lp, draw through st or sp to RS of work.

Cluster (cl): *Yo twice, insert hook in indicated st, yo, draw lp through, (yo, draw through 2 lps) twice, rep from * twice, yo, draw through all 4 lps on hook.

DOILY CENTER
Following manufacturer's instructions, iron butterfly transfer pattern onto center of linen circle, or apply pattern to center of circle using dressmaker's carbon and ballpoint pen or pencil.

Insert linen circle into embroidery hoop. Using photo as a guide, outline pattern with **surface ch** (see Special Stitches) using smaller crochet hook and 2 strands of embroidery floss held tog.

With embroidery needle, embroider **French knots** (see illustration) on butterfly's wings.

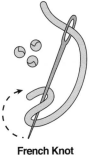

French Knot

Cut away excess linen to within ⅛ inch from edge of hemstitching.

BORDER

Rnd 1: With larger hook, **join** (see Pattern Note) A in any hole around edge of linen circle, ch 1, sc in same hole, *[2 sc in next hole, sc in next hole] 26 times, sc in next hole, rep from * around to last 3 sc, 2 sc in next sc, sc in last sc, join in beg sc, fasten off. (320 sc)

Rnd 2: With RS facing, using larger hook, join B in any sc, ch 1, beg in same st, sc in same st as beg ch-1, sc in each of next 4 sc, *ch 5, sk next 5 sts, (**cl**—see Special Stitches, ch 4, cl) in next st, ch 5, sk next 5 sts**, sc in each of next 5 sc, rep from * around, ending last rep at **, join in beg sc, fasten off.

FIRST PANSY

Rnd 1 (RS): With larger hook and C, ch 7, join in 7th ch from hook to form ring, ch 3 (counts as first dc), (2 dc, ch 7, {3 dc, ch 7} 4 times) in ring, join in beg sc. (5 ch-7 sps)

Rnd 2: Sc in next dc, [{6 dc, 2 tr, ch 1, 2 tr, 6 dc} in next sp, sc in center dc of next 3-dc group] 3 times (3 lower petals made), ch 4, ({**dtr**—see Stitch Guide, ch 1} 11 times, dtr, {tr, ch 1} twice, dc, ch 1, dc) in next sp, sc in center dc of next 3-dc group, ({dc, ch 1} twice, {tr, ch 1} twice, {dtr, ch 1} 11 times, dtr) in next sp, ch 4 (2 upper petals made), join in beg sc. Fasten off.

2ND PANSY

Rnd 1 (RS): With larger hook and D, rep rnd 1 of First Pansy.

Rnd 2: Sc in next dc, ({6 dc, 2 tr, ch 1}, **dropped lp join**—see Special Stitches—in next ch-1 sp on 3rd lower petal of previous Pansy, {2 tr, 6 dc}) in next ch sp on working Pansy, ({6 dc, 2 tr, ch 1}, dropped lp join to center sc of 5-sc group on rnd 2 of Border, {2 tr, 6 dc}) in next ch sp on working Pansy, ({6 dc, 2 tr, ch 1, 2 tr, 6 dc} in next sp, sc in center dc of next 3-dc group), ch 4, ({dtr, ch 1} 11 times, dtr, {tr, ch 1} twice, dc, ch 1, dc) in next sp, sc in center dc of next 3-dc group, ({dc, ch 1} twice, {tr, ch 1} twice, {dtr, ch 1} 11 times, dtr) in next sp, ch 4 (2 upper petals made), join in beg sc. Fasten off.

REMAINING 18 PANSIES

Rnds 1 & 2: Alternating C and D for each pansy, rep rnds 1 and 2 of 2nd Pansy, joining first lower petal of last Pansy to 3rd lower petal of previous Pansy and 3rd lower petal to first lower petal of First Pansy.

EDGING

With RS facing, using larger hook, join A in sc between 2 large petals at top of any Pansy, ch 1, sc in same st, *[ch 3, sc in next ch-1 sp] 15 times, ch 3, sc in next ch-4 sp on same Pansy, ch 1, sc in first ch-4 sp on next Pansy, [ch 3, sc in next ch-1 sp] 15 times, ch 3**, sc in sc between same petal and next petal, rep from * around, ending last rep at **, join in beg sc, fasten off. ▪

The Art of Swedish Embroidery

The origins of this unique Scandinavian embroidery style are clouded by the rarity of surviving artifacts and documentation by the ancient Vikings who fashioned the earliest forms of the needlework we know today as Swedish embroidery.

Also called "Swedish weave," or "huck embroidery" (taken from huckaback fabric), Swedish embroidery uses thread or yarn woven through the raised threads, referred to as floats, in the weave of fabric. Repeated geometric patterns are used most often in these designs.

The vertical and horizontal threads of crochet stitches lend themselves to be used as the floats on the finished fabric. For example, in the Swedish Embroidery Baby Blanket pattern included here, the designer's combination of two basic stitches created the floats necessary to execute Swedish embroidery on the surface of the crocheted afghan.

Most Swedish embroidery designs are worked in rows, starting at the bottom of the piece and working up. The first row is usually started at the center and worked out toward the edges. This makes it easy to keep the overall design symmetrical. With the first row as a guide, the remaining rows can be worked from edge to edge.

The stitching is worked in a right-to-left direction. The basic stitch movements used are straight (passing the yarn under floats that will keep it in a straight or diagonal direction), offset (passing the yarn under floats that will create a stairway or zigzag directions), open loops (passing the yarn under floats that will create loops with an open bottom) and closed loops (passing the yarn under floats that will close the bottom of a loop).

For a neat finish, always keep the twist of the yarn intact. It tends to unwind as you work, so remember to periodically release the tapestry needle and allow the original twist to return.

The fun and relaxing simplicity of Swedish embroidery has made it a popular needlecraft for centuries. It has experienced renewed interest in recent times by being integrated with other needle arts such as crochet. It's an interesting technique that adds eye-catching detail to virtually any type of needlecraft.

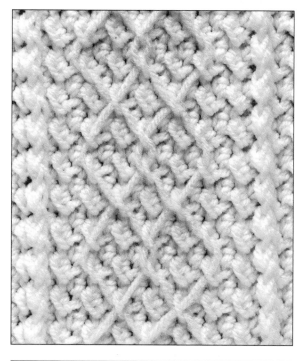

SWEDISH EMBROIDERY PASTEL STRIPES

SKILL LEVEL

EASY

FINISHED SIZE
50 x 54½ inches, excluding Fringe

MATERIALS
- Fine (sport) weight yarn:
  2,400 yds white
  800 yds pink
  500 yds each green and yellow
- Medium (worsted) weight yarn:
  200 yds light green
- Tapestry needle
- Size I/9/5.5mm crochet hook or size needed to obtain gauge

GAUGE
4 sts = 1 inch; 7 rows worked in pattern = 2 inches

PATTERN NOTES
Leave 6-inch end at beginning and end of each row to be worked into Fringe.

Use sport-weight yarn unless otherwise stated.

Join with slip stitch unless otherwise stated.

AFGHAN
Row 1: With white, ch 200, sl st in 2nd ch from hook, [hdc in next ch, sl st in next ch] across, turn. Fasten off. *(199 sts)*

Row 2: Join *(see Pattern Notes)* yellow in first st, ch 2, [sl st in next st, hdc in next st] across, turn. Fasten off.

Row 3: Join white in first st, [hdc in next st, sl st in next st] across, turn. Fasten off.

Rows 4–13: Working in color sequence of pink, white, green and white, ending with white, [rep rows 2 and 3 alternately] 5 times.

Row 14: With yellow, rep row 2.

Row 15: Rep row 3, **do not fasten off.**

Row 16: Ch 1, sc in each of first 2 sts, ch 4, sk next 3 sts, sc in next st, **turn**, sc in each of 4 chs just made, **turn**, working in front of ch-4 sp, sc in each of 3 sk sts on last row, *ch 4, sk next 3 unworked sts, sc in next st, **turn**, sc in each of 4 chs just made, **turn**, working in front of ch-4 sp, sc in each of 3 sk sts on last row, rep from * across to last st, sc in last st, **do not turn.** Fasten off.

Row 17: Rep row 3.

Rows 18–31: Rep rows 2–15.

Row 32: Working this row in **front lps** *(see Stitch Guide)* only, sl st in first st, [hdc in next st, sl st in next st] across, **turn.**

Row 33: Working this row in rem lps 2 rows below, sl st in first st, [hdc in next st, sl st in next st] across, **do not turn.** Fasten off.

Rows 34–47: Rep rows 2–15. At end of last row, **do not turn.** Fasten off at end of last row.

Row 48: Working this row in front lps only, join white in first st, [hdc in next st, sl st in next st] across, **turn.**

Row 49: Working this row in rem lps 2 rows below, sl st in first st, [hdc in next st, sl st in next st] across, **turn.** Fasten off.

Rows 50–63: Rep rows 2–15.

Rows 64 & 65: Rep rows 32 and 33.

Rows 66–79: Rep rows 2–15. At end of last row, **do not turn.** Fasten off at end of last row.

Rows 80 & 81: Rep rows 48 and 49.

Rows 82–95: Rep rows 2–15. At end of last row, **do not turn.** Fasten off at end of last row.

Row 96: Join white with sc in first st, sc in next st, ch 4, sk next 3 sts, sc in next st, **turn**, sc in each of 4 chs just made, **turn**, working in front of ch-4 sp, sc in each of 3 sk sts on last row, *ch 4, sk next 3 unworked sts, sc in next st, **turn**, sc in each of 4 chs just made, **turn**, working in front of ch-4 sp, sc in each of next 3 sk sts on last row, rep from * across to last st, sc in last st, **turn**. **Do not fasten off.**

Row 97: Ch 1, sl st in first st, [hdc in next st, sl st in next st] across, **turn**. Fasten off.

Rows 98–111: Rep rows 2–15. At end of last row, **do not turn**. Fasten off at end of last row.

Rows 112 & 113: Rep rows 48 and 49.

Rows 114–127: Rep rows 2–15.

Rows 128 & 129: Rep rows 32 and 33.

Rows 130–143: Rep rows 2–15. At end of last row, **do not turn**. Fasten off at end of last row.

Rows 144 & 145: Rep rows 48 and 49.

Rows 146–159: Rep rows 2–15.

Rows 160 & 161: Rep rows 32 and 33.

Rows 162–175: Rep rows 2–15.

Rows 176 & 177: Rep rows 16 and 3.

Rows 178–191: Rep rows 2–15. Fasten off at end of last row.

FRINGE

For **each Fringe**, cut 3 strands each white, green and pink each 14 inches long. Holding all strands tog, insert hook in end of specified row, draw fold through, draw all loose ends through fold including 6-inch ends at beg and end of each row, tighten. Trim ends.

Add Fringe to every 4th row across short ends of Afghan.

EMBROIDERY

Sections between white trim are embroidered by weaving yarn through **back bar of hdc** (*see close-up photo on page 216*).

With tapestry needle and light green worsted-weight yarn, embroider every other section according to Chart A.

With tapestry needle and light green worsted-weight yarn, embroider remaining sections according to Chart B. ■

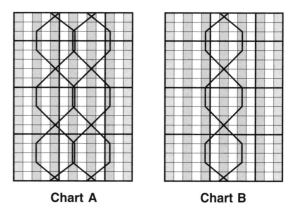

Chart A   Chart B

Note: Each square on charts equals 1 stitch.

Crocheting on Fabric

Crocheting lace onto fabric is a great way to add decorative elegance to everyday items in your home. The basic steps for creating this technique are simple and easy to follow.

The first thing you need to do is prepare the fabric by washing and pressing it. This pre-shrinks the fabric and avoids any warping of the finished crochet work.

Next, hem any raw edges by folding them under once or twice and tacking them in place with a basting stitch. For curved edges, **cut notches** (*see illustration*) to remove fullness when folding the edge under. The more delicate the fabric, the narrower the hem should be (about ¼ inch for medium-weight cottons, about ⅛ inch for lightweight cottons and a narrow, rolled 1/16 inch for sheers). Purchased items will usually have finished edges, eliminating this step.

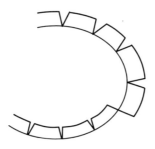

Cutting Notches on Fabric

To minimize the size of the hole made when working stitches into the fabric, the end of the crochet hook used should be small enough to easily go through the fabric and still catch the thread as you work.

For the foundation stitches, which are usually single crochet stitches, place a slip knot on the hook, hold the thread over the edge of the fabric, insert the hook through the front of the fabric at the base of the hem (do not catch the folded edge of the hem), yarn overand draw a loop up to the outer edge of the hemmed fabric, yarn over and draw through both loops on the hook. Continue working stitches, spacing them an even distance apart.

One method of spacing is to calculate the number of stitches per inch needed for the desired pattern. Mark the edge of fabric with pins at 1-inch intervals, and space the stitches per inch between the pins. Remove the pins when you're finished with the foundation stitches.

When working a specific number of stitches on the edge of square fabric, divide the total number by four and space that number across each quarter of the fabric edge. For round or oval edges, fold the fabric into quarters and place pins at each quarter point and space stitches between the pins.

Try these tips with your favorite lace patterns. You can create an almost endless variety of beautiful projects by adding the beauty of crochet to fabric pieces, like this lovely Zinnias Doily. It's a great project to practice some of the techniques discussed in this article, and when you're done, you'll have a beautiful floral piece to dress up your home.

ZINNIAS DOILY

SKILL LEVEL

INTERMEDIATE

FINISHED SIZE

14½ x 18 inches

MATERIALS

- Size 10 crochet cotton:
    350 yds each cream and spruce
    300 yds variegated yellow
- Size 7/1.65mm steel crochet hook or size needed to obtain gauge
- 1 yd beige linen fabric
- Sewing needle
- Coordinating sewing thread

GAUGE

Small Zinnia = 1³/16 inches in diameter

Take time to check gauge.

PATTERN NOTES

Weave in loose ends as work progresses.

Join rounds with a slip stitch as indicated
   unless otherwise stated.

SPECIAL STITCHES

Picot: [Sc, ch 3, sc] in indicated st.

Joining chain-6 (joining ch-6): Ch 3, remove
   hook from lp, insert hook from RS to WS in
   indicated ch-6 sp on previous motif, pick up
   dropped lp, draw through ch-6 sp, ch 3.

LINEN RECTANGLE
MAKE 4.
Cut 5 x 7-inch linen rectangle. On each edge, turn under 1/8 inch, then 1/4 inch. Hemstitch in place.

FIRST MOTIF
Rnd 1: Attach cream with a sl st approximately 1/4 inch from edge at right-hand corner of either longer edge of any linen rectangle, ch 1, *3 sc in corner, 51 sc evenly sp across to next corner, 3 sc in corner, 31 sc evenly sp across to next corner, rep from * around, **join** (see Pattern Notes) in beg sc.

Rnd 2: Ch 1, sc in same st as joining, *ch 5, sk next corner sc, sc in 3rd corner sc, ch 3, sk next sc, sc in next sc, [ch 5, sk next 2 sc, sc in next sc, ch 3, sk next sc, sc in next sc] rep across to first sc of next 3-sc corner group, rep from * around, ch 3, join in beg sc.

Rnd 3: Sl st in first ch of first ch-5 sp, ch 1, beg in same sp, *(**picot**—see Special Stitches, ch 6, picot) in corner sp, [ch 6, picot in next ch-5 sp] across to last ch-5 sp before next corner ch-5 sp**, ch 6, rep from * around, ending last rep at **, ch 3, dc in beg sc to form last ch-6 sp.

Rnd 4: Ch 1, picot in sp just formed, *ch 6, (picot, ch 6, picot) in corner ch-6 sp, [ch 6, picot in next ch-6 sp] rep across to last ch-6 sp before next corner ch-6 sp, rep from * around, ch 3, dc in beg sc to form last ch-6 sp, fasten off.

Rnd 5: With RS facing, attach variegated yellow with sl st in top of dc just made, ch 1, picot in sp just made, ch 6, picot in next ch-6 sp, *ch 6, (picot, ch 6, picot) in corner ch-6 sp, [ch 6, picot in next ch-6 sp] across to last ch-6 sp before next corner ch-6 sp, rep from * around, ch 3, dc in beg sc to form last ch-6 sp, fasten off.

Rnd 6: With RS facing, attach cream with sl st in first corner ch-6 sp after joining st, beg in same sp, *(picot, ch 6, picot) in corner ch-6 sp, [ch 6, picot in next ch-6 sp] across to last ch-6 sp before next corner ch-6 sp, ch 6, rep from * around, join in beg sc, fasten off.

2ND MOTIF
Rnds 1–5: Rep rnds 1–5 of First Motif.

Rnd 6: With RS facing, attach cream with sl st in first corner ch-6 sp after joining st, picot in same sp, **joining ch-6** (see Special Stitches) to corresponding corner ch-6 sp on previous Motif, picot in same sp as last picot made, [joining ch-6 to next ch-6 sp on previous Motif, picot in next ch-6 sp on working Motif] across to last ch-6 sp on working Motif before next corner ch-6 sp, joining ch-6 to last ch-6 sp on previous Motif before corner ch-6 sp, picot in corner ch-6 sp on working Motif, joining ch-6 to corner ch-6 sp on previous Motif, picot in same corner ch-6 sp on working Motif as last picot made (1 side joined), continue around as for rnd 6 of First Motif.

REMAINING 2 MOTIFS
Rnds 1–6: Rep rnds 1–6 of 2nd Motif, joining on as many sides as necessary to form a rectangle of 2 rows of 2 Motifs each.

BORDER
Rnd 1: With RS facing, attach cream with sl st in ch-6 sp at upper right corner, (picot, ch 6, picot) in same sp, *[ch 6, picot in next ch-6 sp] 14 times*, ch 6, picot in joining ch-6, rep from * to *, ch 6, (picot, ch 6, picot) in corner ch-6 sp, **[ch 6, picot in next ch-6 sp] 10 times**, ch 6, (picot, ch 6, picot) in joining ch-6, rep from ** to **, ch 6, (picot, ch 6, picot) in corner ch-6 sp, rep from * around, ch 6, join in beg sc, fasten off.

Rnd 2: With RS facing, attach spruce with sl st in ch-6 sp at upper right corner, ch 1, *(picot, ch 6, picot) in corner ch-6 sp, ch 6, [picot in next ch-6 sp, ch 6] across to next corner ch-6 sp, rep from * around, join in beg sc, fasten off.

Rnd 3: With RS facing, attach cream with sl st in any ch-6 sp, ch 1, sc in same sp, *ch 2, [dc, ch 3, hdc in top of last dc made, dc] in next picot, ch 2**, sc in next ch-6 sp, rep from * around, ending last rep at **, join in beg sc, fasten off.

SMALL ZINNIA
MAKE 4.

Rnd 1: With variegated yellow, ch 2, 6 sc in 2nd ch from hook, **join** (*see Pattern Notes*) in beg sc. (*6 sc*)

Rnd 2: Ch 1, sc in same st as joining, ch 2, [sc in next sc, ch 2] around, join in beg sc. (*6 ch-2 sps*)

Rnd 3: [Sl st, ch 2, 3 hdc, ch 2, sl st] in each ch-2 sp around, **do not join.** (*6 petals*)

Rnd 4: Working behind petals of last rnd, sc in beg sc of rnd 2, ch 3, [sc in next unworked sc of rnd 2, ch 3] around, join in beg sc. (*6 ch-3 sps*)

Rnd 5: [{Sl st, ch 3, 2 dc, ch 3} twice, sl st] in each ch-3 sp around, fasten off. (*12 petals*)

LARGE ZINNIA

Rnds 1 & 2: Rep rnds 1 and 2 of Small Zinnia.

Rnd 3: (Sl st, ch 3, 3 dc, ch 3, sl st) in each ch-2 sp around, **do not join.** (*6 petals*)

Rnd 4: Rep rnd 4 of Small Zinnia.

Rnd 5: ({Sl st, ch 4, 2 tr, ch 4} twice, sl st) in each ch-3 sp around, do not join. (*12 petals*)

Rnd 6: Working behind petals of last rnd, sc in beg sc of rnd 4, ch 4, [sc in next unworked sc of rnd 4, ch 4] around, join in beg sc. (*6 ch-4 sps*)

Rnd 7: ({Sl st, ch 4, 3 tr, ch 4} twice, sl st) in each ch-4 sp around, do not join. (*12 petals*)

Rnd 8: Working behind petals of last rnd, sc in beg sc of rnd 6, ch 5, [sc in next unworked sc of rnd 6, ch 5] around, join in beg sc. (*6 ch-5 sps*)

Rnd 9: ({Sl st, ch 5, 3 dtr, ch 5} twice, sl st) in each ch-5 sp, do not join. (*12 petals*)

Rnd 10: Working behind petals of last rnd, sc in beg sc of rnd 8, ch 5, [sc in next unworked sc of rnd 8, ch 5] around, join in beg sc, fasten off.

LARGE LEAF
MAKE 6.

With spruce, ch 8, 2 sc in 2nd ch from hook, *dc in next ch, tr in next ch, 2 tr in next ch, tr in next ch, dc in next ch*, 3 sc in last ch, working on opposite side of foundation ch, rep from * to *, sc in same ch as beg sc, join in beg sc, sl st in center of any unworked ch-5 on rnd 10 of Large Zinnia.

LARGE STEM
MAKE 4.

With spruce, ch 66, sl st in 2nd ch from hook and in each rem ch across, fasten off.

SMALL STEM
MAKE 4.

With spruce, ch 41, sl st in 2nd ch from hook and in each rem ch across, fasten off.

LEAF PAIR
MAKE 8.

With spruce, ch 7, *sc in 2nd ch from hook, dc in next ch, 2 dc in next ch, dc in next ch, sc in next ch*, sl st in next ch, ch 6, rep from * to *, sl st at base of first leaf, fasten off.

SMALL LEAF
MAKE 20.

With spruce, ch 6, sc in 2nd ch from hook, dc in next ch, 2 dc in next ch, dc in next ch, sc in next ch, fasten off.

FINISHING

Press doily. With sewing needle and thread, using photo as a guide, sew Zinnias, Stems and Leaves to Doily. ■

Cross-Stitch on Crochet

Cross-stitch is a style of embroidery that is the perfect accompaniment to crochet. The designs that can be created using this technique range from simple geometrics to florals to elaborate scenes that depict stories.

Cross-stitch embroidery on crochet is done much the same way as counted cross-stitch on a woven-thread background. The rows of crochet stitches form a gridlike fabric that can be used to anchor the diagonal straight stitches used to create cross-stitch designs. Single crochet is best suited for the foundation fabric because of the almost square symmetry of the stitch.

The palette of colorful yarns, threads and flosses available today allows us to be as elaborate as our imagination permits. Usually, same or similar fibers are used to embellish a crochet piece. For example, worsted-weight yarn cross-stitches are worked on worsted yarn crochet. When combining different types of fibers, such as floss on cotton thread or perle cotton on yarn, experiment with a swatch of the two together before starting the project to become familiar with how to handle the different textures together.

The tool needed to work cross-stitch on crochet is simple—just a tapestry needle in the correct size needed for the type of yarn or thread you are using. Needle sizes 16 to 18 are best for worsted- and sport-weight yarns. Smaller needle sizes like 22 to 24 work well with cotton threads and flosses.

It is important to keep an even tension on the embroidery yarn or thread as you work to prevent warping and other distortions in the crochet fabric. The stitches should blend and lay smoothly over the surface of the crochet work. Stitches that have been pulled too tightly will make unsightly holes in the finished piece. If they are too loose, the piece can become snagged more easily and damage your beautiful handiwork.

In working cross-stitches, it is important to make sure that the direction of the stitching is done the same throughout for a consistent look to your stitch work. In the illustration below, you'll see that, in the correct version, the stitches are all crossed in the same direction. In the incorrect version, the stitches vary in the directions in which they are crossed.

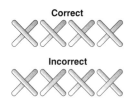

It is best to work with a length of yarn or thread that is no more than 18 inches long. Longer lengths are difficult to handle and tend to tangle and knot up as they are pulled through the work. Also, as you work, the movement of the stitching can make the strand overtwist. It is best to stop periodically, release the strand and allow it to unwind.

Cross-stitches can be worked in two ways. As shown in the illustrations below, the first half (the bottom stitch) of the crosses can be stitched in a row, and then the second half (the top stitch) of the crosses can be worked on the return pass for the same row. This method works well when you have a group of stitches to work using the same color of yarn or thread.

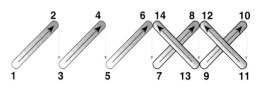

Cross-stitches can also be completed one at a time. This method works best when the stitches of the design are scattered over the piece.

To begin, using the "knotless" method, leaving about a 2-inch end on the wrong side of the work, bring the strand through to the front of the crochet piece. Hold the 2-inch end along the back of the piece and work over it as you make the first several cross-stitches. This secures and hides the end at the same time. Trim away the excess end. When the last stitch is made, bring the strand to the wrong side of the work and weave it through the back of several stitches with a tapestry needle before cutting the excess end.

For a durable anchoring method on items that may receive more wear and tear, make one or two tiny tacking stitches as you weave the strand through the back of the crochet stitches when you begin and also when you end.

For crocheters who are not familiar with working cross-stitch on crochet, here is a pretty and practical pot-holder pattern that will let you practice the technique and create a lovely gift at the same time. Discover how much fun doing cross-stitch on crochet can be. It will open up a whole new world of decorative possibilities in your crochet projects.

HEART POT HOLDER

SKILL LEVEL
■■□□
EASY

FINISHED SIZE
8¾ inches x 9½ inches

MATERIALS
- Medium (worsted) weight cotton yarn: **4 MEDIUM**
  - 150 yds white
  - 75 yds green
  - 15 yds yellow
  - 11 yds rose pink
- Size G/6/4mm crochet hook or size needed to obtain gauge
- Tapestry needle

GAUGE
4 sc = 1 inch; 4 sc rows = 1 inch

PATTERN NOTE
Join rounds with slip stitch as indicated unless otherwise stated.

SIDE
MAKE 2.

Row 1: With white, ch 30, sc in 2nd ch from hook and in each ch across, turn. *(29 sc)*

Rows 2–32: Ch 1, sc in each st across, turn. At end of last row, fasten off.

CROSS-STITCHING

For Front, with tapestry needle, work **cross-stitch** *(see illustration)* design on 1 Side according to Cross-Stitch Chart.

EDGING

Rnd 1: Hold Sides tog, with Front facing. Working through both thicknesses, join green with sc in first st on row 32, sc in each st across top of Pot Holder, *working in ends of rows along side, 2 sc in end of first row, sc in end of each of next 30 rows, 2 sc in end of last row**, working in rem lps on opposite side of beg ch on row 1, sc in each ch across, rep from * once, ending rep at **, **join** *(see Pattern Note)* in first sc, fasten off. *(126 sc)*

Rnd 2: Join yellow with sc in first st, sc in each st around, working 3 sc in each corner, join in first sc. Fasten off. *(134 sc)*

Rnd 3: Sk first st, join green with sc in next st, (ch 1, sc) in same st as join, sk next st, *(sc, ch 1, sc) in next st, sk next st, rep from * 5 times, sc in next st, for **hanger**, ch 8, sl st in **left bar** *(see illustration)* of last sc made, sc in same st, [sk next st, (sc, ch 1, sc) in next st] around, join in first sc. Fasten off.

Left Bar of Single Crochet

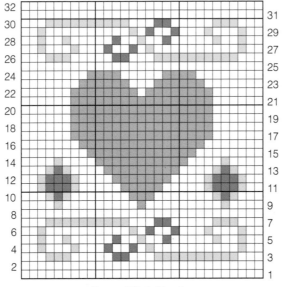

Cross-Stitch Chart

COLOR KEY
- Pink
- Yellow
- Green

From Batt to Beautiful

The wide array of exotic fibers available on the market today offers a wonderland of experiences for the fiber enthusiast. Silk, wool, alpaca, camel and mohair are just a few in the cornucopia of choices. Not only can you find these fibers already spun, plied and labeled for your convenience, but you can also find these fibers available in unspun form. Using the fibers in their unspun form can make it very affordable to crochet and knit with exotic fibers to create hats, scarves, sweaters and more.

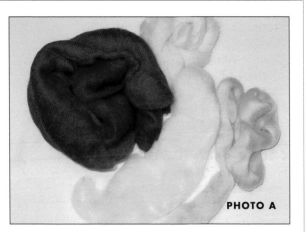

PHOTO A

Working with these fibers in unspun form comes with a bit of a learning curve, but it is well worth the experience. It really gives you a great sense of accomplishment because you are involved with the entire process from creating your fiber to making your project.

First, let's explain what unspun means. When you purchase yarn, you are purchasing fibers that have been spun or twisted into strands, which are then usually plied together with other spun strands to form a yarn or thread. Conversely, unspun fibers are those that have not yet gone through the spinning and plying process. Once you know how to handle and work with these fibers, you can use them instead of yarn or thread in a crochet or knit project. You can also use unspun fibers and a yarn or thread of a contrasting color. Some combinations of thread and unspun fiber are simply beautiful.

After the sheep have been sheared, the wool is washed and combed to remove the debris commonly referred to as "VM" or vegetable matter. The remaining fiber is then run through a carding process and then formed into batts, roving or "top."

Top is a long piece, approximately 2–4 inches in diameter. It requires a complex process that involves extensive combing and drawing of the wool to keep the individual fibers parallel. It is shown in the far right of Photo A.

Roving is also a long piece, approximately 2–4 inches in diameter, with the fibers lying in random directions. It is shown in the center of Photo A.

Batts are large pieces of roving laid out flat. As with roving, the fibers lay in random directions. The initial shape is thinner in depth than roving and can be quite long and wide, like a quilt batt. It is shown in the top left of Photo A.

A batt was used for the instructions in this article, but you would use the same process for roving or top. The fiber used is carded Corridale Cross from DyakCraft (formerly known as Grafton Fibers).

The first step in creating unspun fiber from a batt is to separate the fiber into a manageable strip. Open the batt and gently pull away a strip about 2 inches wide from one end (*see Photo B*). If you are using roving, pull off a hank about 3–4 feet in length and separate the hank into 1-inch-wide strips.

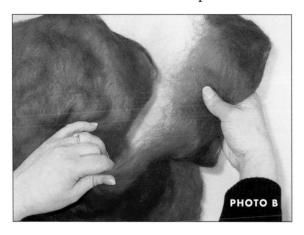

PHOTO B

Before drafting the wool with which you will crochet or knit, you need to determine staple-fiber length and how far to pull the fibers. The staple fiber is the length of the hair, which is important because the individual hairs hold on to each other by friction. You can only draft or pull the fiber to half the length of the staple fiber; pulling further causes the fiber to pull apart as there is not enough friction between the hairs to hold it together. Some fibers will hold together if drafted slightly longer; however, a good rule of thumb to remember is to draft only half the length of the staple.

Find the staple length by gently pulling a thin strand from the fiber. Now place that thin fiber strand between the thumb and forefinger of one hand and gently pull the strand with the opposite thumb and forefinger until you have only a few strands in your fingers that are a single length. Holding the length between the thumb and forefinger of each hand, you can see the length of the staple fiber (see Photo C). In this case the staple fiber is approximately 4 inches long, which means that I can only pull the fiber half that length, or 2 inches, before it falls apart.

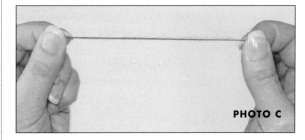

PHOTO C

Drafting the fiber takes a bit of practice, but it will go rather quickly for you after you get the feel of it. Taking the strip you separated from the batt, gently hold the fiber in your nondominant hand with the end you are going to pull from between your thumb and forefinger. Now, using the thumb and forefinger of your dominant hand, pull the tip of the strand out and away from the strip in light, short strokes making sure that you are only drafting the fiber half the length of the staple. In this instance, I can

pull about 2 inches of fiber before stopping and repositioning my hands and fingers to pull again.

You will be using a pulling action, but do not yank the fiber and do not hold the fiber with too much pressure. Not only will this result in hanks of fiber coming away from the source, it will also hurt your fingers and hands. Always use gentle pressure and draft using a smooth, easy rhythm.

The thickness of the draft depends on the amount of fiber you hold between your thumb and forefinger to draft out from the strip. As you can see in Photo D, holding only a narrow section of fiber, about ¼ inch in width, in my right hand, and the fiber coming from the source in my left hand is forming a nice, thin triangle coming out from the strip and drafting into a nice and even strand that I can work with. I like to pull my fiber from about ¼ inch in width to as fine as slightly less than ⅛ inch in width (see Photo D). Continue to draft the fiber until you come to the end of your strip, allowing it to pool in a loose pile.

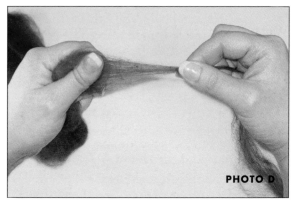

PHOTO D

Once you have some fiber drafted, you need to wind it so that you can crochet or knit with it. Unspun wool is extremely difficult to wind onto a wool winder, since it can fall apart as you wind it. Instead, try using a smooth, coated mailing tube that is about 6 inches in length and about 2 inches in diameter. Holding the tube, place the end of the fiber onto the tube and hold it there with your thumb. Tightening up very gently, wrap the drafted fiber around the tube in slightly crisscross wraps, allowing the fiber to flow through your fingers and onto the tube (*see Photo E*).

This gentle tension on the fiber allows it to wrap around the tube without felting or adhering to itself too much. Do not pull hard or tighten up too much or the fiber will pull apart. Wind the fiber in the center of the tube about 3 inches wide. Do not wind up and down the entire length of the tube or the fiber will adhere to itself. Mark your tube with a permanent marker if you need to and stay within the lines.

When you get to the end of the drafted strand that you have wrapped, leave a tail of about 4–6 inches. Draft another strand, and then fuse the end of the new strand to the tail on the tube by laying the strands in the palm of your hand with their lengths overlapping each other about 2–3 inches. Place the palm of your opposite hand over the strands and rub the strands together in one direction only. Do not rub back in the opposite direction or you will untwist the fuse. You can also apply a little bit of moisture to the strands if you choose. Wind this strand onto your tube and continue on with drafting.

Crocheting or knitting with your unspun wool fiber is, relatively speaking, the same as working with yarn. Crocheting with unspun wool is usually much easier than knitting because you can normally apply tension very loosely over one finger when crocheting

as long as you don't pull on the fiber (*see Photo F*).

Remember that the fiber has not been spun or twisted and is very delicate. If you are having difficulty, try holding the fiber in your hand and wrapping it around the hook without tensioning the fiber around or over your finger.

CRANBERRY CLOCHE

SKILL LEVEL
◼◼◻◻
EASY

FINISHED SIZES
Instructions given fit woman's size small/ medium; changes for large/X-large are in [ ].

FINISHED MEASUREMENT
Circumference: 18½ inches (*small/medium*) [20¼ inches (*large/X-large*)]

MATERIALS
- 100 percent wool or wool/blend roving: 4 oz/200 yds/113g burgundy
- Sizes F/5/3.75mm and H/8/5mm crochet hooks or size needed to obtain gauge
- 6-inch coated mailing tube, 2–3 inches in diameter
- Stitch markers

GAUGE
Size H hook: 15 sc = 4 inches; 19 sc rows = 4 inches

PATTERN NOTES

Draft wool to ⅛–¼-inch thickness comparable to light worsted–weight yarn and wind onto center section of coated mailing tube.

If wool seems to be too thick, you can thin the wool as you crochet with it.

Join with slip stitch as indicated unless otherwise stated.

CLOCHE
CROWN

Rnd 1: With size H hook, ch 3, **join** (see Pattern Notes) in first ch to form ring, ch 1, 6 sc in ring, **do not join rnds,** mark first st of each rnd. (6 sc)

Rnd 2: 2 sc in each st around. (12 sc)

Rnd 3: [Sc in next st, 2 sc in next st] around. (18 sc)

Rnd 4: [Sc in each of next 2 sts, 2 sc in next st] around. (24 sc)

Rnd 5: [Sc in each of next 3 sts, 2 sc in next st] around. (30 sc)

Rnd 6: [Sc in each of next 4 sts, 2 sc in next st] around. (36 sc)

Rnd 7: Ch 1, sc in each st around.

Rnd 8: [Sc in each of next 5 sts, 2 sc in next st] around. (42 sc)

Rnd 9: Ch 1, sc in each st around.

Rnd 10: [Sc in each of next 6 sts, 2 sc in next st] around. (48 sc)

Rnd 11: Sc in each st around.

Rnd 12: [Sc in each of next 7 sts, 2 sc in next st] around. (54 sc)

Rnd 13: Sc in each st around.

Rnd 14: [Sc in each of next 8 sts, 2 sc in next st] around. (60 sc)

Rnd 15: Sc in each st around.

Rnd 16: [Sc in each of next 9 sts, 2 sc in next st] around. (66 sc)

Rnd 17: Sc in each st around.

LARGE/X-LARGE SIZE ONLY

Rnd [18]: [Sc in each of next [10] sts, 2 sc in next st] around. ([72] sc)

BOTH SIZES

Rnd 18 [19]: Sc in each st around.

BODY

Rnd 1: [(Sc, dc) in next st, sk next st] around.

Rnd 2: [(Sc, dc) in next sc, sk next dc] around.

Next rnds: Rep rnd 2 until Cloche measures 7–7½ [8½–9] inches from beg.

LOWER EDGE

Rnd 1: Sc in each st around. (66 [72] sc)

Rnd 2: With size F hook, ch 3, dc in each st around.

Rnd 3: *Fpdc (see Stitch Guide) around next st, bpdc (see Stitch Guide) around next st, rep from * around.

Rnds 4 & 5: Rep rnd 3. At end of last rnd, fasten off. ■

Crocheting With Thrums & Locks

Crocheting bits of fiber known as thrums and locks into your fashions and accessories can give them a unique look and luxurious pile for added warmth. But what, exactly, are thrums and locks, and where do they come from?

Originally a bit of unspun wool that workers were allowed to take home from the mill or spinner's basket, thrum means a piece of waste wool. The use of thrums is thought to have originated in European countries, especially Scandinavian areas, (although evidence of this technique is also seen in Peru and Tibet), where peasants stuffed raw wool into knits for added warmth. Settlers brought this technique with them to North America. Skiers, hikers and fishermen have long used the extra warmth of thrums.

Thrum knitting works these pieces or bits into the fabric of jackets, vests, mittens, socks or slippers as an easy way of forming a soft, plush pile for cozy warmth in the garment. This technique is easily applied to crochet, using twisted lengths (thrums) of carded unspun fiber (roving). The bit of roving forms a V on the outside, while the ends of the thrum inside the garment form a fluffy inner lining that felts with wear.

FIBERS FOR THRUMS & LOCKS

When first working with thrums, Corriedale is one of the friendliest fibers to use. Some other excellent fibers for thrums include bluefaced Leicester, merino and mohair. Almost any soft, fine to medium wool would be ideal. Do not use superwash as it tends to fall apart and will not felt. You can get absolutely decadent results using alpaca, llama, camel down, cashmere, yak or qiviut.

Fiber blends or novelty rovings, such as Coopworth/mohair with Angelina® (a glittery polyester and metal fiber), can create beautiful effects. A merino/silk blend can produce wonderful results. However, stay away from fibers with noil or neps. Noil and neps are little nubby bits of fiber that tend to have a nasty habit of pilling off when used for thrums.

Individual staple length (hair length) is not important. Remember, our ancestors used whatever they took home from the mill, which in most cases, was small bits and pieces. Combed together, these small bits became workable lengths. Back in the day, thrums were normally short strands of fiber; however, now we create cute little bow ties with the fiber.

Locks are curls from mohair goats, or from Suri alpaca or sheep (such as Wensleydale) that can be dyed and used not only as decorative embellishments, but also as thrums. When used as thrums, leave them as a lock—do not create a bow tie. Who wants to lose those cute little curls? The curls hang on the inside of the work and eventually felt into a beautiful wavy fabric inside your garment.

MAKING A THRUM

Begin with a workable piece of roving about 18 inches or so in length. Never cut the roving; hank it off by placing your hands several inches apart and pulling. Split the piece in half lengthwise (see Photo A).

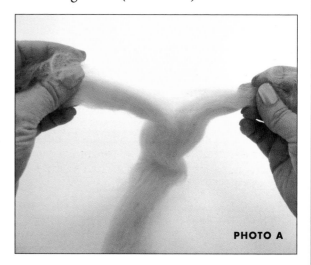

PHOTO A

Now split each piece until the strips are about ½ inch in width.

Lay a thinned section of roving along a ruler. Place thumb and forefinger of your left hand at the 7-inch mark, and thumb and forefinger of your right hand about 3 inches up, and pull piece in half (see Photo B).

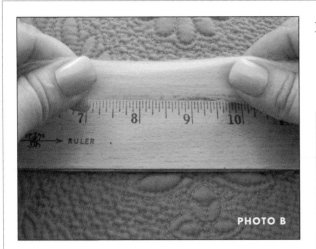

PHOTO B

Your two pieces will be about 8½–9 inches in length. You do not want them shorter than 8 inches.

Split the piece lengthwise into strips of about ⅛ inch in thickness for crocheting with worsted weight yarn, or the diameter of a (U.S.) crochet hook size G/6/4mm to H/8/5mm. You do not want the piece too thick, because once the thrum is formed, it will be twice the thickness at the center. For thinner yarn, make thinner thrums; for thicker yarn, make thicker thrums.

Note: *If your piece of roving is just slightly shorter than 8–8½ inches, place thumb and forefinger of each hand about 1 inch in from each end. Pull very gently, carefully stretching the piece.*

Bring each end of the thrum toward the middle of the piece, overlapping the ends slightly (see *Photo C*).

PHOTO C

Roll thrum between your thumb and forefinger at the center point. You now have a cute little bow tie. You want your finished bow tie to be about 3¾–4 inches in length (see *Photo D*).

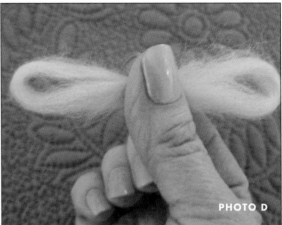

PHOTO D

Make a good-size pile of thrums before beginning your project, placing them in a paper bag, box or a lined basket.

CROCHETING WITH THRUMS

Insert hook into "V" of next single crochet two rows/rounds below (see *Illustration and Photo E*).

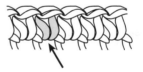

"V" of Single Crochet

PHOTO E

Loop thrum in half over hook and pull through stitch *(see Photo F)*.

You now have two loops on the hook (yarn loop and thrum) *(see Photo G)*.

Insert hook into both loops of next stitch to be worked in current row (stitch behind thrum) *(see Photo H)*.

Bring loops of thrum up toward top of work, yarn over hook bringing yarn across the back of the thrum and pull through the stitch *(see Photo I)*.

You now have three loops on the hook (yarn loop, thrum, yarn loop) *(see Photo J)*.

Keeping loops of thrum toward top of work and bent slightly left, yarn over hook, again bringing yarn across the back of the thrum and pull loop through all three loops on hook in the order they are on the hook (yarn loop, thrum, yarn loop) *(see Photo K)*.

This forms the decorative "V" with the thrum *(see Photo L)*.

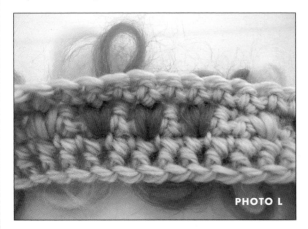

Pull down on the thrum at the back of the work to secure.

CROCHETING WITH LOCKS

Crocheting with locks is the same as thrums, however, in most cases, you will want the locks to be on the right side of the work as an embellishment, thereby crocheting them into the wrong side of the work. Preparing the locks is different because although you thin the locks apart, you do not form them into bow ties. You want the curly waves to remain *(see Photo M)*.

Once you have separated your locks into the preferred width, crochet them into your project the same as you would a thrum.

THRUMMED HAT & GAUNTLETS

SKILL LEVEL
INTERMEDIATE

FINISHED SIZES
Hat: Instructions given fit 19-inch head *(small/medium)*; changes for 22-inch head *(large/X-large)* are in [ ].
Gauntlets: Instructions given fit hands 7 inches long *(small)*; changes for 8¼ inches *(medium)* and 9½ inches *(large)* are in [ ].

MATERIALS
- Brown Sheep Co. Nature Spun medium (worsted) weight wool yarn (3½ oz/245 yds/100g per ball): 2 balls #N04 blue knight
- Wool roving:
  2 oz fuchsia
  1 oz each pink and dark mauve
- Mohair locks:
  1 oz periwinkle
- Sizes H/8/5mm and I/9/5.5mm crochet hooks or sizes needed to obtain gauge
- Tapestry needle
- Stitch markers
- Row counter *(optional)*

GAUGE WITHOUT THRUMS

Size H hook: 18 sts = 4 inches; 21 rows = 4 inches

Size I hook: 15 sts = 4 inches; 20 sc rows = 4 inches

PATTERN NOTES

Make thrums from wool roving per instructions on pages 232 and 233, and set aside.

Separate locks into workable pieces about ⅛-inch in thickness and set them aside for Brim.

Work in continuous rounds, do not turn or join unless otherwise stated.

Join rnds with sl st as indicated unless otherwise stated.

Mark first stitch of each round.

HAT
THRUM COLOR SEQUENCE

Rnd 4: [Fuchsia, pink, fuchsia, dark mauve] around.

Rnd 8: [Fuchsia, dark mauve, fuchsia, pink] around.

BODY

Rnd 1: With size I hook and blue knight, ch 73 [85], working in **back bar of ch** (*see illustration*), sc in 2nd ch from hook and in each rem ch around, being careful not to twist ch, **join** (*see Pattern Notes*) in beg sc. (*72 [84] sc*)

Back Bar of Chain

Rnds 2 & 3: Sc in each st around, **do not join** (*see Pattern Notes*).

Rnd 4: [Insert hook in **"V" of sc** (*see illustration*) 2 rnds below and work a thrum, sc in each of next 2 sc] around alternating colors of thrums per Color Sequence.

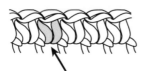

"V" of Single Crochet

Rnds 5–7: Sc in each st around.

Rnd 8: [Insert hook in "V" of sc 2 rnds below and work a thrum, sc in each of next 2 sts] around, alternating colors of thrums per Color Sequence.

Rnds 9–11: Sc in each st around.

Next rnds: Rep rnds 4–11 consecutively until Hat measures 5 [6] inches from beg, ending with an even-numbered rnd and dec 0 [4] sts on last rnd by working **sc dec** (*see Stitch Guide*) in next 2 sts. (*72 [81] sts*)

CROWN

Next rnd: *Sc in each of next 7 [8] sts, sc dec in next 2 sts, rep from * around. (*64 [72] sc*)

Next rnd: Sc in each st around.

Next rnds: Rep last 2 rnds alternately, working 1 less sc between each sc dec and continue to work thrums on appropriate thrum rnds until you have 8 sts.

Last rnd: [Sc in next sc, thrum in next st 2 rnds below] around. Leaving long end, fasten off.

Weave long end through top of sts, pull to close. Secure end.

FOLD-UP BRIM

Rnd 1: With RS of Hat facing, working in starting ch on opposite side of rnd 1 on Body and with size H hook, join blue knight with sc in first ch, sc in each ch around, **do not join**. (*72 [84] sc*)

Rnd 2: Sc in each st around.

Rnd 3: [Sc in each of next 2 sts, insert hook in "V" of sc 2 rnds below and work lock] around.

Rnds 4 & 5: Sc in each st around.

Rnd 6: Sc in next st, [insert hook in "V" of next st 2 rnds below, work lock, sc in each of next 2 sts] around to last 2 sts, insert hook in "V" of next st, 2 rnds below and work lock, sc in last st.

Rnds 7 & 8: Sc in each st around.

Rnds 9–11: Rep rnds 3–5. At end of last rnd, fasten off.

Fold Brim up and tack to Body 4 times evenly sp around.

Fluff up locks around Brim.

GAUNTLET
MAKE 2.
THRUM COLOR SEQUENCE

Rnd 3: [Fuchsia, pink] around.

Rnd 7: [Fuchsia, dark mauve] around.

CUFF

Row 1: With size H hook and blue knight, ch 9, working in **back lps** *(see Stitch Guide)*, sl st in 2nd ch from hook and in each rem ch across, turn. *(8 sl sts)*

Row 2: Working in back lps, ch 1, sl st in each st across, turn.

Next rows: Rep row 2 until piece measures 6 [7¼, 8½] inches from beg.

HAND

Rnd 1: Working in ends of rows on Cuff, ch 1, evenly sp 30 [36, 42] sc across, **join** *(see Pattern Notes)* in beg sc to form circle.

Rnd 2: Sc in each st around, **do not join** *(see Pattern Notes)*.

Rnd 3: [Insert hook in **"V" of sc** *(see illustration on page 237)* 2 rnds below and work a thrum, sc in each of next 2 sc] around alternating colors of thrums per Color Sequence.

Rnds 4–6: Sc in each st around.

Rnd 7: [Insert hook in "V" of sc 2 rnds below and work a thrum, sc in each of next 2 sts] around, alternating colors of thrums per Color Sequence.

Rnds 8–10: Sc in each st around.

Rnds 11–14: Rep rnds 3–6.

Next rnds: With size I hook, rep rnds 7–10.

Next rnds: Rep rnds 3–6. At end of last rnd, fasten off.

Sew first and last rows of Cuff tog. ■

Putting on the Dog

Have you ever had a special dog in your life that had a beautiful, downy-soft coat, and you thought to yourself, *This would make some incredible yarn!* With a little know-how and understanding of pet-hair fibers, it's easy to create your own unique blend of pet-hair yarn from the fur of a beloved friend.

WHY PET HAIR?

First, it's not practical for most people to keep traditional fiber animals like sheep or llamas, but it is practical to have a dog that, in addition to loving companionship, will provide you with a ready source of fiber to spin. Second, long after a beloved friend is no longer here, a knitter or crocheter will have a pair of cozy socks or a cute, fuzzy hat as a memento.

A special canine companion posing with some socks created with her hair.

DOESN'T IT SMELL?

While some dogs smell more "doggy" than others, once the yarn has been washed it usually doesn't have a noticeable smell. There are exceptions, however. Hair from a wolf-dog hybrid will usually reek, even after multiple washings.

WHAT KINDS OF PET HAIR CAN YOU SPIN?

You can spin almost any hair as long as the hairs are at least 1½ inches long. Most dogs are double-coated with stiff, coarse guard hairs outside and a soft, downy undercoat next to the skin. For dogs, a slicker brush works well to collect the undercoat without getting a lot of the guard hairs too. Some excellent favorite breeds to spin are sheltie, husky and Samoyed. You can also spin hair from breeds without a double coat, such as poodle and Afghan hound. Longhair cats work well too.

HOW DO YOU TURN THE HAIR INTO YARN?

There are a number of steps involved in processing hair into yarn.

1. COLLECT THE HAIR

Naturally shed hair is best. If you brush your dog, collect the hair from the brush and keep it in a bag. Using clipped hair is not recommended. Hair clipped from double-coated breeds will have a lot of guard hairs in it that will have to be picked out.

Some state and federal laws prohibit processing, buying or selling anything made from domestic cat or dog. These laws are designed to prohibit the killing of pets for their flesh or pelt. However, the wording of some laws is broad enough to include items made from shed or clipped hair. It's a good idea to check the dog- and cat-protection laws in your area, especially if you plan to spin pet hair for other people either privately or commercially.

2. PICK THE CARD

"Picking" the fiber is sorting through the hair to separate the usable from the unusable. The three-bag method works well for most. Begin with three paper grocery bags: one for the collected hair, one for the guard hairs, twigs, matted clumps, etc. that get picked out, and a third bag to hold the hair for spinning.

"Carding" uses a pair of paddles with rows of small, bent-wire teeth to comb the hair so that all the hairs run parallel to each other. Sometimes the picking process will make the hair fluffy enough that it doesn't need carding. If you want to blend the pet hair with another fiber, like wool, to modify the properties of the resulting yarn, you would need to card the different fibers together.

The "picking" process to clean a dog's brushed and collected fur of debris allows her to still enjoy one of her favorite pastimes— playing in the leaves!

3. SPIN

Spinning twists the hairs together to form a ply (single strand). Two common spinning tools are the drop spindle and the spinning wheel. A drop spindle has a weight at one end of the shaft. You set the spindle turning in the same way that you would spin a top. A spinning wheel has a foot treadle to keep the wheel turning continuously. With both tools, it's the rotation that supplies the twist.

Two things control the thickness of the yarn: the amount of hair twisted into an individual ply and the number of plies in your final yarn. A single ply will coil back on itself and is very difficult to work with. You generally need at least two plies to make a workable yarn. You make yarn by spinning two or more plies together, in an opposite direction from which they were originally spun. For example, if your individual plies were spun clockwise, when you ply them together to make yarn you would spin the spindle or wheel counterclockwise.

4. WASH, SET & DRY

Wind the plied yarn into a hank by wrapping the yarn around and around, hand to elbow, the way you might coil a long extension cord or phone cable. Tie the hank loosely in about four places with lengths of string or other yarn to keep the hank from getting tangles.

Submerge the hank in very warm, soapy water. Add a healthy amount of an inexpensive shampoo directly to the water for most house-pet hair yarns. If the hair is particularly dirty, or if it's from an oily-coated breed of animal, you can use grease-cutting dish soap. Don't agitate the yarn or it might felt. Just let it soak for 10–15 minutes, and then drain. If the water was very dirty, repeat the soaking process.

Rinse the hank by submerging it in clean water that is at least as hot as the water you soaked it in. Continue the submerge-and-drain process until all trace of soap is removed. Gently squeeze as much water as you can from the hank. Never wring it. Roll the hank in a towel to blot out more water.

Hang the damp hank somewhere out of the way with good air circulation until it is completely dry. Don't use anything made of metal (it may rust a bit and stain your yarn) or wood (it may be damaged by the moisture). Hang a weight from the bottom to straighten the hank. When the yarn is completely dry, wind it into a ball and it's ready to use.

WHAT IS THE YARN LIKE?

That depends on the fiber you used, and how you processed it. Dog undercoat yarn is very soft and fuzzy; in fact, some people mistake it for angora. Yarn made from single-coated breeds like Afghan hound will be smoother and not have the fuzzy "halo" that an undercoat yarn has. Cat-hair yarn, Persian or Himalayan for example, will be very soft and drape well. Since pet hair doesn't have the crimp that wool does, it tends to be inelastic. Some pet-hair yarns, such as Afghan hound, will felt and others like the Samoyed won't, so be careful which yarns you mix in a project.

WHAT CAN YOU DO WITH IT?

Pet-hair yarn is virtually as versatile as most other types of yarn. As with commercial yarns, each yarn has its own characteristics and you need to pair a project with a suitable yarn.

One final thing to keep in mind: Dog hair is much, much warmer than wool. This characteristic makes it much more suitable for smaller projects such as ear bands, hats, mittens or socks.

DOG-HAIR TAM

SKILL LEVEL

INTERMEDIATE

FINISHED SIZE

One size fits most

MATERIALS

- Hand-spun dog hair/wool-blend novelty yarn or similar light (light worsted) weight wool or wool-blend yarn: ¾ oz/160 yds/21g natural color of fiber being used
- Size D/3/3.25mm crochet hook or size needed to obtain gauge
- Tapestry needle

GAUGE

5 sc = 1 inch

PATTERN NOTE

Join with slip stitch as indicated unless otherwise stated.

SPECIAL STITCH

Triple treble (trtr): Yo hook 4 times, insert hook in indicated st, yo, draw up a lp, [yo, draw through 2 lps on hook] 5 times.

TAM
HEADBAND

Row 1: Ch 6, sc in 2nd ch from hook and in each of next 4 chs, turn. *(5 sc)*

Row 2: Ch 6 *(counts as first trtr)*, **trtr** *(see Special Stitch)* in each rem sc across, turn. *(5 trtr)*

Row 3: Ch 1, sc in each trtr across, turn. *(5 sc)*

Next rows: [Rep rows 2 and 3 alternately] until headband fits snugly around head at temples, ending last rep with row 2.

Next row (joining row): Holding last row and first row tog, working through both thicknesses, sl st last row to opposite side of foundation ch of row 1.

CROWN

Rnd 1: Working in ends of rows, *ch 5, sc in end of next trtr row, ch 5**, sc between same trtr row and next sc row, rep from * around, ending last rep at **, **join** *(see Pattern Note)* in first sc *(see Fig. 1)*.

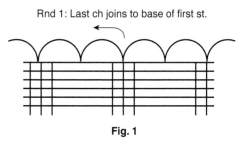

Rnd 1: Last ch joins to base of first st.

Fig. 1

Rnd 2: [Ch 7, sc in 3rd ch of next ch-5] around, ch 3, join in 4th ch of beg ch-7 *(see Fig. 2)*.

Rnd 3: [Ch 9, sc in 4th ch of next ch-7] around, ch 9, join at base of beg ch-9 *(see Fig. 3)*.

Rnd 4: [Ch 11, sc in 5th ch of next ch-9] around, ch 5, join in 5th ch of beg ch-11.

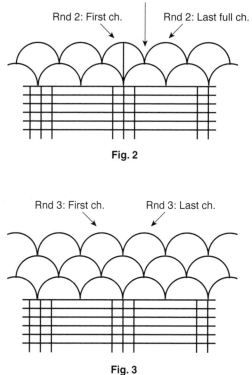

Rnd 2: Half ch connects to center of first ch.

Rnd 2: First ch.

Rnd 2: Last full ch.

Fig. 2

Rnd 3: First ch.

Rnd 3: Last ch.

Fig. 3

Rnd 5: [Ch 9, sc in 6th ch of next ch-11] around, ch 9, join at base of beg ch-9.

Rnd 6: [Ch 9, sc in 5th ch of next ch-9] around, ch 4, join in 5th ch of beg ch-9.

Rnd 7: [Ch 7, sc in 5th ch of next ch-9] around, ch 7, join at base of beg ch-7.

Rnd 8: [Ch 5, sc in 4th ch of next ch-7] around, ch 3, join in 3rd ch of beg ch-5.

Rnd 9: *[Ch 5, sc in 3rd ch of next ch-5 sp] twice, ch 5, [insert hook in 3rd ch of next ch-5 sp, yo, draw up a lp] twice, yo, draw through all 3 lps on hook, rep from * around until 4 ch-5 sps rem. Fasten off, leaving 10-inch length for finishing.

FINISHING

With tapestry needle and length left for finishing, sew centers of last 4 ch-5 sps tog. ▪

chapter thirteen
crochet care

When you put a lot of time, effort and love into your crochet projects, you want them to look their best for a long time. We'll show you how to properly care for your crocheted items, fix stitching mishaps and make safer, longer-lasting toys.

Tender Loving Care for Crochet

In our wash-and-wear culture, many of us are at a loss to understand how to properly launder and care for our handcrafted items. Proper care can make your hard work last longer and look better. There is nothing more disappointing than to spend hours painstakingly crocheting a special project only to see it lose its beauty. By following these helpful suggestions, you can keep your lovingly handcrafted projects looking their best for years to come.

LAUNDERING BASICS

First, here are some basic tips to help ensure the best laundering care for your crocheted items:

• Read and follow the care instructions on the yarn label. These will often be represented by certain symbols (*see the Universal Laundering Symbols Chart on page 247*). You may discover that your item requires dry cleaning.

• Make a swatch of your pattern, and wash it to see if it turns out as expected before risking your completed item.

• Be sure all ends are securely woven in and trimmed before washing to eliminate snagging in the wash.

• If your piece has buttons, make sure they are washable. Some buttons are not made to be washed or dry-cleaned. If that is the case with the buttons on your project, remove them before washing the project.

• Don't use bleach.

WASHING YOUR PROJECT

For crocheted projects made with washable yarn, most gentle commercial soaps and detergents are suitable. A mild shampoo or a wool detergent is best for washing angora, mohair, wool or wool blends. Stronger detergents can be used on synthetics or cotton. When using powdered detergents, be sure to fully dissolve the powder in water before adding the item. Whether machine- or hand-washing your project, cold or tepid water is recommended, especially for natural fibers, as hot water may damage the fiber content of the yarn or cause shrinkage.

If the piece is being machine-washed, machine-dry it as well. Machine-washable yarn usually regains its "bounce" in the dryer. Place the item in a mesh laundry bag and use the gentle cycle for both washing and drying. High heat can melt synthetics, so always use the lowest setting possible.

To hand-wash your crocheted piece, create lather by running water into a basin with a small amount of gentle soap or detergent. The yarn label should indicate the water temperature, but if it doesn't, use tepid water. Squeeze the suds gently through the fabric. Rinse well and lift the item carefully from the water, taking care to support the piece so that the heavier weight does not stretch it out of shape (*see Photo A*). Roll the piece between two clean towels, squeezing gently to blot out excess water (*see Photo B*). Do not wring or twist! If you prefer, briefly run the

PHOTO A

PHOTO B

piece through the gentle spin cycle on the washing machine. Lay the piece out to block and dry (see Photo C).

Brush garments made with fluffy yarns lightly when dry to restore the plush texture. Any pilling from wear should be carefully plucked off.

DRY CLEANING

Some yarns labeled "dry-clean" are done so only to protect the manufacturer against complaints, but can indeed be carefully hand-washed. Test your "dry-clean only" yarn by stitching a small swatch and then hand-washing it. If you are not happy with the results, then dry-clean only.

Some yarns are labeled "do not dry-clean." Heed this warning—these yarns are ruined by exposure to dry-cleaning chemicals.

EMBROIDERED OR BEADED PIECES

Because embroidered projects usually contain several colors of thread and fabric together, they should be hand-washed in cold water in a mild shampoo or gentle detergent to prevent the colors from bleeding or fading. Use just enough water so the garment can move freely and rinse thoroughly. If you have hard water, add two tablespoons of white vinegar per quart of rinse water to restore softness and brighten colors. Insert plastic wrap between the front and back of the garment to prevent the damp fabric from sticking to the embroidery as it dries.

Beaded or sequined garments usually cannot be washed. To find out if they are washable, test some of your extra beads or sequins by washing them in cold water with mild soap. Let dry and rub with your thumb to see if the surface of the bead or sequin remains intact.

COLORFASTNESS

Colorfastness refers to the tendency of dyes to run when wet. Sometimes washable yarns are used in color combinations in which lack of colorfastness is a problem. To test for colorfastness, thoroughly wet a test swatch, squeeze out excess moisture and place on a paper towel to dry. If any color bleeds onto the paper towel, it may run onto other colors in the finished project. Dry cleaning may be your best option, or choose a different yarn and/or colors.

STORAGE TIPS

Taking care when storing your crocheted pieces can be just as important as proper cleaning. Here are a few helpful suggestions:

Fold crocheted garments and store in drawers—don't hang them. Zippered, under-the-bed blanket or garment boxes also make excellent storage containers for all types of crocheted pieces. To protect items from the acid in the wood or cardboard, wrap pieces in acid-free tissue paper or pure white cotton muslin. This will help prevent discoloration and deterioration in the fiber content of the clothing.

Clean items before storing them. Body oils from wearing or handling crocheted pieces actually accumulate dirt—spots that will show up later.

To guard against mildew, do not store items while they are still damp—include baking soda and/or activated charcoal with stored clothing to absorb atmospheric moisture such as humidity.

Use moth repellent for natural fibers. Items made from wool or wool-blend yarn should be placed in a special garment bag made to protect them from moths and carpet beetles.

Occasionally refold items stored for long periods of time to prevent weak spots from developing along the folds. To help prevent unsightly fold lines in stored items, try rolling them loosely.

Avoid putting clean items in airtight plastic bags that prevent fibers from breathing. Use a garment bag or storage box, or wrap in a clean sheet.

CROCHETED GIFTS

Before giving a crocheted item as a gift, it should be washed and dried following the instructions on the yarn label. To help insure that the recipient can keep the item looking beautiful for years to come, include a yarn label or a card that gives the washing instructions for the project. It's also a good idea to add a small bundle of the yarn for any future repairs that might become necessary.

A great way to personalize a crocheted gift is to sew on a fabric label, like those shown at right, identifying the item as being specially made for the recipient by you. It adds a nice personal touch and professional finish to the gift. ∎

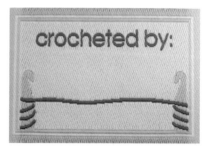

UNIVERSAL LAUNDERING SYMBOLS

Machine Wash, Normal

Machine Wash, Cold

Machine Wash, Cold

Machine Wash, Warm

Machine Wash, Warm

Machine Wash, Hot

Machine Wash, Hot

Machine Wash, Hot

Machine Wash, Hot

Machine Wash, Hot

Machine Wash, Hot

Machine Wash, Hot

Machine Wash, Permanent Press

Machine Wash, Gentle or Delicate

Hand Wash

Hand Wash, Cold

Hand Wash, Warm

Hand Wash, Hot

Do Not Wash

Dry-Clean

Dry-Clean, Any Solvent

Dry-Clean, Petroleum Solvent Only

Dry-Clean, Any Solvent Except Trichloroethylene

Dry-Clean, Short Cycle

Dry-Clean, Reduced Moisture

Dry-Clean, Low Heat

Dry-Clean, No Steam

Do Not Dry-Clean

Bleach When Needed

Non-Chlorine Bleach When Needed

Do Not Bleach

Tumble Dry, Normal

Tumble Dry, Normal, Low Heat

Tumble Dry, Normal, Medium Heat

Tumble Dry, Normal, No Heat

Tumble Dry, Normal, High Heat

Tumble Dry, Permanent Press

Tumble Dry, Gentle

Do Not Tumble Dry

Do Not Dry

Line Dry

Drip Dry

Dry Flat

Dry In Shade

Do Not Wring

Iron, Any Temperature, Steam or Dry

Iron, Low

Iron, Medium

Iron, High

Do Not Steam

Do Not Iron

Crochet Mishaps

It's a known fact that "to err is human." Everyone makes mistakes, and crocheters are no exception. Of course, not every crochet mistake or miscalculation can be fixed or corrected, but there are fixes for some common problems.

LOOSE RIBBING

When the bottom, lower sleeve or neck ribbing of a crochet garment is too loose, the result can be a shapeless mess. Due to the way crochet stitches are formed, they have more stretch than do knit stitches, which are less elastic. Knowing this in advance means you can compensate from the beginning to avoid fit problems in the end.

FIX #1 PLAN-IN-ADVANCE

Create ribbing that fits better by simply changing the size of hook used for the ribbing. Use a hook one or two sizes smaller than the hook used to stitch the main body to work a sample 4 x 4-inch swatch **before** beginning a garment using a hook one or two sizes smaller than used for the main body pieces to determine the finished look you desire. This method can be applied whether each body piece begins with ribbing or the ribbing is added on after each body piece is completed or assembled.

FIX #2 AFTER-THE-FACT FIX

Simply thread clear elastic thread into a sewing needle and run three or more rows of loose running stitches through the back of several evenly spaced stitches. Draw stitches to desired width.

JACKET IS TOO TIGHT AROUND THE BUST

There are simple ways to add extra width to a jacket that is a bit too tight to fit comfortably.

Work several extra rows in single crochet along the front bands of the jacket.

If the jacket has overlapped front bands with buttonholes worked into the right-side band, omit the buttonholes. If the problem is discovered after completing the band, unravel back to the row prior to making the buttonholes and finish the required number of rows, even adding extra rows for that extra room needed. Instead of buttonholes, sew on toggles or frog closures, or make button loops on the last row by working the required number of chain stitches to fit snuggly around your buttons. Both of these methods then allow the buttons to be placed on the outside edge of a band, instead of in the center and provide extra room.

Note: Adding extra rows or stitches to each front actually provides for a better fit anyway, because of the structure of the human female anatomy.

SPLIT STITCH OR SNAG
FIX #1 (BEST FIX)

Insert a yarn needle into the damaged stitch and gently push and pull on it trying to even out the snag. Then, gently pull on the stitches to the left and right of the same stitch to place the stitch or part of a stitch back into its proper position. Nine times out of 10 the problem can be fixed in this way.

FIX #2

Using a smaller hook than used for the garment, pull the snag to the back or inside of work. Sew that loose section or strand of yarn into a hiding position using matching sewing thread.

FIX #3

When all else fails, using a small crochet hook, pull the damaged stitch tightly to the inside of the garment. Thread a yarn needle with matching yarn and insert yarn from back to front of work, draw yarn **over** the offending stitch, duplicating the crochet stitch (or portion of the stitches used), hiding the damaged stitch, push needle to back of work and secure ends.

STAINS

When it comes to stains, there are the all-too-obvious *fixes* such as crocheting a pocket or flap of any size or shape to cover the offending stain, or you can crochet a flower or other motif. When the stain is placed in certain areas, this kind of fix can be used to create a design element that actually enhances a garment.

However, when it comes to those stains that are in odd places, there are two **super-secret** products that almost always eliminate stains: liquid Tide® detergent and Dawn® dishwashing liquid. For best results, use Dawn® for any stain that is greasy. Pour a generous amount of either liquid over the eyesore and allow to rest at least one hour to overnight so the liquid can work its magic and then launder. Sometimes a second treatment is required if washing doesn't get the stain out the first time.

EDGING PROBLEMS

Tip! When edging garments, begin at a seam (underarm, shoulder or sleeve) and then work around, join and continue as instructed. Using this technique avoids drawing the eye to a joining at a corner of the neck or lower front.

EDGING BEGINS TO FLARE SLIGHTLY

The easiest fix for this problem is to use a crochet hook one size smaller than that used for the body of the project. Using the smaller hook, work as stated in the pattern. Doing so would form smaller stitches, which, in turn, will pull the flared area back in line.

EDGING IS DISTORTED

This problem seems to show up most frequently when instructions say to work "evenly placed sc (single crochet)" along or around a piece. The way to solve this problem is to understand how to place your stitches evenly because when stitches are not worked evenly, the edging can become distorted and unattractive. If the stitches are too far apart, the edging begins to strain and pull together, conversely, when the stitches are placed too closely together, the edging begins to ripple—either way the end result is likely to be somewhat puckered in appearance.

This technique works especially well for garments, particularly when it comes to the fronts of a jacket where it is essential that the number of stitches worked on each front is exactly the same. If they don't match, buttonholes will not line up properly or one front may be slightly longer or shorter than the other and look off-kilter.

When working around a large surface, such as the outer edges of a jacket or an afghan, you may be told to work a specific number of stitches either around the entire piece, or from one point to another, such as from the bottom to the top. To ensure those edging stitches are even, fold the piece in half and place a plastic marker at the halfway point. Then, fold from the marker to the ends on each side of marker just placed to create quarter lengths and again place markers. If the piece is large enough, divide the quarters into eighths by folding again. Divide the number of stitches given for this section by the number of marked segments to determine how many stitches to work within each segment.

PLAIN EDGING ROLLS TO FRONT

When you work three or more rounds of single crochet to edge the outer edges of a garment, sometimes, the edging begins to roll a bit toward the front, losing the flat, crisp finish desired. When this happens, work the last round in reverse single crochet. The added bulk tends to correct the problem easily.

EDGING CORNERS

Generally speaking, when instructions call for several rounds of single crochet, three single crochet stitches are worked into each corner stitch. However, sometimes you'll find the corners begin to splay and lose that sharp, neat corner angle. Try working one round even without any corner increases, then increase on the next round. If this takes care of the problem, continue to work corner increases, every other round instead of every round.

MISSING STITCHES

If you discover that you accidentally skipped a double crochet on your previous row of work, or have an odd-looking shell, popcorn or cluster farther back in your work that's missing a stitch, try these fixes before ripping out a large amount of work.

SKIPPED DOUBLE CROCHET FROM PREVIOUS ROW

Work current row until it is in line with skipped double crochet, then work one more double crochet. Yarn over, and insert hook again into same stitch as last double crochet and pull yarn through (three loops on hook). Now work a double crochet in the skipped stitch as follows: yarn over, insert hook into skipped double crochet and pull yarn through, (five loops on hook), yarn over, pull yarn through two loops twice. Return to last stitch worked on current row. Yarn over and again pull yarn through two loops twice to compensate for skipped double crochet. The stitch just made to close the gap made by the skipped stitch looks similar to a treble crochet. Stop and determine whether the look is satisfactory. If it is, secure the ends on the wrong side of the work. If not, rip your work back and work the offending row correctly.

SKIPPED STITCH OF SHELL, POPCORN OR CLUSTER BELOW

Leaving a tail, make a slip stitch. Remove hook, holding slip stitch on back of work, using crochet hook, pull hook through stitch used for shell, popcorn or cluster to front of work into center of shell, popcorn, or cluster. Now, work matching stitch (double crochet, half double crochet or single crochet) until one loop remains on hook. Fasten off, leaving a tail, and pull to back of work, nudging new stitch into position. Inspect your work to determine whether this fix looks OK. If so, remove the hook after completing the stitch, and thread the end of the yarn or thread into the yarn needle. Insert your hook into either the top of the next stitch of a group of stitches or into the stitch that closes the group of stitches together and pull yarn to back of work. Gently remove slip stitch. Secure ends.

BUTTONHOLE BAND MADE ON WRONG FRONT

Here's a quick remedy for this all-too-common mistake. For a woman's garment, the buttonholes should be on the *right* front, while a man's garment has the buttonhole band placed on the *left* front. Instead of ripping out the bands when this glaring mistake is discovered, simply sew the buttons evenly spaced to right front. Sew snaps to wrong side, one behind each button, and the other half of each snap set to the left front. Clear plastic snaps are available, and make the snaps less noticeable. To ensure perfect alignment of buttonholes and buttons, work buttonholes on both right and left front bands. Then sew buttons over buttonholes on the opposite band.

Obviously, not every crochet mistake can be corrected, but any of the above fixes can help save time and effort in successfully completing your crochet projects, despite the human-error factor! ■

Tips for Making Safer, Longer-Lasting Toys

Photo of toys for illustrative purposes only; patterns are not available.

Many crocheters love making cute, stuffed crocheted dolls and toys for babies and young children. Soft, cuddly toys are tailor-made for giving to little ones, but it's always wise to carefully consider making these special gifts as safe as possible, especially for children under age 3.

The face is generally the most appealing part of a doll or toy, but it is also the most potentially dangerous. Never attach anything to a small child's or baby's toy or doll that can be pulled or chewed off and swallowed. Cut features out of felt or crochet them with yarn rather than using buttons or other potentially dangerous items.

Use a tiny amount of washable fabric glue to place the features as desired and then sew them securely in place. Carpet thread is a good choice as it is stronger than regular sewing thread. The safest option of all, however, is to embroider the facial features. They can be stitched using embroidery floss, crewel yarn or the yarn used in the item.

If your doll or toy pattern calls for a stick or dowel, use plastic canvas rolled and stitched into a similar-size tube instead. It's also better to use plastic canvas in place of cardboard. Plastic canvas is safe and washable. Chenille stems are not recommended for small children's or babies' toys because the sharp wire ends can work through the stitches.

Lots of crochet toy or doll patterns can be converted into smaller toys or rattles for baby, but again, keep safety in mind. If jingle bells are used, tie several together and insert them into the middle of the stuffing inside. Or put dried beans or unpopped popcorn kernels into a small plastic container, securely sealed with duct tape, and place it deep inside the doll or toy. If you want to weight down a toy or doll so it will sit better, try pouring dried beans into a zip-shut plastic bag, wrapping it completely in duct tape and placing it in a pocket inside the stuffing.

Crocheted toys will last longer if they are properly cared for. Keeping a toy or doll in good repair and laundering it with care can help extend its life and give the recipient many more hours of enjoyment. Keep in mind, however, that if cardboard, tape, dried beans or other non-washable materials are used in an item, it can't be laundered (except, perhaps, with some light surface wiping that does not soak into the piece).

To launder a washable crocheted toy, first mend it as needed. Then, if it is extremely dirty, spray it thoroughly with a laundry prewash. Immerse the toy in cool, mild sudsy water, pressing down gently to saturate, and let soak for about 30 minutes. Rinse gently in cool water. Place the toy on thick towels and roll the towels gently over the toy to remove excess water. Arrange the toy on more dry towels and let dry completely.

After the toy is dry, replace stuffing as needed by poking very small bits of stuffing through the crochet stitches with the blunt end of a small crochet hook. Smooth and pinch openings in the stitches closed after stuffing. You can also use the crochet hook to adjust any stuffing that has shifted during washing to reshape areas where needed.

When giving a doll or toy as a gift, it's always helpful to include safety information and washing instructions. If the item is non-washable, this should be specified. It's also a nice touch to include extra crocheted clothing with a doll or stuffed animal for the recipient's added enjoyment.

When putting the time and care into making a special doll or toy for a child, following these suggestions will help you produce a finished project that you can feel good about giving, and the recipient will enjoy using. ■

Photo of toys for illustrative purposes only; patterns are not available.

chapter fourteen
getting organized

It's easier to work more effectively when your crochet supplies are organized and readily accessible. Learn how to store all those patterns, books, magazines, catalogs, yarn skeins and crochet tools in such a way that it helps your projects go more smoothly and efficiently.

No More Crochet Chaos

Most crocheters have a lot more than just yarn stashed about. If you're like most crocheters, your "crochet stuff" probably is a wide variety of crochet-related items. Whether or not your "stuff" is organized, you might benefit from a few "anti-chaos" tips.

THREE TYPES OF "STUFF"

Usually, other than yarn, you're most likely to have at least one of the following three kinds of crochet "stuff":

• Crochet pattern and reference books.

• Crochet tools: hooks, scissors, plastic stitch markers, small scissors, small calculator, pincushion, knitting gauge, yarn needles, etc.

• Things saved: magazine clippings, favorite patterns, sizing information for loved ones, etc.

It takes little money, time or effort to organize your "stuff," and the payoff is huge in terms of knowing where all that stuff resides at any given time. There are solutions to organizing your three kinds of crochet stuff in decorative ways.

MAGAZINES, PATTERN & REFERENCE BOOKS

Most crocheters gradually add to their collection of magazines, and pattern and reference books. But as a collection grows, it somehow gets placed in different locations (most likely wherever space is available), whether by yourself or a family member. Before you know it, the next time you need a certain pattern to make a special gift for someone, you may not be able to find the particular book or magazine you're looking for, no matter how hard or long you search.

Magazine holders are not only great for keeping your magazines nicely organized, they're also a simple solution to storing crochet books and are available in all kinds of looks. Choose the look that best complements and blends in with the decor of the room where you spend your time crocheting. From the plainest of

plastic to classy leather, holders are available in a wide variety of styles and finishes that range from businesslike and high-tech to novelty and the exotic.

Buy two or three matching holders for starters, even if you don't have enough materials to fill them all. Crochet libraries tend to grow rapidly, and you may not be able to match holders unless you buy several at one time. Placed side by side on a bookshelf, they look nice and easily stand out from other books so you can quickly find them—another time-saver!

CROCHET TOOLS

Buy a decorative box with a hinged lid to hold all those little tools and necessities for crochet work. Choose a box to complement your room's decor. When you've finished working, simply place everything in your box and close the lid. Voilà! No muss, no

fuss, and, best of all, your box appears to be nothing more than something of beauty that completes the look of your room. Whether you select a box with a sleek, enameled finish, one with a vintage look, one with hammered copper detailing or one with floral accents, if you choose with your decor in mind, it can add a nice finishing touch to any room.

A decorative box is a great gift for new crocheters. You can include the little things a new crocheter isn't likely to have already. Here are some ideas:

- Colored-ball pins: These work well with crochet work due to their bright colors and their larger heads that aren't easily enmeshed in a stitch or cause snags.

- Crochet hooks: Most new crocheters don't have a wide variety of sizes, so some of the larger- and smaller-size hooks will be greatly appreciated.

- Retractable tape measure: Some type of measuring tool is a must, and most straight rulers don't fold easily if at all.

- Small pincushion: Crocheters will need someplace to store their colored-ball pins.

- Plastic markers and/or plastic marker safety pins: These are very valuable when it comes to counting the number of stitches or rows required in a pattern or when the armhole and neck shaping of a garment need to be marked.

- Yarn needles: Large-eye steel or plastic needles are necessary for weaving in the ends.

GET A NOTEBOOK

The easiest and cheapest way (less than five dollars) to begin a crochet notebook is with an inexpensive ring binder that can be purchased in office-supply stores and in many general-merchandise chain stores. Get one with three rings that snap open and that has pockets inside both the front and back covers. Simply write "Crochet Stuff" on the spine, and you can put it on a handy bookshelf. If you'd like to make it a little more professional looking, print out a title sheet and insert it in the front cover plastic opening.

While you're at the store, get two other inexpensive items: snap-in clear sheet protectors and dividers with large, customizable write-on tabs.

There isn't any right or wrong way to categorize your materials; simply divide up your binder-bound patterns in a manner that will suit you and your needs. Write the categories on the tabs of your dividers and snap them into your notebook. Organize your materials into stacks according to category. Now, simply insert those stacks of materials behind the right divider. No doubt you'll be amazed at how quickly all that chaos is suddenly transformed into an organized system. When you sit down and survey your neatly organized room, you'll feel proud of what you accomplished in so little time, not to mention feeling more calm and serene.

Want a decorative look? Cover your notebook with pretty paper and trims or, better yet, crochet a cover. Add little motifs, bits of crochet lace or whatever you like to embellish the outside.

FOLD-OUT FILING SYSTEM TOTE

These beauties are just the ticket to add another decorative touch, as well as organize take-along projects. Easy to carry about, whether from room to room or on a trip, filing totes will keep your crochet materials organized ever so efficiently.

The one shown here features a faux-suede finish; others can be found in slick leather, wild florals, plaids, shiny metals or whimsical prints. Our tote has oodles of folders and was found in the paper-crafting section of a local craft store. Self-adhesive, brightly colored index tabs (with paper inserts) were attached to the top of each section for easy identification.

You can substitute the tote for your notebook or make use of both systems—it's up to you!

SWATCHES

If you're like me, you develop crochet yarn favorites. Regardless of which yarns you prefer, here's a tip that will save you countless time when you're ready to begin another crochet project. Make and save a swatch in half double crochet. Use mounting tape to attach your newly made swatch to a sheet of paper or card stock. Write the hook size and the resulting gauge (number of stitches and rows per inch over at least 4 inches) directly on the paper or card stock. If you use the same yarn and use single crochet, half double crochet or double crochet to make any future crochet projects, your gauge (stitches and rows per inch) will remain the same, so you won't have to make a new swatch.

Repeat this process for your favorite yarns in other weights so you'll be ready for other crochet projects (afghans, baby items, garments, etc.) you're likely to make more than once. Of course, these swatches should go in your crochet stuff notebook for future reference.

Don't fall into the trap of thinking that all yarns of the same weight are sure to swatch at the same gauge! There are three factors that are apt to cause problems should you fall into the trap of thinking this might be true. First, many yarns today are imported from European mills. And in Europe, there are DK-weight (double-knit weight) yarns that are in between a medium (worsted) and a light (light worsted) weight, yet are labeled as medium-weight yarn for the American market. The diameter of a DK-weight yarn, therefore, will not swatch the same as either a true medium or light yarn.

Second, did you know dyes can affect the true weight and diameter of yarns? When using dark-color yarn, work another swatch because dark-color yarns are most likely to thicken during the dyeing process. This difference may or may not affect your gauge, but to ensure the proper fit of a garment, it's always best to work a swatch.

Third, all fibers have natural characteristics and tendencies that could possibly affect gauge. For example, cotton yarns are usually stiff and stitches worked with cotton yarn tend to be more distinct and separated than other yarns. Many of today's yarns are blends of various fibers, and thus, have individual characteristics that are dependent upon the percentages of fibers blended together. When in doubt, take the time to swatch!

You don't need to make a new swatch to check gauge as long as you use the same yarn, the same size of hook and the same stitch or fancy stitch. However, if you plan to crochet a jacket in the same yarn but are using a different pattern stitch, like a shell pattern, you then must work a new swatch. Any time you make a swatch with a yarn that you're likely to use again, save that swatch to save time in the future.

Using any of these creative techniques can make your crochet relatively "anti-chaotic" in a remarkably short amount of time! ■

Storing Your Yarn Scraps

Crocheters store their yarn scraps in all manner of ways, from bags or containers stuffed in whatever closet has room to a variety of creative storage bins made from buckets, boxes, crates or totes. For maximum efficiency, easily accessible cubicle-style storage units make it much easier to sort, store and locate scrap yarn colors when needed. Plastic crates make great storage units. They come in a variety of sizes, easily stack on top of each other and are a relatively inexpensive storage option.

Before setting up your choice of yarn bins, be sure to select a wise location, preferably in an unobtrusive place in your home where it's cool, dry and clean. While you want the location to be handy for you, you do not want it to be accessible to pets and small children. Avoid places like an unfinished basement that can be vulnerable to water leakage or mold or a garage that houses dirty machinery, chemicals or little critters that might decide to nestle in or chew on your yarn.

Once you have selected a good location and set up your preferred type of storage-bin unit, you need to sort your yarn scraps by color and value. A color wheel can be a great tool to help you do this. In order to see the true colors, lay the scraps out on a white or neutral-color carpet or sheet. In looking at the color wheel shown here, you'll notice that the colors are arranged in "families" by value, from lightest to darkest, so you should sort your yarn scraps in the same manner. Put each multicolored yarn in the pile with its predominant solid color. Put black, white, off-white and gray yarns in their own separate piles.

Once you have all of your color groups sorted, store them in the cubicles in whatever manner makes the most sense to you or is most workable for you. One way is to put the darkest-value shades of each color in the cubicles across the bottom row. Leave the column of cubicles on the right or left end free for the black, white, off-white and gray yarns.

In the corresponding cubicles across the next row, put the next darkest shade of each color—and so on—with each row, ending with the lightest-value shades in the top row (similar to how the color groups are arranged on the color wheel). If you have only a small amount of several colors, they may be able to share cubicles.

With a small investment in time and effort and a relatively low cost, you can have a well-organized system for efficiently locating specific colors in your leftover yarns when you need them. In addition, being able to view all those wonderful colors in various shades at a glance will be sure to inspire lots of crochet creativity when planning your projects! ■

Projects for Odd Balls

No, this isn't about strange people who crochet, but small amounts of yarn! Now that you've got your yarn stash organized and user-friendly, it will be easy to locate just the right "odd ball" or partial skein of yarn or crochet thread to whip up a quick, last-minute gift.

There are many types of projects that you can whip up in a relatively short amount of time and that are perfect for using up scraps or leftover balls of yarn and crochet thread. Here are some project suggestions:

- Hats
- Mittens
- Hand/wrist warmers
- Scarves/neck warmers
- Ear warmers/headbands
- Belts
- Easy slippers/socks
- Leg warmers
- Facecloths (add a back scrubby and soap sachet and make it a spa set)
- Hot pads/oven mitts
- Dishcloths
- Pot holders
- Coasters (give with a personalized mug and some packets of tea or coffee!)
- Tea cozies
- Pillows
- Rugs (especially those made with bulky or multi-strand yarn and large hooks)
- Sachets filled with potpourri (make them in holiday colors and use seasonal scents!)
- Small gift bags
- Holiday ornaments
- Small purses
- Small clutch bags with decorative button closures (perfect to use as tissue holders, makeup bags, coupon keepers or cozies for slide phones and other mini electronics)
- Coin purses/money pouches
- Simple jewelry
- Bookmarks
- Package trims
- Small, simple toys (for kids or pets)
- Hair decorations (scrunchies, barrettes, ties, headbands, ponytail holders)

Check out your stash of yarns, crochet cotton and patterns, and see how many great gifts you can create. Here are a couple of fun, easy patterns that are perfect for making from a yarn stash.

NORTH COUNTRY CAPS

SKILL LEVEL
■ □ □ □
BEGINNER

FINISHED SIZES
Child: One size fits most
Adult: One size fits most

FINISHED GARMENT MEASUREMENTS
Child: 21 inches in circumference, unstretched
Adult: 22 inches in circumference, unstretched

MATERIALS
- Medium (worsted) weight yarn:
  Child: approximately 250 yds MC
  small amount CC
  Adult: approximately 300 yds MC
  100 yds CC
- Sizes H/8/5mm and J/10/6mm crochet hooks or sizes needed to obtain gauge
- Yarn needle
- 5-inch square cardboard

GAUGE
Size H hook: 9 sc = 2 inches; 4 sc rows = 1 inch
Size J hook: 7 sc = 2 inches; 3 sc rows = 1 inch

Take time to check gauge.

PATTERN NOTES
Weave in loose ends as work progresses.

Use larger hook for adult-size Cap and smaller hook for child-size Cap.

BRIM

Row 1: With MC for child's and CC for adult's, ch 13, sc in 2nd ch from hook, sc in each rem ch across, turn. *(12 sc)*

Row 2: Working in **back lps** *(see Stitch Guide)* only, ch 1, sc in each st across, turn.

Rows 3–75: Rep row 2.

CAP

Row 1: Ch 1, working across side edge of Brim rows, work 1 sc in each row, for child's Cap, turn, for adult's Cap, fasten off CC, attach MC, turn. *(75 sc)*

Row 2: Ch 1, sc in each sc across, turn.

Rows 3 & 4: Rep row 2.

Row 5: Ch 1, sc in same st as beg ch-1 and in each of next 22 sts, **sc dec** *(see Stitch Guide)* in next 2 sts, *sc in each of next 23 sts, sc dec in next 2 sts, rep from * once, turn. *(72 sc)*

Rows 6 & 7: Rep row 2.

Row 8: Ch 1, sc in same st as beg ch-1 and in each of next 9 sts, sc dec in next 2 sts, *sc in each of next 10 sts, sc dec in next 2 sts, rep from * across, turn. *(66 sc)*

Rows 9–13: Rep row 2.

Row 14: Rep row 8. *(60 sc)*

Rows 15–17: Rep row 2.

Row 18: Rep row 8. *(54 sc)*

Rows 19–22: Rep row 2.

Row 23: Rep row 8. *(48 sc)*

Rows 24–26: Rep row 2.

Row 27: Rep row 8. *(42 sc)*

Rows 28–30: Rep row 2.

Row 31: Rep row 8. *(36 sc)*

Rows 32–36: Rep row 2.

Row 37: Rep row 8. *(30 sc)*

Rows 38–41: Rep row 2.

Row 42: Rep row 8. *(24 sc)*

Rows 43–47: Rep row 2.

Row 48: Rep row 8. *(18 sc)*

Rows 49–55: Rep row 2.

Row 56: Rep row 8. *(12 sc)*

Rows 57–66: Rep row 2.

Row 67: Rep row 8, fasten off. *(6 sc)*

ASSEMBLY
With matching yarn, sew Brim and Cap seams. Fold Brim upward onto Cap.

TASSEL
Cut 2 lengths of CC yarn and set aside. Wrap CC around cardboard until desired thickness. Pass a length under bundle of wrapped yarn at center top, tie ends securely tog and knot. Cut opposite end of Tassel strands and remove cardboard. Wrap 2nd length of yarn around Tassel approximately 1½ inches from top of Tassel. Trim ends as desired. Attach Tassel to row 67 of Cap.

BABY ANIMAL TRIMS

SKILL LEVEL
EASY

FINISHED SIZES
Duck: 2 x 2½ inches
Bear: 2 x 3 inches
Bunny: 2 x 3½ inches
Frog: 3 x 3 inches

MATERIALS
- Medium (worsted) weight yarn: 1 oz/50 yds/28g each yellow, orange, light blue, white, pink, black and olive
- Sizes D/3/3.25mm and G/6/4mm crochet hooks or size needed to obtain gauge
- Tapestry needle
- ¼-inch white pompoms: 2
- Pink mini pompom
- Hot glue or tacky craft glue
- Stitch markers

GAUGE

Size G hook: 4 sc = 1 inch

PATTERN NOTES

Head is worked in continuous rounds.

Do not join rounds unless specified; mark beginning of rounds.

SPECIAL STITCH

Popcorn (pc): 5 dc in place indicated, drop lp from hook and insert hook in first dc made, pull dropped lp through.

TRIMS

DUCK

BODY

Rnd 1 (RS): With size G hook and yellow, ch 6, sl st in first ch to form ring, ch 1, 12 sc in ring, join with sl st in beg sc.

Rnd 2: Ch 1, 2 sc in first sc, (sl st, ch 3, dc, ch 2, sl st in 2nd ch from hook) in next sc, (dc, hdc, sc) in next sc, 2 sc in each of next 6 sc, (sc, hdc, dc, ch 2, sl st in 2nd ch from hook) in next sc, (dc, ch 3, sl st) in next sc, 2 sc in next sc, join with sl st in beg sc. Fasten off.

HEAD

Rnd 1 (RS): With yellow, ch 2, 5 sc in 2nd ch from hook, **do not join** (see Pattern Notes).

Rnd 2: 2 sc in each sc around. (10 sc)

Rnd 3: [Sc in next sc, 2 sc in next sc] 5 times, join with sl st in beg sc. Leaving 12-inch end for sewing, fasten off. (15 sc)

BEAK

With D hook and orange, ch 5, sl st in 2nd ch from hook, sc in each of next 2 chs, sl st in last ch. Fasten off.

FINISHING

Sew Head to Body. For top tuft, cut 3 strands of yellow 1½-inches long. Sew to top of Head.

Fold Beak in half. With orange, sew fold to Head as shown in photo.

With **straight stitch** (see illustration) using black, embroider eyes as shown in photo.

Straight Stitch

BEAR

BODY

Rnd 1 (RS): With size G hook and light blue, ch 6, sl st in first ch to form ring, ch 1, 12 sc in ring, join with sl st in beg sc. (12 sc)

Rnd 2: Ch 1, 2 sc in each of first 2 sc, **pc** (see Special Stitch) in next sc, 2 sc in each of next 2 sc, pc in next sc, 2 sc in next sc, pc in next sc, 2 sc in each of next 2 sc, pc in next sc, 2 sc in last sc, join with sl st in beg sc. Fasten off.

HEAD

Rnd 1 (RS): With size G hook and light blue, ch 2, 4 sc in 2nd ch from hook, **do not join** (see Pattern Notes).

Rnd 2: 2 sc in each sc around. (8 sc)

Rnd 3: Sc in next sc, 2 sc in next sc, sc in next sc, (sc, ch 3, sl st) in next sc, sc in next sc, (sc, ch 3, sl st) in next sc, sc in next sc, 2 sc in next sc, join with sl st in beg sc. Leaving 12-inch end for sewing, fasten off.

SNOUT

With size D hook and white, ch 3, 5 hdc in 3rd ch from hook, join with sl st in first hdc. Fasten off.

FINISHING

Sew Head to Body.

Sew Snout to Head as shown in photo.

With **straight stitch** (see illustration above) using black, embroider eyes, nose and mouth as shown in photo.

BUNNY

BODY

Rnd 1 (RS): With size G hook and white, ch 6, sl st in first ch to form ring, ch 1, 12 sc in ring, join with sl st in beg sc. (12 sc)

Rnd 2: Ch 1, 2 sc in first sc and in next sc, **pc** (see Special Stitch) in next sc, 2 sc in each of next 2 sc, pc in next sc, 2 sc in next sc, pc in next sc, 2 sc in each of next 2 sc, pc in next sc, 2 sc in last sc, join with sl st in first sc. Fasten off.

HEAD

Rnd 1 (RS): With white, ch 2, 5 sc in 2nd ch from hook, **do not join** (see Pattern Notes).

Rnd 2: 2 sc in each sc around. (10 sc)

Rnd 3: [Sc in next sc, 2 sc in next sc] twice, sc in next sc, *(sc, ch 5, sc in 2nd ch from hook, hdc in each of next 2 chs, sc in next ch, sc) in next sc (ear), sc in next sc, (sc, ch 5, sc in 2nd ch from hook, hdc in each of next 2 chs, sc in next ch, sc) in next sc (ear), sc in next sc, 2 sc in next sc, join with sl st in beg sc. Fasten off.

INNER EAR
MAKE 2.
With size D hook and pink, ch 3.

Fasten off.

FINISHING
Sew Head to Body.

Sew Inner Ears to Ears.

With **straight stitch** (see illustration on page 262), using black, embroider eyes as shown in photo.

Glue white pompoms to Head for cheeks and glue pink mini pompom between cheeks for nose as shown in photo.

FROG
BODY
Rnd 1 (RS): With size G hook and olive, ch 6, sl st in first ch to form ring, ch 1, 12 sc in ring, join with sl st in beg sc.

Rnd 2: Ch 1, 2 sc in each of first 2 sc, (sc, ch 6, sl st in 3rd ch from hook, ch 2, sl st in same ch as last sl st made, sl st in each of next 3 chs, sc) in next sc (arm), 2 sc in next sc, *(sc, ch 6, sl st in 3rd ch from hook, ch 2, sl st in same ch as last sl st made, sl st in each of next 3 chs, sc) in next sc (leg), 2 sc in each of next 3 sc, (sc, ch 6, sl st in 3rd ch from hook, ch 2, sl st in same ch as last sl st made, sl st in each of next 3 chs, sc) in next sc (leg), 2 sc in next sc, (sc, ch 6, sl st in 3rd ch from hook, ch 2, sl st in same ch as last sl st made, sl st in each of next 3 chs, sc) in next sc (arm), 2 sc in last sc, join with sl st in beg sc. Fasten off.

HEAD

Rnd 1 (RS): With olive, ch 2, 5 sc in 2nd ch from hook.

Rnd 2: 2 sc in each sc around. (10 sc)

Rnd 3: [Sc in next sc, 2 sc in next sc] 5 times, join with sl st in beg sc. Leaving a 12-inch end for sewing, fasten off. (15 sc)

EYE
MAKE 2.
With size G hook and white, ch 2, 5 sc in 2nd ch from hook, join with sl st in beg sc. Fasten off.

FINISHING
Sew Head to Body.

Sew Eyes to top of Head as shown in photo.

With **straight stitch** (see illustration on page 262), using black, embroider pupils on eyes and mouth as shown in photo. ▪

chapter fifteen
teaching kids to crochet

It isn't just showing children how to do the basic stitches that makes teaching them how to crochet a success. Rather, it's how to engage their interest and make it meaningful to them with fun, creative results they can be proud of.

Chain, Chain, Chain!

Crocheters often want to know how they can successfully teach their children, grandchildren, students or youth groups at church how to crochet. Passing on the love of crochet to a child could be a gift that lasts a lifetime.

The good news is kids are naturally curious and love to learn new things. One important key to successfully teaching children something new is to make what you're teaching meaningful to them and to have the result be something fun and creative.

When teaching kids to crochet, it's generally best to use a larger size crochet hook (I, J or K) and a medium- or bulky-weight acrylic or wool yarn in a light or bright color, and a smooth texture. The lighter color and smooth texture of the yarn will make the stitches easier to see, and the larger hook is easier for small hands to grip.

Naturally, learning to crochet starts with the simple chain. As kids get the hang of chaining, it's wonderful to see them beam with pride over their accomplishments. Once kids feel comfortable with their chaining skills using the smooth yarn, you can then introduce them to other yarns in different weights, darker colors and interesting textures.

Once your students discover what fun and cool things they can make—even with those simple to learn chains, they will be even more excited about learning more about crochet. Thanks to the flexibility of the crocheted chain, it can be used just about anywhere you might use a piece of string or cord.

Kids can turn longer chains into necklaces, which can be embellished with beads, buttons, charms, medals or school awards. Shorter chains are perfect for bracelets, anklets or even rings. Chains can also be made into cute hair decorations or colorful ties for holiday packages. With some cardboard, short chains and a hole punch, kids can make hanging tags to match any package!

For a personal, one-of-a-kind style, kids can string their shoes with their own unique crocheted chains, made to the same length as the original shoelaces. Colorful chains can also be shaped into pretty flowers and scrapbook embellishments or used to create simple bookmarks. Two or three long chains braided together make a cool-looking belt. The creative designs made possible by the simple crocheted chain are virtually endless!

Not only will children enjoy putting their new crochet chaining skills to good use, but, teaching crochet chains can also help you use up your yarn scraps in the process. What's more, after the children see how much fun they're having just making chains, they will be eager to learn the next step: single crochet. ▪

Crochet Squared

Once a child has mastered the basics of simple crochet chains, he or she is ready to move on to the next step—single crochet. This stitch is very easy to master, and your students will be surprised by the variety of useful projects they can make with this one basic stitch.

The best place to start is with a single-crochet square. You may not think you can do much with plain squares, but they can become many different finished items. Sew or single-crochet two blocks together around three sides and add a simple single-crochet strap to create a little purse. Crochet two blocks together all the way around to make a useful pot holder (cotton yarn is best for items that will be exposed to heat).

By stuffing a pot holder with fiberfill before joining the last sides together, you get a cute little mini pillow that can be decorated with crochet-chain embellishments, buttons, ribbon, lace, flowers—almost anything! A group of these little pillows would be cute on a child's bed. You can also crochet squares together into larger pieces, creating a regular-size pillow, a doll blanket or even a full-size afghan.

To get students started on making a basic single-crochet square, use a smooth worsted weight yarn and a size J/10/6mm hook. Have them make a chain as long as the desired width of their finished square. For example, a chain 10 inches long will result in a square approximately 10 inches wide, but gauge is not crucial for these pieces. Show your students how to work single crochet stitches back and forth in rows until the piece is as long as it is wide, making a square.

Encourage kids to experiment with color variations. Have them make squares in different colors and then single-crochet them together with a unifying color for a patchwork mat or blanket. Show them how to alternate yarn colors on rows to create stripes. Color variations help keep single crochet from getting boring!

Now that your students have mastered the single crochet stitch, encourage them to use their new skill to make blocks they can join into simple projects for charity, such as pet mats for animal shelters, lap robes for patients in nursing homes and veterans' hospitals, or blankets for homeless shelters. It will be a wonderful lesson for them to learn to use their crochet talents for the benefit of others.

Having accomplished the technique of single crochet, kids should easily be able to continue progressing to other basic stitches, such as half double crochet and double crochet, with only a little guidance, and as always, lots of encouragement. ■

chapter sixteen
the business of crochet

If you're feeling confident enough in your crochet skills to take it from a hobby to a business, this chapter has some important tips to help you follow the right path to success, whether you want to be a designer or simply sell your crocheted wares.

Submitting Designs to Publishers

Many designers are hesitant to submit any of their original designs to publishers for one or more of three major reasons.

First, the designers don't understand the submission process, and just aren't sure how to go about effectively getting their designs into a publisher's hands. It seems confusing and complicated to them.

Second, the designers are afraid of feeling intimidated by editors. In actuality, most editors are pretty friendly, down-to-earth, ordinary people who really enjoy discovering and working with aspiring designers and seeing what great new talent lurks beyond their doors.

And last, but certainly not least, the fear of having their work rejected deters many of these promising new designers from submitting their projects to publishers. The fact that design rejection is a very real expectation on their part is an important issue unto itself.

Submission requirements can vary among publishers, so it's always a good idea to call or write for a publisher's submission guidelines and editorial calendar. Here are some basic suggestions for making a submission presentation that most editors will likely appreciate. Keeping it simple, but professional, is the key.

If you choose to send the completed article of your design to a publisher, make sure it is clean, well-made and packaged securely against possible damage. An editor will not be likely to review a project that is soiled, sloppy or damaged.

In lieu of finished items, you can submit photos, swatches and sketches by mail or e-mail. This is more cost effective, easier for editors to deal with, and eliminates the risk of your articles being lost or damaged in shipping.

Project or swatch photos must be high quality and clearly show details and features of the design. Swatches should be accompanied by a sketch that will give the editor a good, clear visual of what the finished piece, or pieces, will look like. You don't have to be an artist by any means—even a rough sketch showing as much detail as possible is better than no sketch at all.

When submitting photos, swatches and sketches of unfinished projects, always do so in a great presentation! It's important to remember that your design is not in its complete form yet, and showing the editor as much detail and providing as much information as possible is a key factor in your design getting the highest possible consideration for acceptance.

While it's true that a great design speaks for itself, it's always a good idea to include a brief, but complete, description of your design in your presentation so the editor will be able to fully evaluate its benefits. Editors can receive literally hundreds of design submissions for just one publication's review, so supplying the editor with an impressive, stand-out presentation that's easy for an editor to review quickly and easily is extremely important.

On the opposite page are two submission examples that resulted in *Crochet!* magazine accepting and publishing the Petals & Plaid Baby Set and the Fringed Shell Skirt. Key details the editor needs to know about the submitted projects, such as proposed pieces, sizes, suggested yarns and colors, and actual stitched samples of the designs, can be easily seen, almost at a glance, in the two open pages of these informative portfolio presentations.

When mailing photos, swatches, sketches or completed projects, make sure to include adequate return postage for your submission package. Be sure to tag or label each item in your submission with your name, address, phone number and e-mail address. Correspondence can often become separated from submitted items, so it's extremely important that each item is labeled and readily identifiable.

Completed instructions should be included with finished items. It's very helpful for an editor to have them already on hand with the project should it be accepted for publication.

Once your design has been submitted to a publisher, be patient! That can be hard to do, especially when you're just starting out. But, unfortunately, the wheels of the publishing world grind slowly, and it generally takes weeks, even months, before most submissions can be reviewed and decisions made. Despite the editor's best efforts, scheduled design reviews sometimes have to be delayed due to other critical deadlines.

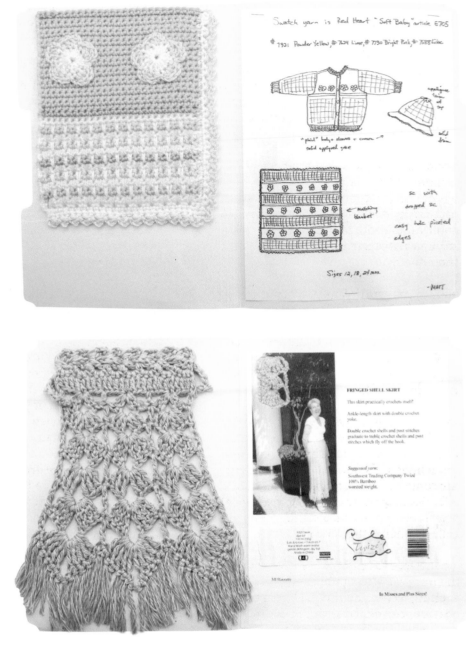

It can often be less of a waiting game for you if you submit a number of different designs to different editors simultaneously on a consistent basis. Never submit the same design to more than one editor at a time, even editors within the same publishing company. It's considered unprofessional and most editors simply won't review a design if they know other editors are looking at it at the same time.

Submitting your original creations to publishing companies can be an exciting experience— not at all scary or complicated. Keeping the process simple and professional simply makes it work better for everyone involved. ▪

When Your Design Is Rejected

You've submitted your very first original crochet design to a publisher, and then you get it back with a very nice letter of rejection. So, is this the end? Do you say, "My work is obviously not good enough to be published, so there is no reason to pursue this further?" Absolutely not. Rejection is a part of life, even in the publishing world, but it doesn't necessarily mean that your creative crochet work of art isn't publication-worthy.

The discouragement of a first design rejection can cause some very gifted individuals to doubt their designing talents. It can make them want to throw in the towel on what could possibly be a promising and prosperous crochet design career—given time, dedication and perseverance. One would have to wonder just how many bright, talented crochet designers' work the world never had the pleasure of seeing simply because it all ended with the pain of that first rejection. Too many, most likely.

So, why is a design rejected? There can be a number of reasons, the first and most obvious being that it is simply a poor design that was not well planned or well executed. When submitting a design to a publisher, be your own worst critic and make a detailed evaluation of your design before sending it. Is it a well-thought-out concept that results in a well-crafted design? Is the style of your design timely for the current marketplace? Is it a design that crocheters would enjoy and appreciate, and that a publisher would find valuable for its customers? If the design is in completed form, is it well-made, eye-catching and nicely finished?

Detach yourself from your creation. Yes, it's your "baby" but you need to be able to review it with a critical, impartial eye. Ask other people, crocheters and non-crocheters (whose opinions you value because you know they will be honest), to evaluate your design as well. You have to feel good about your design before you can expect a publisher to appreciate it.

If you have thoroughly assessed your design and are confident of its quality and appeal, then believe in your work and in yourself! It still may be rejected by a publisher, but this rejection most likely won't be because they thought it was a poor design.

It may be that you submitted a project that really didn't fit the concept of the company's publication. For example, you submitted designs for kitchen pot holders or bathroom accessories to a crochet magazine that primarily features high-end fashions. They may be really cute, clever designs, but obviously your pot holders or bath items aren't a good fit for that particular magazine. Take the time to study various crochet publications and see what types of designs they generally tend to feature and submit accordingly. The shoe has to fit!

Another reason your design may be rejected simply comes down to a matter of timing. You need to submit appropriate projects to a particular publisher when they're looking for specific designs at certain times. That's why it's a good idea to contact a publisher and ask them for their crochet editorial calendar (or schedule of design reviews). This will let you know what types of designs they are looking for and when they will be reviewing them.

The old adage "timing is everything" is very true when it comes to getting the right design into an editor's hands at the right time. If you submit a home-decor item to an editor when he or she is looking for fashions, toys or baby items, your design stands a good chance of being passed over. But don't hesitate to resubmit the same design to the same publisher at a later time when they are in need of that type of project. The right timing on your second try just might pay off.

If you keep having the same design rejected over and over by different publishers, perhaps it's time to take a closer look at your design and reevaluate it. There may be a good reason why several publishers have rejected this particular design (aside from poor quality, bad timing or inappropriate concept for their publication needs). You (and others) may have deemed it a very good design, but perhaps something is "missing" or not quite "right" in the overall design. Can you change or add to the design in order to enhance its appeal? It might be something as simple as changing the color scheme or type of yarn, or adding some embellishment. It can really be worth the effort!

When your first design rejection happens (and it will), don't despair, and above all, don't take it personally. A design rejection is not a publisher's personal affront to you, the individual who submitted the design. A project is reviewed and critiqued solely on the merits of its quality and appeal.

The best therapy for the pain of design rejection is a good dose of perseverance. Again, if you are confident that you have a high-quality design with strong customer appeal, then chin up. Square those shoulders and immediately submit your design to another publisher. If it comes back, send it to another publisher. It's a likely bet that some editor, somewhere, at some point in time, will find your design perfect for his or her publishing needs. If you know your work is good, and you feel that it's worthy of publication, it's a good bet there is an editor somewhere who will too.

Never lose belief in yourself or your capabilities. Even the most talented designers are on shaky ground when they lack the confidence and fortitude to "hang in there" and persist in their efforts to get publishers to sit up and take notice of their work. It WILL happen!

Feeling better? Good … now go and submit that wonderful crochet work of art that will likely, sooner or later, be just right for an editor's publishing needs. ■

When Your Design Is Accepted

Your first design has been accepted. (Happy dance! Happy dance!) Now what? As the song says, you probably "feel like dancing," but there is still serious work to be done! After a quick celebratory "woo-hoo!" it's time to dig in and complete the process that will put you among the ranks of published designers.

Needless to say, your excitement is understandable. For a new designer, there is nothing quite like the thrill of having that first design accepted for publication. It validates your creative talents and gives you professional credibility. But you can dance later … the submission process is not quite complete.

Once you have been notified by an editor (or associate editor, in some cases) that your design has been accepted, the first order of business is agreement upon a price for your work. Prices for same or similar-type designs can vary widely among publishers. For example, one publisher may pay $300 for an afghan while another might pay as much as $500.

As you submit more and more designs for publication, you will become more and more familiar with the average fees from different publishers. When you're just starting out in the submission process, however, it's a good idea to do a little homework and find out from various publishers—and other designers— what fees are being paid for the types of crochet designs you are submitting. That way you won't be totally in the dark when an editor calls and wants to purchase your design.

Some editors will automatically offer a specific fee for your design while others will request your asking price. If you've done some research, you will have a reasonably good idea if the payment an editor is offering is fair, or know what fee to ask for without undercutting yourself. Always ask for the maximum fee within reason. If a publisher cannot or will not meet this price, most are willing to negotiate a payment on which you both can agree.

Once the fee has been agreed upon, the next order of business is to provide the editor with the completed project and pattern manuscript. Of course, if your initial submission was the completed item and pattern, then you're good to go. If you submitted a swatch, sketch or photo for a still-to-be-completed design, the editor will give you a date when the finished article and instructions must be received.

It is critical that you meet this deadline. Most editors reserve the right to ultimately refuse a design for publication if a designer fails to meet the deadline for the completed project and instructions. However, sometimes "life happens" and throws a monkey wrench into our carefully planned schedules. Unavoidable circumstances can arise that prevent a designer from meeting a project deadline.

In this case, it is extremely important to contact the editor as soon as possible and explain the situation, and find out if there is any possibility of an extension on the deadline. Always ask for the minimum length of time possible while still allowing yourself adequate time to do a quality job on your project. A rushed project rarely generates positive results. Most editors are willing to work with a designer who occasionally needs an extended deadline and will allow as much extra time as their production schedules will permit (which often isn't very much).

Now, let's talk about your pattern manuscript. For many new designers, this is often the scariest part of the whole process. Even though, as crocheters, they are familiar with general pattern formats, many often feel (and are) inexperienced in the fine points of pattern writing.

Look at recently published copies of your editor's crochet publications, study the pattern format used, and then write yours accordingly. While it's true that most publishers rewrite designers' patterns into their own respective styles, they much prefer working with designers who have taken the time and care to send them well-written and complete instructions that have been formatted as closely to the editor's style as possible.

Two elements are vital in a designer's pattern instructions: completeness and correctness. In today's highly competitive and fast-paced publishing world, publishers simply don't have the time to deal with the production delays that incomplete or incorrect patterns can cause.

While it's advisable to follow your publisher's pattern format, generally speaking, any well-written pattern should include the following:

Title: This should be a logical, creative name for your project that reflects the nature of the design. Don't use names that are too general, like "Pink Doily" or "Short-Sleeve Top." Let your project's name express its positive qualities!

Byline: Place the name by which you want to be published after the title of the project so that proper credit can be given.

Design description: Editors really appreciate designers who include a brief, descriptive blurb about their project. You, the designer, know your project better than anyone else, so let the editor know what's great about it and why crocheters would love it. Is it made in an unusual yarn or color? Is it a versatile design that can have multiple uses? Is it a great style that can be made in a range of sizes? Point out the positive!

Skill level: Include the skill level you feel best fits your design.

Finished size(s): Always be sure to give the finished size(s) for any project. If the design is a garment, finished garment measurements also need to be given as a separate entry following the finished size(s).

Materials list: It is extremely important to be sure that everything used in the making of your project is included in your materials list. Be very specific about brand names of products used, quantities, colors and sizes. Yarn quantities should always include ounces, yards and grams, since most manufacturers are now including these on their packaging. Quantities for crochet cotton are generally only given in yards, both on manufacturers' packaging and in patterns.

List your materials in the logical order used: yarn or thread, crochet hook(s), finishing needles (tapestry, yarn, beading, etc.), crocheting helps (stitch markers, safety pins, etc.) and final embellishment or finishing materials (ribbon, beads, flowers, stiffening agent, etc.).

Gauge: Many new designers often overlook including this important piece of information. The gauge determines the finished size of the project. It's especially critical for any type of fitted item. If your project uses more than one hook size, be sure and specify the hook size(s) for which the gauge is being given.

Notes: Special procedures should be clearly explained so that even less-experienced crocheters can follow them.

Special stitches: List the nonstandard crochet stitches along with the abbreviation for each stitch and the instructions for how to work the stitch.

Instructions: Editors prefer typed instructions, double-spaced. Many editors will no longer accept any handwritten patterns. It's costly and time consuming for the publisher to have them redone in typed format for editing.

Instructions should be written in a logical, step-by-step order, keeping them as concise as possible, but not at the expense of clarity. Be sure to use correct crochet terminology and abbreviations, and try to make your abbreviations publication specific.

Patterns for garments should always include applicable schematics. These drawings generally do not have to be professionally rendered. As long as they clearly and accurately show the necessary information, even rough sketches can be acceptable. Many publishers will not accept garment designs—no matter how fabulous they are—if the instructions cannot be provided with schematics.

Proofread your instructions at least three times to make sure they are correct and that nothing has been omitted (instructions for a teddy bear with missing arms or legs wouldn't be a good thing). If possible, have an experienced crocheting friend proof your pattern as well.

Make sure each page is numbered and includes your name and contact information.

Copyright notice: Always include your copyright notice at the end of your pattern manuscript. A "work" is automatically copyrighted by its author upon its completion, so make sure that your "stamp of identity" is clearly noted. Once you have signed the contract with the publisher to sell full rights for your design, your copyrights are legally transferred to them.

Once you have sent in your completed item and instructions, and the editor gives final approval to the project, you will be sent a contract for the agreed-upon price for your design. The time at which you will be sent this agreement varies among publishers, so don't hesitate to ask your editor when to expect your contract, or how long it usually takes to receive payment once you have returned the signed contract.

With the completed contract and payment in hand, you are now recognized as a "professional" designer, with your foot in the proverbial door to bigger and better things. But don't rest on your laurels; it will take continued hard work and perseverance to keep your design career growing. On the other hand, a happy dance around the house now and then is definitely in order! ■

Can Designing Be a Profitable Business?

A successful business not only enhances the lives of those who work within it, but it also enriches the lives of all those it touches. This is definitely true of crochet designing because it's a wonderful thing to get paid to do what you most enjoy. While the love of crochet and the fulfillment it gives can provide rich rewards for the heart and soul, can designing be a profitable way to earn a living?

The answer to that question will depend on many things, first and foremost being the time, commitment and perseverance that you are willing to devote to becoming a successful designer. The road to success may be littered with numerous publishers' rejections of your work before your first design is accepted for publication. However, once that wonderful day arrives, your confidence in your creative talents will get a major boost.

The validation of being a published designer will not only work wonders for your self-esteem, but will also help increase your professional appeal to other publishers who review your work. The recognition gained from one publishing success can lead to another, and then another, and so on, until you eventually become a "known" name, recognized and respected by editors throughout the industry. That's when the potential for profitability in designing begins to feel like a reality.

This progression doesn't happen overnight. As with most endeavors, there is an initial "paying your dues" period during which you are learning the ropes and gaining valuable experience on the road to success. This "payment period" can vary in duration, depending on the time and effort you devote to getting as much of your work into editors' hands as quickly as possible. Submitting one design here and there won't accomplish much.

In addition to the obvious fact that you must produce quality work, you must also create it in very large quantity. A major key to successfully having your work accepted for publication on a consistent (and thus profitable) basis is to continually have a vast volume of different submissions concurrently in the hands of many editors. This not only increases your chances for design acceptance, but also helps familiarize editors with your name throughout the industry.

At the same time, make sure the designs you are submitting to each editor are the types of designs common to that particular editor's publication. You're pretty much beating a dead horse if you submit yarn afghan designs to a publisher who only specializes in fine thread pieces. Do some research and study the publications of the various editors to whom you plan to submit your work to see what types of designs are suitable for each. Many editors periodically issue editorial calendars or design schedules that specify the types of patterns they are looking for, and when they will need that particular type of design. If you aren't sure, don't hesitate to get in touch and ask.

Another important element in a successful crochet design career is the use of contract labor. As your success grows, and more and more of your designs are accepted for publication, there comes a point when it becomes illogical to think that you can stitch all of the crocheted pieces yourself. The smart designer realizes when it's time to enlist the help of contract crocheters to stitch his or her publishers' models. Yes, part of your publisher's fee will have to be paid to the contract stitcher, but it is so well worth it. Why? All of the time you would be spending to crochet the models yourself can instead be used to create many more new designs that can be submitted and sold, thus adding to your profitability.

Each publishing success can become a stepping-stone to a profitable designing career. Providing quality designs to publishers on a steady basis and working with editors in a conscientious, professional manner are important factors in obtaining success as a designer. It's hard work, but the profits can be great—for both the heart and the pocketbook. ■

Selling Your Crochet (or Crafts): Tips for Success

Many crocheters and other crafters sell their handmade items through various outlets such as craft fairs, church bazaars, retail stores and online retailers. After you make the decision to sell your items, you may need to rethink your crafting focus. Up to this point, you've probably been viewing your designs as more of a hobby than a business, and in order to change that thinking pattern, you need to answer the following business-related questions.

- Who is in your target market?

- Where are you planning on selling your items in order to reach your target market?

- What are the best items to sell based on your target market and chosen selling location?

- How are you going to price your items?

- Should you rotate your inventory of projects (i.e. sell different items in a particular season, or around a particular holiday)?

- What are you going to include with your finished product?

- How are you going to promote and/or present your products?

- Other than selling your products, how can you influence your own profitability?

Leaving these questions unanswered, can result in considerably less profit than would have been possible had you taken the time to answer or at least consider the questions.

Define your product, customer base, market venue and selling price: Show samples of your items to a broad spectrum of friends, family, co-workers and other acquaintances, and get feedback on which items have the most appeal (translation: salability!). Based on this information, you should have a pretty good idea what items will sell best for you, and which type of consumer your products are best suited for, and what venue would be the best medium to sell your products. One other point to keep in mind when developing your product line is to try and offer items of various sizes. This will not only help you more efficiently use up leftover materials, therefore helping keep your costs down, but it will also allow you to offer products that vary in price and thus appeal to a wider range of customers.

One of the biggest questions in selling your products is how much to sell them for. Pricing your handcrafted items can be a tricky affair, full of puzzles and variables. With a bit of research, you'll likely find numerous "formulas" for determining the proper retail price for goods. One popular pricing formula is to figure two or three times the cost of materials, depending on how many expenses you have. Expenses include things like cost of materials, overhead, labor and selling expenses (such as travel, booth rental costs, etc.).

Another big question that usually arises is how much to charge for your labor. How much is your time worth? A general rule of thumb among crafters when it comes to charging for their time when producing their items is a minimum of $10 per hour, although it can be higher depending on the complexity involved in producing the product.

Do some research to see what other crafters are charging for similar items online, at craft exhibits, in retail shops and other venues. This will help give you a good idea of how competitively you can (or should) price your product, but when it comes right down to it, only you can determine a feasible price that will be both profitable for you and reasonable for your customer.

Coming up with an ideal price that makes your items neither too cheap nor too expensive must be carefully thought out and perhaps even market-tested first among a few potential customers. You'll soon discover that if your price is too cheap, you may sell more items, but you'll see little or no profit for your hard work. Potential customers will also likely be turned off by cheap prices, wondering what might be wrong with the product. And most certainly, pricing too high will dissuade customers. Ultimately, you should set a price on each of your products that fairly, and within reason, reflects both the work you put into it and the quality of the materials. People generally recognize quality when they see it and are usually willing to pay for it.

Sell a complete product: When thinking along the lines of quality, you need to make sure your products are sold complete and need no additional items to make them usable. Selling your beautiful crocheted jewelry without findings, for example, is pretty much a self-defeating endeavor.

Are your items seasonal? Holiday products, especially Christmas, are always popular, but selling only seasonal items can be very limiting. Most consumers want and need products that can be used year-round for many and varied purposes. In crochet, for example, baby items are always top sellers. Babies aren't going out of style, so there is a demand year-round for quality baby products. Also popular are things that will make nice gifts, such as jewelry and other accessories, as well as pretty and practical things for the home. Most people frequent boutiques and shops with gift buying in mind. However, depending on the time of year, including some holiday items with your product line can work very well.

Items to include or provide: Make sure to include extra "niceties" that project a more professional image. When selling your items at exhibits, fairs, bazaars, etc., make sure all of your items are properly tagged with the price, and where appropriate, any additional information that will be helpful to the customer when using the items, such as care instructions for crocheted garments or afghans, for example. Display a guest book for visitors to sign. This can be invaluable for creating a customer database and contact list.

You'll also need to have the following items on hand at shows where you'll be setting up a display away from home or work:

- Secure cash box and plenty of small bills and change. Be prepared for customers to use $20s and $50s. A word of advice about your cash box: do not keep large amounts of money in the box. Have a plan and place the cash in your car trunk or other secure place.

- Receipt book and current tax table

- Blank pricing labels or stickers

- Calculator

- Plenty of pens

- Copy of your state tax certificate; many states require that this be on display where you are selling your crafts so be sure and keep the copy in your cash box.

- Toolbox for putting displays together or making unexpected repairs

- Refreshments, if allowed by the show. Who can resist candy treats or delectable cookies? A container of water is also recommended.

What not to bring: Don't bring young children who need constant supervision, pets, a book or anything else that will distract you from interacting with potential customers.

Promotion and presentation is important: Have business cards and brochures on hand to give customers and other visitors. Many shop owners and other retailers often visit craft exhibits looking for fresh new products to offer in their stores, so be ready to put your information in their hands! Package your customers' purchases properly. Don't use old plastic grocery bags, but then again, don't overdo it with expensive, profit-cutting packaging, either. Some relatively inexpensive packaging choices include plain white paper bags or clear plastic bags that you can dress up with a bit of ribbon and colored tissue paper.

Boost your profitability. Profit, of course, is one of the main reasons you're in the business of selling your handcrafted items in the first place. To make a profit, you must have a product line that has a big salability factor, and you must keep your production costs to a minimum. Purchase your raw materials at the lowest possible prices, usually wholesale. You will need to obtain a sales tax number. In some states, there is no charge for acquiring a sales tax number, and in other states it is available for a relatively small fee, often under $50.

One way to influence your profitability is to shop around for your materials and get price comparisons from a number of wholesalers before buying. Buyers are not created equal, and some will not give you the same amount of materials for your dollar! Also, keep in mind that in some cases, with a little detective work, you can even find real bargains on good materials at retail outlets like discount stores, "odd lot" stores and flea markets, as well as stores' after-season, pre-season or closeout sales. Taking advantage of these resources may help you reduce your production costs by allowing you to stock up on materials when prices are down.

Another way you can influence your profitability is by making sure you are able to produce your products in quantity, and as quickly and efficiently as possible. Be prepared to meet customer demand. Making only a few of your items isn't very cost effective in the use of your materials. Pay others to stitch, or involve family and friends where possible to help produce inventory.

These are just a few tips to consider when venturing into the wonderful world of selling your handcrafted items. There is much more information available from a variety of published sources (check your local library and online), and from simply talking with others who are pros at selling their crafts and learning from their experiences. Selling what you make can be fun and fulfilling, but it should be profitable as well. ▪

chapter seventeen
tips from the pros

It's always a good thing to benefit from the experience of others. In this chapter, we'll share with you some great advice from a number of crochet professionals who have developed a variety of creative tips and tricks that may be able to help your crochet projects go more smoothly.

Tips From the Pros

No matter what our crochet projects may be, we all want them to start out great, go smoothly and end satisfactorily. Through years of creating crochet patterns for publication, professional crochet designers have naturally developed a variety of tricks that help them produce their work more efficiently and effectively. Here are some of their great tips that will help make your projects more enjoyable and successful.

YARN

Brand is important: All yarns are not created equal. There can be differences among yarn brands in fiber content, density, number of yarn plies, twist, care instructions and other important factors. If a pattern specifies the brand to use, for best results, always try to use that brand throughout. If that isn't possible, choose a yarn with the same weight, fiber characteristics and care requirements. You might want to make a swatch with the substitute yarn to make sure it will work satisfactorily before purchasing the entire amount.

Don't come up short: Dark-color yarns can be thicker due to the heavier dye, so be sure and purchase a little extra for safety's sake.

Color schemes: Use current home-decorating magazines and catalogs to help in determining successful color schemes for afghans and other home-decorating accents.

Know the numbers: Always check dye-lot numbers when purchasing yarn and purchase the full amount needed plus an extra skein or two.

Different dye lots: If you cannot buy enough of one dye-lot for an entire project, or if you run out and can't match it, use the new dye lot for less conspicuous areas such as borders or when assembling.

Nearing the end: When you are approaching the end of your ball of yarn and start to wonder how many rows you can still get from it, fold the remaining yarn in half and tie a loose over-hand knot at the halfway point. Stitch a row. If you reach the knot before you finish the row, you will not have enough yarn to complete a second row. If, however, you finish the row before reaching the knot, you can complete another row with the remaining yarn.

A weighty issue: If you forget how many skeins you used in a project and it was made in one yarn and one color, weight it. Convert the project pounds to ounces and then divide the total number of ounces by the number of ounces per skein for the yarn you used. Example: if your project weighs 3 pounds, this equals 48 ounces. If your yarn has 6 ounces per skein, you used 8 skeins.

Label leftovers: So you will have a record of the brand and color, when rewinding leftover yarn, use the label as a bobbin. Fold the label several times then wrap the yarn around it, leaving at least one end of the label exposed. Slip the label out when ready to use.

Yards to ounces: If your pattern lists the quantity of yarn needed in ounces only, you can easily figure if you have enough yarn on hand to do the project with this simple equation: it takes about 50 yards of worsted (medium) weight yarn to equal 1 ounce *(see conversion information on page 28)*.

Grams to ounces: To convert grams to ounces and vice versa, remember that 100 grams equals approximately 3½ ounces. Divide the number of grams by 28.35 to get the number of ounces you need. To convert ounces to grams, multiply the number of ounces by 28.35 to find the number of grams needed *(see conversion information on page 27)*.

Signs of aging: To avoid "splotchy" colors, if you suspect the yarn you are about to purchase may have been on the shelf for some time, look at the portion of the skein that has been covered by the label for tell-tale signs of discoloration.

THREADS

Know the size: If the labels on your balls of crochet thread have been removed, use a simple color-coding system to keep track of thread sizes. Place colored stickers inside the cardboard tubes of your crochet thread to designate the size (i.e. red for size 10, green for 20, etc.).

Take a stand: Freestanding paper-towel holders work well for holding balls of thread and make it easy to work with more than one color at a time.

Thread substitute: If you need only a small amount of crochet thread, embroidery floss is an excellent substitute. Use six strands when substituting for size 5 crochet cotton; four strands for size 10 crochet cotton; two for size 20 crochet cotton; and one for size 30 or 40 crochet cotton.

Common threads and their equivalents: If you're not sure the thread you have will work as a substitute for your pattern:

Size 5 crochet cotton = No. 3 or 5 pearl/perle cotton

Size 10/bedspread-weight cotton = No. 8 pearl/perle cotton

Size 20 crochet cotton = No. 12 pearl/perle cotton

Size 30 crochet cotton = No. 12 pearl/perle cotton

Size 40 crochet cotton = tatting thread

MAKING GREAT AFGHANS

Motifs made faster: If making an afghan comprised of motifs that have several color changes, you may find that an "assembly-line" method helps the process of completing the motifs go more quickly. Work all of the motif centers first, then all of the next colors in the pattern around each motif, and so on, to complete all of the motifs simultaneously rather than working each complete motif separately. After working just a few motifs in this manner, you will know the pattern for each color section by heart, and you will be able to work it much more quickly without having to refer to notes or instructions.

Same-size pieces: If making an afghan that has numerous blocks or motifs that need to be the same size, be sure to measure each newly completed piece to previously made pieces to be sure all are consistent in size.

Non-twisting motifs: When making individual motifs and afghan borders, try to figure a way to work one or two rounds with the wrong side facing (by turning at the end of a round, rather than continuing the next round with the right side facing). This "change of direction" on one or two rounds prevents the motif from twisting in one direction and helps keep the border from curling up.

Mixed motifs: When joining motifs of a lighter color to those of a darker one, use the lighter color for seams.

Fuzzy yarn: If your afghan is made with a yarn that is fuzzy or nubby, purchase a skein of smooth yarn in the same color to make seaming easier.

Counting tip: To stay on track when making afghans that require many blocks or motifs, stack the pieces in groups of 10 as they are completed and run a length of contrasting yarn through the center of each group, tying them together loosely. This not only eliminates the need to continually count (and recount) your motifs as work progresses, but it helps keep all your pieces secured in neat, manageable groups that take up less space in your work bag.

Starting a new color: Rather than tying on a new color when making color changes (especially on large projects like afghans), fasten off the last color used and begin the new one by drawing up a loop in the specified stitch and then chain the necessary number of stitches to begin the next row or round. It's faster than tying on a new color, and the pattern is always sharper with no color bleed-through.

Taming loose yarn ends: Yarn ends tend to pop out more easily on large, heavy items like afghans. After carefully weaving in the tails of yarn (as discussed on page 59), sew them down with matching thread. This takes a little extra time, but it makes for a very finished look, with a wrong side that looks almost as good as the right side and yarn ends that virtually never pop out.

No bumps: When working with two or more strands of yarn held together, weave ends in separately to avoid an unsightly bump.

Joining large sections: Save the plastic clips which are used to keep new shirts folded in their package. Use the clips to hold afghan sections together while you join. These clips work better than pins, which tend to slip out. However, if using clips, use two clips instead of one, crisscrossing them to help keep them in place.

Take the long view: When choosing colors for an afghan you plan to make for your own home, work up swatches in several possible color combinations. Look at them from a distance rather than close up, and preferably in a location where you plan to use the afghan. You will get a more realistic view of how the color combination will look and which combinations you prefer.

A fine finish for ripple afghans: Most single-crochet ripple afghans call for you to work in back loops only across. However, one way to obtain a great finished look in ripple afghans is to work through both loops in each of the first three stitches at the beginning of each row, through the back loop only in all stitches across to the other end and then work in both loops in each of the last three stitches. This will reinforce the side edges to keep them from stretching and help keep the shape of the afghan for many years.

Avoid those holes: When working motifs that begin with a chain joined into a ring, if you don't like the appearance of a hole in the middle of the first round, leave a 4- to 6-inch length of yarn at the beginning and work your stitches over it while working into the ring. At the end of the round, pull the yarn end tightly to close the hole and weave in the end securely on the back side. Doing this on all your afghan motifs will give a nice, consistent look.

A second method is to begin with a chain-two instead of the ring if the pattern begins with single crochet. Work the required number of single crochet into the second chain from the hook, using it as the "ring." If the pattern begins with double crochet, begin with a chain-four instead of the ring and work the required number of double crochet into the fourth chain from the hook to form the ring.

Easy sewing: When working with blocks, motifs or strips that will be sewn together later, leave a tail of yarn approximately twice the length of the seam to be sewn when fastening off. This will eliminate the need to tie on additional yarn for sewing and result in fewer ends to work in when you are done.

Care instructions: When making an afghan for a gift, be sure and include a small card, or the label from the yarn used, with the laundering instructions. This will help ensure that the recipient can keep his or her afghan looking beautiful for years to come.

MISCELLANEOUS TIPS FOR THIS & THAT

Small stuff: Stuff small items with yarn scraps of the same color.

Temporary threader: When you don't have a needle threader handy, cut a 1/4-inch x 3-inch strip of paper, fold it over the yarn end and insert through the eye of the needle.

Trouble makers: If you run across a bad spot in the yarn you are using, cut it out. Working it into your project will only cause problems later.

Damaged goods: Save damaged pieces of yarn and separate the plies to use for embroidery when thinner yarn is needed.

To "dye" for: If a doily or tablecloth becomes stained, tea-dying will add a rich antique look and help cover the stain.

Lose the lumps: Add new skeins of yarn at the beginning or end of a row or round to prevent unsightly lumps in your work.

In the bag: Attach a metal eyelet (available at craft stores) to the edge of your crochet bag. Thread the end of your yarn through the eyelet before starting your project and your yarn will stay securely in the bag.

Ease eyestrain: To help ease eyestrain, when working with light-color yarn or thread, place a dark cloth over your lap. If working with dark yarn or thread, use a light-color cloth.

Tight spots: Keep a slightly smaller hook than the one you are using handy for pulling yarn or thread through tight spots like beginning chains.

Stiff stuff: When making an item that says to use cardboard inserts, use plastic canvas instead. It's much more durable.

Carrying case: Eyeglasses cases make great "tool chests." Use them to hold needles, threaders, small scissors, tape measures and a few crochet hooks.

Hold it!: Fold your pattern book or magazine open to the page you need, then slip inside a plastic zip-shut bag and seal for an instant pattern holder.

Simple storage: Reusable plastic drinking cups that have snap-on lids with straw holes make great holders for smaller balls or skeins of yarn and thread.

A little goes a long way: Instead of using expensive potpourri for stuffing sachets, try using polyester fiberfill or cotton balls sprinkled with less expensive potpourri oil. A few drops will last a long time and the scent can easily be refreshed by adding more oil.

Chain a few more: When stitching a foundation chain, crochet a few more chains than you'll need. That way, if you counted wrong, you'll be able to use the extra chains. Extra chains not used can be pulled out later.

Clip it: The little clips that hold buttons to display cards make great stitch markers.

Write it down: If you are modifying a pattern, write down your changes. You may want to make the project again at a later time and you'll likely not remember what you did.

A second look: Things that look like mistakes at 11:00 p.m. may not look like mistakes at 9:00 a.m. the next day. And even if they are still mistakes, it is a lot easier to correct them in the clear light of day.

Take a step back: When you're working on a garment, regardless of whether you're following a pattern or creating an original design, it's important to step back and take a look at the overall effect. Do this often. You'll be able to see if the proportions and the yarn you're using look good, whether you've made any major mistakes in the pattern stitches and whether your tension has been consistent. Your work looks very different from an arm's length or across the room than it does while you're working on it.

Butterfly bobbins: Instead of using purchased bobbins, make your own yarn butterflies. Open your left hand in a V, with forefinger and middle finger together, and ring and pinkie fingers together. Holding the end of the yarn between your left thumb and palm, wrap the yarn in a figure-8 around the fingers until you have pulled off enough yarn for your needs. Cut the yarn, leaving a 5-inch tail, and wrap the tail several times (not too tightly) around the center of the figure-8 of yarn and secure. You can now pull on the starting end to release yarn as you need it, but your little butterfly will continue to hold the remainder of the yarn in place.

Matching Tunisian crochet edges: To produce matching selvedges in Tunisian crochet, work the last stitch of every forward row (regardless of the stitch pattern) in to the last vertical thread *plus* the thread just behind it. This makes your work more attractive and simplifies finishing.

STITCH GUIDE
FOR MORE COMPLETE INFORMATION, VISIT **FREEPATTERNS.COM**

STITCH ABBREVIATIONS

beg	begin/begins/beginning
bpdc	back post double crochet
bpsc	back post single crochet
bptr	back post treble crochet
CC	contrasting color
ch(s)	chain(s)
ch-	refers to chain or space previously made (i.e., ch-1 space)
ch sp(s)	chain space(s)
cl(s)	cluster(s)
cm	centimeter(s)
dc	double crochet (singular/plural)
dc dec	double crochet 2 or more stitches together, as indicated
dec	decrease/decreases/decreasing
dtr	double treble crochet
ext	extended
fpdc	front post double crochet
fpsc	front post single crochet
fptr	front post treble crochet
g	gram(s)
hdc	half double crochet
hdc dec	half double crochet 2 or more stitches together, as indicated
inc	increase/increases/increasing
lp(s)	loop(s)
MC	main color
mm	millimeter(s)
oz	ounce(s)
pc	popcorn(s)
rem	remain/remains/remaining
rep(s)	repeat(s)
rnd(s)	round(s)
RS	right side
sc	single crochet (singular/plural)
sc dec	single crochet 2 or more stitches together, as indicated
sk	skip/skipped/skipping
sl st(s)	slip stitch(es)
sp(s)	space(s)/spaced
st(s)	stitch(es)
tog	together
tr	treble crochet
trtr	triple treble
WS	wrong side
yd(s)	yard(s)
yo	yarn over

YARN CONVERSION

OUNCES TO GRAMS		GRAMS TO OUNCES	
1	28.4	25	7/8
2	56.7	40	1 2/3
3	85.0	50	1 3/4
4	113.4	100	3 1/2

UNITED STATES		UNITED KINGDOM
sl st (slip stitch)	=	sc (single crochet)
sc (single crochet)	=	dc (double crochet)
hdc (half double crochet)	=	htr (half treble crochet)
dc (double crochet)	=	tr (treble crochet)
tr (treble crochet)	=	dtr (double treble crochet)
dtr (double treble crochet)	=	ttr (triple treble crochet)
skip	=	miss

Reverse single crochet (reverse sc): Ch 1, sk first st, working from left to right, insert hook in next st from front to back, draw up lp on hook, yo, and draw through both lps on hook.

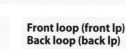

Chain (ch): Yo, pull through lp on hook.

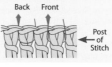

Single crochet (sc): Insert hook in st, yo, pull through st, yo, pull through both lps on hook.

Double crochet (dc): Yo, insert hook in st, yo, pull through st, [yo, pull through 2 lps] twice.

Front loop (front lp) Back loop (back lp)

Front Loop   Back Loop

Front post stitch (fp): Back post stitch (bp): When working post st, insert hook from right to left around post st on previous row.

Back   Front

Post of Stitch

Half double crochet (hdc): Yo, insert hook in st, yo, pull through st, yo, pull through all 3 lps on hook.

Double treble crochet (dtr): Yo 3 times, insert hook in st, yo, pull through st, [yo, pull through 2 lps] 4 times.

Slip stitch (sl st): Insert hook in st, pull through both lps on hook.

Chain color change (ch color change) Yo with new color, draw through last lp on hook.

Double crochet color change (dc color change) Drop first color, yo with new color, draw through last 2 lps of st.

Treble crochet (tr): Yo twice, insert hook in st, yo, pull through st, [yo, pull through 2 lps] 3 times.

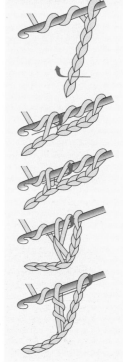

Single crochet decrease (sc dec): (Insert hook, yo, draw lp through) in each of the sts indicated, yo, draw through all lps on hook.

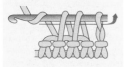

Example of 2-sc dec

Half double crochet decrease (hdc dec): (Yo, insert hook, yo, draw lp through) in each of the sts indicated, yo, draw through all lps on hook.

Example of 2-hdc dec

Double crochet decrease (dc dec): (Yo, insert hook, yo, draw lp through, yo, draw through 2 lps on hook) in each of the sts indicated, yo, draw through all lps on hook.

Example of 2-dc dec

Treble crochet decrease (tr dec): Holding back last lp of each st, tr in each of the sts indicated, yo, pull through all lps on hook.

Example of 2-tr dec